PASSENGER ARRIVALS

at the

Port of Charleston
1820–1829

PASSENGER ARRIVALS

at the

Port of Charleston

1820–1829

Transcribed by
BRENT H. HOLCOMB

INTRODUCTION

Passenger lists are among the most sought-after records in all of American genealogy. Unfortunately, they do not exist in a complete and unbroken series, and for some ports of entry they do not exist at all. For the port of Charleston, South Carolina such records exist only for the years 1820–1829.

I began publishing the Charleston customs collector's copies of the passenger lists from National Archives microfilm, Microcopy 575, Roll 2, serially in the *South Carolina Magazine of Ancestral Research* in 1989 with plans to make a volume of them eventually. In *American Passenger Arrival Records* by Michael Tepper (Genealogical Publishing Company, 1993), I learned of the existence of eight volumes of State Department Transcripts of ships' passenger lists at the National Archives, in Record Group 36. Dr. Tepper's book explains that the original passenger lists were prepared on board ship and deposited with the collectors of customs at the various ports. The collectors of customs (in the case of Charleston, J.R. Pringle) prepared copies of these lists and sent them quarterly to the Secretary of State. Transcripts of these copies, prepared at the State Department (thus State Department Transcripts), were recorded in nine volumes (Volume 2 is missing) and are now in the National Archives.

According to Dr. Tepper, these transcripts were made "when the returns were crisp and unblemished, the ink fresh, and the style of handwriting familiar." While the information given is often abbreviated and/or incomplete, the transcripts are legitimate records and useful for comparison in cases where the customs collector's copies are in poor condition, illegible, or missing. The book *Passenger Arrivals 1819–1820* (Genealogical Publishing Company, 1967), a reprint of an 1821 government publication, contains a published version of the State Department Transcripts for Charleston for the year 1820, but even here there are discrepancies with the original transcripts. Therefore, I have used both the customs collector's copies and the original State Department Transcripts in putting together this compilation of Charleston passenger arrival records.

My thanks to Mrs. Norma Gransee for her help in locating these volumes and having the appropriate pages microfilmed for this project. I have also viewed the original volumes at the National Archives to check for names which were not clear or not visible on the microfilm. A checklist of the extant transcripts and copies follows:

Date	Transcripts	Copies	Date	Transcripts	Copies
1st Quarter 1820	yes	yes	1st Quarter 1825	yes	yes
2nd Quarter 1820	yes	yes	2nd Quarter 1825	yes	no
3rd Quarter 1820	yes	yes	3rd Quarter 1825	yes	no
4th Quarter 1820	yes	yes	4th Quarter 1825	yes	no
1st Quarter 1821	no	no	1st Quarter 1826	yes	yes
2nd Quarter 1821	no	no	2nd Quarter 1826	yes	no
3rd Quarter 1821	no	no	3rd Quarter 1826	yes	yes
4th Quarter 1821	yes	yes	4th Quarter 1826	yes	yes
1st Quarter 1822	yes	yes	1st Quarter 1827	yes	yes
2nd Quarter 1822	yes	yes	2nd Quarter 1827	yes	yes
3rd Quarter 1822	yes	yes	3rd Quarter 1827	yes	yes
4th Quarter 1822	yes	yes	4th Quarter 1827	yes	yes
1st Quarter 1823	yes	yes	1st Quarter 1828	yes	yes
2nd Quarter 1823	yes	yes	2nd Quarter 1828	no	yes
3rd Quarter 1823	yes	no	3rd Quarter 1828	yes	yes
4th Quarter 1823	no	yes	4th Quarter 1828	no	no
1st Quarter 1824	no	yes	1st Quarter 1829	yes	no
2nd Quarter 1824	yes	yes	2nd Quarter 1829	yes	yes
3rd Quarter 1824	yes	yes	3rd Quarter 1829	no	yes
4th Quarter 1824	yes	yes	4th Quarter 1829	no	no

My transcriptions of the copies of the lists are found on pages 1–85; my transcriptions of the State Department Transcripts on pages 86–148. I have tried to maintain the format and order of the originals as much as possible. The lists are in columnar format, but as it was impractical to reproduce the headings exactly as they appeared on the lists, some headings had to be abbreviated. The headings on the original lists are as follows: Name of Vessel/Passengers Name/Age/Sex/ Date of Arrival/Occupation/Where from/Country to which they belong/Country of which they intend to become inhabitants/Died on the voyage.

The researcher is reminded that these are lists of passengers arriving at the port of Charleston from foreign ports. Lists of passengers from ships coming from other American ports (such as Philadelphia and New York) were not recorded. Additionally, not every person arriving in Charleston from a foreign port was an immigrant. Some persons had merely been on a passage and were returning home to Charleston. Others were traders whose names we find nearly every year, one being Anthony/Antoine Aymar. It is my hope that this volume will be a useful addition to the growing literature of passenger arrivals at American ports.

Brent H. Holcomb
June 30, 1994

PASSENGER ARRIVALS

at the

Port of Charleston
1820–1829

PASSENGERS ARRIVING AT THE PORT OF CHARLESTON 1820-1829

Date arrival	Name of vessel	Where taken on board	Passengers' names	Age	Sex	Occupation	Country- belong	Country- inhabit
January 1 1820	Schooner Margaret	St. Augustine	Joseph Coppinger	18	Male	Merchant	Spain	Charleston
	"	"	Joseph Guadarama	18	do	do	do	do
			Manuel Guere	30	do	do	do	do
"	Sloop Connecticut	Havanna	Michael Maslerson	30	do	do	U States	New York
		"	Thomas Herbert	25	do	Carpenter	do	Salsbury
6	Brig Columbia	Dublin	Mary Ann Eagan	25	Female	Lady	Britain	Baltimore
	"	"	Margaret Eagan	under	do		do	do
	"	"	John Eagan	nine	Male		do	do
	"	"	William Eagan	years	do		do	do
	"	"	Therisa Eagan		Female		do	do
	"	"	Eliza Eagan		do		do	do
	"	"	Mary Moss		do	Servant	do	do
"	Brig Angelina	Belfast	Thomas Moorhead	23	Male	Farmer	do	So Carolina
	"	"	Eliza English	36	Female		do	do
	"	"	John English	32	Male	Farmer	do	do
	"	"	Lawrence English	3	do		do	do
	"	"	Andrew English	3	do		do	do
	"	"	George Weir	22	do	Farmer	do	do
	"	"	Martha Weir	21	Female		do	do
	"	"	John Weir	1	Male		do	do
	"	"	Thomas Smith	31	do	Farmer	do	do
	"	"	Mary Smith	26	Female		do	do
	"	"	Rebecca Smith	4	do		do	do
	"	"	Bess Smith	2	do		do	do
	"	"	Issabella Smith	4	do		do	do
	"	"	Hugh Moore	16	Male		do	do
	"	"	William Fox	21	do		do	do
	"	"	Margarett Fox	19	Female		do	do
	"	"	Mary Fox	50	do		do	do
	"	"	Ellen McCarren	7	Female		do	do
	"	"	Margarett Woods	55	do		do	do
14	Sloop Ann	Matanzes	James Emery	27	Male	Merchant	U States	New York
17	Schooner Adventure	do	Patrick Dillon	28	do	do	do	Charleston
		"	Thomas McGowan	30	do	Marriner	do	do
		"	Gibbert	28	do	do	do	do
		"	Thomas Barnard	35	do	do	do	do
21	Brig Edw'd D. Douglas	St. Thomas	William Parkham	43	do	Carpenter	do	do
"	Sloop Jay	Bermuda	Issadore Grognet	23	do	Merchant	France	France
	"	"	Charlotte F. Grognet	18	Female	Lady	do	do
	"	"	Emel Marc Mandet	25	Male	Merchant	do	do
	"	"	Joane Anto Enie	20	do	do	do	do
	"	"	Edward E Bringeon	13	do	do	do	do

PASSENGERS ARRIVING AT THE PORT OF CHARLESTON 1820-1829

Date arrival	Name of vessel	Where taken on board	Passengers' names	Age	Sex	Occupation	Country- belong	Country- inhabit
January 22 1820	Schooner Mary Ann	Havanna	William Miller	25	do	do	U States	Charleston
			George Crombelholm	30	do	do	do	do died 19 Jany
25	Brig Columbia	Havanna	Samuel Mitchell	51	do	do	U States	New York
			John F. Fortune	23	do	do	do	Charleston
29	Schooner Comet	do	Ann Charties	20	Female	do	do	do
		"	Anthony Moore	30	Male	Marriner	Spain	Havanna
		"	Garrer	25	do	do	do	do
		"	Thomas Barnet	25	do	Engineer	Britain	Liverpool
		"	John Dies	21	do	Marriner	Spain	Havanna
		"	Granades	35	do	do	do	do
31	ditto Jane	St. Augustine	Anthony Triai	30	do	Merchant	do	St. Augustine
		"	John Pelicia	21	do	do	do	do
"	do Ann	Samanna	John Warton	30	do	Marriner	U States	U States
		"	Andrew Gay	45	do	Merchant	do	do
		"	William Melly	22	do	do	Spain	St. Augustine
		"	Manuel Giano Bly	21	do	do	do	do
February 3	Brig Mary	Colerain	John Kean	47	do	Labourer	Britain	So Carolina
			Patrick Dempsey	20	do	do	do	do
			Ann Burke	50	Female	Spinster	do	do
			Mary Keary	22	do	Mantuamaker	do	do
			Thomas Bourke	17	Male	Labourer	do	do
			Mary Thompson	5	Female	do	do	do
			Eliza Fraizer	23	do	Spinster	do	do
			William Peacock	50	Male	Dancing Master	do	do
5	Schooner Eudora	St. Jago de Cuba	Joseph Sanchez	20	Male	Merchant	Spain	Charleston
"	Brig Catherine	Havanna	Samuel Yates	36	do	do	U States	do
		"	Jane Yates	32	Female	Lady	do	do
		"	E. Farley	26	do	do	do	do
		"	Thomas Frink	22	Male	do	do	do
		"	Bazil Gonsales	35	do	Merchant	do	do
		"	Fontane	36	do	do	France	do
		"	L. H. C. Schutt	32	do	do	U States	do
		"	Isaac Suares	21	do	Servant	do	do
14	Ship Java	Havre de Grass	Lecufer	48	do	Merchant	France	France
15	Schooner Sally	Bermuda	William Arnott	36	do	Mason	Britain	U States
			Prudence Hibbert	22	Female	Lady	U States	Boston
"	do Mary	Matanzes	John P. Lavinciendier	45	Male	Merchant	St. Domingo	Charleston
16	Sloop Laurence	St. Augustine	Jacques Biecies	30	do	Cabinet Maker	do	do
		"	Chapman Levy	35	do	Lawyer	U States	do
		"	Alexander McGilvery	40	do	Auctioneer	do	do
		"	Stephen Lancaster	32	do	Merchant	do	do
		"	Angulo Sante	40	do	do	do	do

PASSENGERS ARRIVING AT THE PORT OF CHARLESTON 1820-1829

Date arrival	Name of vessel	Where taken on board	Passengers' names	Age	Sex	Occupation	Country- belong	Country- inhabit
Feb 1820 18	Ship Elizabeth	Liverpool	Thomas Hindley	38	do		Britain	Britain
	"	"	John Hall	28	do	do	do	do
	"	"	William Mitchell	31	do	do	do	do
	"	"	William Barber	28	do	do	do	Charleston
"	Ship Mars	Greenock	Niel McNiel	18	do			Charleston
20	Scho'r Mary Ann	Havanna	James McNamy	40	do	Merchant	U States	do
			James Hatch	33	do	Marriner	do	do
			John Helfred	21	do	do	do	do
			Lorenzo Henry	34	do	Merchant	do	do
23	Do Margarett	Matanzes	Alexander England	15	do		do	do
			Samuel Porter	22	do	Planter	do	do
24	Brig Perseverance	Havanna	James Mathews	42	Male	Trader	U States	Charleston
	"		Manuel Fernandes	38	do	do	do	do
	"		Joseph Squeber	25	do	Marriner	do	New York
	"		Anthony Gray	48	do	do	do	do
March 1	Schooner Echo	ditto	Luther Whiting	30	do	Merchant	do	do
	"		Francis Jacobus	25	do	do	do	Charleston
	"		Bourke	25	do	do	do	do
	"		Thompson	23	Female		do	do
7	do Charleston Packet	do	James Flemming	45	Male	Merchant	do	do
	"		James P. Ripley	25	do	do	do	Boston
	"		Joseph M. Mayhle	32	do	do	do	New York
	"		Pasquel Macaletti	45	do	Marriner	do	Charleston
11	Ship Montgomery	Liverpool	Sextus Gaillard	19	do	do	do	do
	"		Samuel Gaillard	18	do	do	do	do
	"		James Slegman	30	do	Soap Boiler	Germany	New Orleans
"	Brig Eliza	Havanna	Anthony Yallick	50	do	Marriner	U States	do
	"		Jose Frara	39	do	Merchant	do	Charleston
	"		William Brown	21	do	Shoe Maker	Britain	do
	"		George Burne	19	do	do	do	do
	"		Anthony Morra	25	do	Merchant	Spain	Cadez
	"		Francis Perez	26	do	do	do	St. Cruz
	"		John Senet	25	do	do	Britain	Charleston
	"		John Patterson	24	do	Marriner	U States	do
"	Schooner Mercury	Bermuda	John Morrisson	35	do	Merchant	do	Boston
			Peter Coffin	45	do	Spinster	do	Charleston
"	Brig Harriet	do	Catharine Duncan	27	Female	Farmer	Britain	do
19	do Prince Leopold	Belfast	John Hedley	55	Male	Merchant		do
	"		James Mager	24	do	do		do
	"		John Owens Johnson	24	do	Farmer		do
	"		John McKelvey	47	do	do		do
	"		Robert Harper	45	do	do		do
	"		John Macolm	36	do	do		do

PASSENGERS ARRIVING AT THE PORT OF CHARLESTON 1820-1829

Date arrival	Name of vessel	Where taken on board	Passengers' names	Age	Sex	Occupation	Country- belong	Country- inhabit
Feb 19 1820	Prince Leopold	Belfast	Peter Cad	18	Male	Farmer	Britain	Charleston
	"	"	John Young	63	do	do	do	do
	"	"	Sarah Young	64	Female	do	do	do
	"	"	Jane Young	24	Female	none	Britain	Charleston
	"	"	Ann Young	22	do	"	"	"
	"	"	Margaret Young	20	do	"	"	"
	"	"	John Wilson	25	Male	"	"	"
	"	"	Jane Hare	20	Female	"	"	"
	"	"	Margaret Hare	20	do	"	"	"
	"	"	Alexander Hare	13	Male	"	"	"
	"	"	Samuel Aiken	21	do	"	"	"
	"	"	Nancy Aiken	65	Female	"	"	"
	"	"	Margaret Aiken	30	do	"	"	"
	"	"	Eliza Aiken	25	do	"	"	"
	"	"	Nancy Aiken	23	do	"	"	"
	"	"	John Aiken	5	Male	"	"	"
	"	"	Matilda Crawford	9	Female	"	"	"
	"	"	Alexander Rogers	17	Male	"	"	"
	"	"	John Richardson	23	do	"	"	"
	"	"	Robert Lynn	35	do	"	"	"
	"	"	Daniel McCanty	24	do	"	"	"
	"	"	John Henry	32	do	"	"	"
	"	"	William Shegog	20	do	"	"	"
	"	"	Jane Wilson	21	Female	"	"	"
21	Schooner Comet	Havanna	Joseph Fernandes	40	Male	Marriner	U States	Philadelphia
	"	"	Hugh Rogers	41	do	Merchant	do	Charleston
	"	"	John Lopez	35	do	do	do	do
	"	"	John Dias	44	do	do	Spain	do
22	Ship Octavia	Liverpool	John Shoulbread	25	Male	Surgeon	U States	do
	"	"	Peter Neilson	23	do	Merchant	Britain	do
	"	"	John Tudor	20	do	do	do	do
23	Brig Adeline	Havanna	John Frisbee	35	do	Marriner	U States	New Haven
	"	"	Honb'e Patrick Brown	60	do	Judge	Britain	Nassau
	"	"	Sir Charles Saxton	50	do	Gentleman	do	London
	"	"	Francois	40	do	Servant	France	do
27	Schooner Margarett	Barracoa	Vincent Gonsales	25	do	Marriner	Portugal	Havanna
27	Ship South Carolina	Liverpool	William Ward	27	Male	Merchant	Britain	Charleston
	"	"	Joseph Hodgson	34	do	Mechanic	do	do
	"	"	William Hodgson	11	do	do	do	do
31	Brig Joseph	Gaudaloupe	Richard C. Codman	21	do	Merchant	U States	Boston
"	Schooner Susan	St. Augustine	James Dean	30	do	do	do	Charleston

PASSENGERS ARRIVING AT THE PORT OF CHARLESTON 1820-1829

Name of vessels	Date arrival	Passengers' names	Age	Sex	Occupation	Where from	Country- belong	Country- inhabit
	April 2 1820	Phillip Robinson	38	Male	Merchant	Havanna	U S	Charleston
	"	John De Sylva	33	do	do	"	France	N. York
	"	F. Le Page	21	do	do	"	do	do
	7	Mary Lindsay	39	Female	Spinster	St. Augustine	U S	Charleston
	"	Harriet Frith	17	do	do	"	do	do
	"	Peck	38	Male	Marriner	"	do	N. York
	12	Charles Sully	36	do	Merchant	"	do	St. Augustine
	"	Mrs. Williams	29	Female		Liverpool	Spain	U States
	"	Georgianna Buntin	12	do		"	Britain	do
	"	Jesse Buntin	8	do		"	do	do
	"	William Buntin	7	Male		"	do	do
	13	Arsin Sortie	30	Male	Trader	St. Domingo	France	St. Domingo
	18	Francis Hogg	57	"	Farmer	Greenock	Britain	Britain
	"	William Ireson	30	"	Merchant	"	do	N. York
	"	John Stewart	28	"	Do	"	do	do
	19	James McCully	18	Male	Farmer	Belfast	Britain	U. States
	"	Stephen McCully	17	"	do	"	do	do
	"	Henry Irwin	22	"	do	"	do	do
	"	John Murchie	28	"	do	"	do	do
	20	Lepar Lefleur	21	Female	L. Spinster	Nantz	U States	Nantz
	"	Galbaud	22	do	Servant	"	France	"
	"	P. Machallette	40	Male	Merchant	Havanna	U States	N. York
	"	John Sennett	25	do	Trader	"	Britain	U. States
	"	John Burk	23	do	do	"	do	do
	"	Joseph Barden	28	do	do	"		
	"	Gregory Hexnera	35	do	do	"	Spain	Havanna
	"	Antonio Moro	25	do	do	"	"	"
	24	Aron Lyon	30	do	Physician	St. Jago	U States	Savanna died 12 April 1820
	26	Michael McCobb	35	Male	Labourer	Liverpool	Britain	U States
	"	James Maynard	37	"	Baker	"	do	do
	"	William Maynard	16	"	Barber	"	do	do
	"	George Levan	39	"	Turner	"	do	do
	26	Joseph Gilchrist		"		Matanzes	Spain	St. Augustine
Drew	27	John Durbec	13	Female		do	U States	Charleston
	"	Mrs. Brown	30	Female	Lady	Havanna	Britain	New Providence
	"	Harriott Brown	5)	do		"	"	"
	"	Augustus Brown	3)	Male	children	"	"	"
	"	Caroline Brown	2)	Female		"		
	"	Francis Peyre Jun.	25	Male	Planter	"	U States	Charleston
	"	Robert Child	29	do	Mechanic	"	do	Philadelphia
	"	Joseph Dehagris	30	do	Merchant	"	Spain	New Providence
	"	Harriott	25	Female	Servant	"	Britain	do

5

PASSENGERS ARRIVING AT THE PORT OF CHARLESTON 1820-1829

Name of vessels	Date arrival	Passengers' names	Age	Sex	Occupation	Where from	Country- belong	Country- inhabit
	May 3 1820	Capt. L. Courtois	52	Male	Mariner	Havre de Grass	France	Charleston
	"	Madam Courtois	28	Female	"	"	"	"
	"	Lewis Courtois	6	Male	"	"	"	"
	5	Samuel Cook	37	"	Merchant	St. Augustine	United States	"
	"	Hugh McNary	26	"	do	"	"	"
	"	Thomas Briggs	37		Planter			
	8	Monsieur Martin	25	Male	Doctor	Havre	France	France
	"	Madam Martin	20	Female				
Phoeby	9	Alexander Gregg	24	Male	Baker	Greenock	Britain	Charleston
	"	Gilbert Taylor	24	"	Farmer	"	"	Wilmington
Howland[?]		Henry Janny	60		Labourer	Liverpool	Britain	U States
		Robert Janny	55	"	"	"	"	"
		Mary Janny	46	Female	"	"	"	"
		Harriet Janny	23	"	"	"	"	"
		Louisa Janny	20	"	"	"	"	"
		Mary A. Jenny	17	"	"	"	"	"
		Ellen Jenny	15	"	"	"	"	"
		Elizabeth Janny	13	"	"	"	"	"
		Margaret Janny	12	Female	"	"	"	"
	11	Michael Harvey	32	Male	Mechanic	Havanna	Britain	Charleston
	"	Polly Quick	30	Female	Spinster	"	U States	"
	"	Rebecca Buire	45	"	"	"	"	"
	"	James Chambore	38	Male	Dyer	"	France	"
	15	Andrew Friddle	30	do	Merchant	"	German	"
	"	Nicholas Gardiner	30	"	Marriner	St. Augustine	U States	Rhode Island
	"	John M. Sanchez	22	"	Merchant	"	Spain	Augustine
	"	John Pelliser	26	"	do	"	do	do
	"	George W. Ozden	40	"		"	U States	New York
	"	------ Shaddock	18	"	Marriner	"	do	Charleston
	-- --	------------	--	"	--		Britain	
	22	John Stewart	28	"		Nassau	France	U States
	"	Rachael DePass	28	"		St. Thomas	Britain	"
	23	Adolphus Eschen	18	Female		Havanna	U States	Charleston
	"	Samuel Goodrey	30	Male		"	"	"
	"	John Lopez	24	"		"	"	"
	"	Henry Heldebram	32	"		"	Hambourgh	"
	"	Issabella Heldebram	45	Female		"	do	"
Ceres	24	John Machoen	28	Male	Cabinet maker	Liverpool	Britain	New York
	"	Marshall Luker	23	"	Shoe maker	Havanna	U States	Charleston
	"	George Scott	22	"	Trader	"	"	"
	"	Joseph Mathews	45	"		"	"	"
	29	Seth Austin	48	"	Merchant	Bermuda	U States	New York

PASSENGERS ARRIVING AT THE PORT OF CHARLESTON 1820-1829

Name of vessels	Date arrival	Passengers' names	Age	Sex	Occupation	Where from	Country- belong	Country- inhabit
	29	Jonathan Rathb--	28	Male	Merchant	Bermuda	U States	New York
	"	----- King	15	"	Yeoman	"	Britain	Charleston
	May 29 1820	------ Clark	15	Male	Yeoman	Bermuda	Britain	Charleston
	--	Mrs. Dalton	45	Female	Lady	London	do	do
	"	David Wood	25	Male	Tailor	"	do	do
	"	Two sons	children					
	"	Hugh Levingston	45	Male	Marriner	Greenock[?]	"	"
	"	James Smith	23	"	Clerk	"	"	"
	"	Hugh Olive[r?]	25	"	do	"	"	"
	"	Agnes Olive[r?]	24	Female		"	"	"
	June 1st	William Craig	20	Male	Labourer	Havanna	U States	Kentucky
	"	William Jerry	28	Male	none	"	do	do
	"	L. Blanten	35	"		"	Spain	Cuba
	"	Antonio Garrier	35	"	Trader	"	U S	Bath
	"	Jacob Drummond	32	"	Mariner	"	Holland	N York
	7	William Dustch	28	"	Merchant	Havanna	Spain	"
	"	Manuel Fernandez	60	"		"		"
	"	Peter Pelow	35	"		"		"
	"	Pedres Isazalata	40	Female		"		"
	"	Venison Salsald	55	"		"	U S	"
	"	Mrs. OBrian		Female		"	Spain	"
	8	Ingliso & Servant	58	Males	Labourer	Greenock	Britain	No Carolina
	"	Andrew Munroe	18	Male		"	-------	-------
	"	Christiana Munroe	25	Female		------	-------	-------
	14	James OConnor	35	Male		St. Augustine	U States	-------
	17	Nathaniel Green Clary	32	"	------	"	"	"
	"	Andrew McDowell	30	"	Merchant	"	"	St. Augustine
	"	G. Ward	24	"		"		Columbia
	"	D. Sanchez	25	"		"	Spain	St. Augustine
	"	John Taylor		"		"	U States	"
	"	Deveraux		"		"	Spain	"
	"	Perrier		"		"	"	"
	"	Carrier		"	Marriner	"		
	"	Fortune	24	"	Merchant	St. Domingo	U States	N. York
	"	Francis Burke	24	"	Trader	"	Britain	Trinidad
	"	Asa Harmon	59	"	Mariner	"	U States	Connecticut
	"	Asa Harmon	19	"	Clerk	"	"	"
	23	William Kennau	30	"		Havanna	Britain	Charleston
	"	James Hamelton	28	"	Merchant	"	U States	N. York
	"	Michael Oconnor	38	"	do	"	Britain	Savanna
	"	John Hurting	25	"	----	"	U S	Baltimore
	"	John G. Wade	24	"	----	"	--	-------

Date arrival	Vessels name	Master	Where from	Passengers' names	Sex	Age	Occupation	Country- belong	Country- inhabit
July 4 1820	Sloop Lady Washington	Watterman	St. Augustine	Oliver OHarra	Male	31	Merchant	U States	Charleston
				Charles Sully	"	36	"	"	St. Augustine
				William Travers	"	30	"	"	Charleston
				John Williams	"	24	Marriner		do
				Mrs. McCauley	Female	20		Spain	St. Augustine
				John Carraras	Male	29	Shoe Maker		do
				Bartholomew Janeworth		20			do
				Capt. Walton		27	Marriner	British	do
10	Schooner Mary	Coleman	Matanzes	Madam Chimenard	Female	28	Lady	France	Charleston
				John Oates	Male	60	Shop Keeper	France	"
				John Burke	"	28	"	Breton	"
				Anthony Colingen	"	27	"		"
				William Canuet	"	32	"	France	"
"	Sloop James	Vincent	Fernandina	Major Bird	Male	42	Officer USA	U S	U S
				Lieutenant Leigle	"	20	"	"	"
				Holmes	"	19	"	"	"
				Humphreys	"	19	"	"	"
15	Schooner Comet	N. Forsyth	Havanna	John Barckley	Male	35	Merchant	U S	Havanna
				John Wheeler	"	33	"	"	Charleston
				William Jerrassy	"	30	"	"	
24	Ship Portia	Silliman	----	Bottellier	Male	38	Marriner	France	U S
				Fugerson	"	26	Merchant	Britain	"
				Rachait	Female	--	Seamstress	----	"
26	Schooner Jane	Darling	Florida	Niel Campbell	Male	35	Merchant	U S	U S
27	Schooner Jane	McMillan	Havanna	James Pearson	Male	25	Marriner	Britain	U S
				John Brown	"	44	Marriner	U S	"
				William Marshall	"	25		"	"
30	Ship Arab	Bingham	Liverpool	James M. Mathewson	Male	35	Gentleman	Hambourgh	U S
Aug 2	Brig Christopher	Hayward	Ditto	Pierce Rowe	Male	26	Farmer	Britain	St. Augustine
"	Sloop Gen. Washington	Buckley	St. Augustine	Franklin Goram	Male	35	Merchant	U S	Washington N C
				Joel Dickinson	"	40	do	"	do
4	Lady Washington	Waterman	Ditto	John Andrews	"	30	Marriner	U S	N. York
				Geo. Delespine	"	32	Merchant	Spain	Augustine
				Anthony Tray	"	28	do	"	"
				Joseph Bunnett	"	25	Marriner	"	"
-	Schooner Planter	Osborn	Bermuda	Francis Saltus & Lady	Male	60/50	Merchant	U S	Charleston
				Francis Yates	Male	19		"	"
				Eliza Burch	Female	40		"	"
				Ruthy Righton	do	30		"	"
Aug 4 1820	Sloop James	Vincent	Florida	B. Cooper	Male	45	Marriner	Britain	"
"				James Bentham	Male	33	Merchant	U S	"

PASSENGERS ARRIVING AT THE PORT OF CHARLESTON 1820-1829

Date arrival	Vessels name	Master	Where from	Passengers' names	Sex	Age	Occupation	Country- belong	Country- inhabit
Aug 9 1820	Schooner Mary Ann	Hilliard	Havanna	Joseph Elairo		28	Marriner	Brazil	U S
9	Brig Eliza	Chazell	Ditto	C. Bowman		"	"	Charleston	Charleston
18	Brig Catherine	Wellsman	Do	John Henderson		24	Merchant	U S	N. Orleans
				Bazella Gonzales		30	do	Spain	U S
				John Lopez		36	"	Portugal	Charleston
				William Phillbrick		27	"	U S	Savanna
28	Ship South Carolina	Easterby	Liverpool	William Ward	Male	-7	Merchant	Britain	U S
				Mary Ward	Female	26	Lady	"	"
				Eliza Ann do	do	--		"	"
29	Brig Carolinian	McIntosh	Barracoa	Jack Aiken	Male	--	Servant	U S	Charleston
				Theodore Sheafe	Male	23	Merchant	U S	Portsmouth, N.H.
				Gorham Bassett	"	32	Marriner	"	"
				Hugh Staples	"	23	do	"	"
Sept 3	Schooner Comet	Forsyth	Havanna	Rufus S. Kidman	"	25	Gentleman	U S	U S
				Dr.	"	33	Doctor M.	"	"
				James Bowers	"	34	Merchant	"	"
14	Ship Sybil	Belcher	Liverpool	Mrs. Mary Belcher	Female	32	Lady	U S	U S
				Miss Mary Reed	"	28	"	"	"
				Anna Belcher	"	3		"	"
				Mary Belcher	"	2		"	"
"	Ship Octavia	Wilson	Ditto	Margaret Huise	"	19	Spinster	Britain	"
19	Schooner Alexandria	Smith	Augustine	Samuel Cook	Male	35	Shop Keeper	U S	Charleston
				Joseph Argotie	"	25		Spain	Spain
				Daniel Gaillard	"	21	Gentleman	U S	Charleston
				William Parker	"	25	"	"	"
24	Brig Susan	Pollock	Belfast	James Magie	"	19	Farmer	Britain	U S
				Mary McGuire	Female	18	Spinster	do	do
				Lucy Buntin	do	14	do	do	do
25	Ship Fama	Barry	Liverpool	John F. Walker	Male	23	Merchant	do	Charleston
				Henry Knust	"	47		do	"
				William H. Capers	"	19	Marriner	U S	"
				Mrs. Smith	Female	26	Spinster	Britain	"
				her Two Children				"	"
				Michell	"	24	"	"	"
26	Brig Commerce	Messer--	Hav--	Emills		18	Clerk	--	Charleston
				F. Monbrun		20	"	France	"
				M. Brodut		27	"	"	"
28	Ship Charles & Henry	Carsdoff	Amsterdam	Mr. Vanhaldren	Male	38	Tailor	Holland	Charleston
				Mrs. Vanhaldren	Female	28	"	"	"
				Michael Vanhaldren	Male	5		"	"

PASSENGERS ARRIVING AT THE PORT OF CHARLESTON 1820-1829

Name of vessel	Passengers names	Age	Sex	Date of arrival	Occupation	Where from	Country- belong	Country- inhabit
Schooner Hokee	Peter Larguerelle	?	Male	October 2d 1820	Silver Smith	St. Augustine	France	U. S.
Schooner Jane	Capt Hunt	43	do	" 1	Marriner	Havanna	U. S.	Charleston
	Edward Morris	22	do	"	Merchant	"	"	"
	S. Boshee	28	do	"	"	"	"	"
Brig Hero	J. G. Doberney	26	do	" 4	Gentleman	"	France	"
	Adolphus J Laboindette	25	"	"	"	"	"	"
	Domingo Groadino	42	"	"	Marriner	"	Spain	"
	Thomas Temanes	45	"	"	"	"	"	"
Brig Catherine	Anthony Yorlick	60	"	" 14	Merchant	"	"	"
	John Lopez	35	"	"	"	"	"	"
	Adam Miller	40	"	"	Free person of color	"	"	"
Brig Comely	James McDonnell	18	"	" 17	Baker	Dundee	Britain	"
Brig Phoeby	James Maron	22	"	" 20	Labourer	Greenock	"	"
	William Hanna	20	"	"	Farmer	"	"	"
	William Richman	23	"	"	Clerk	"	"	"
	Charles Fergerson	20	"	"	Farmer	"	"	"
	William Barker	21	"	"	"	"	"	"
	George Robertson	30	"	"		"	"	"
	James Dow	30	"	"		"	"	"
	David Oswald	20	"	"		"	"	"
	James Bill	19	"	"		"	"	"
	James Barr	20	"	"		"	"	"
	James Findley	38	"	"		"	"	"
	John McNeill	23	"	"		Dundee	"	"
Brig Trafalgar	James Hayden) 8 children	47	Female	" 23		"	"	"
	Elizabeth do) children	45	Male	"		"	"	"
	James Holstock	28	Male	" 24	Labourer	"	"	"
Schooner Mary	John Decamp	56	"	"	Planter	Havanna	"	"
	Mrs. Decamp	40	Female	"	Lady	"	"	"
	John Marshall	55	Male	"	Merchant	"	"	"
	James Poyas	55	"	"	Gentleman	"	"	"
	Clara Dechamp	14	Female	"		"	"	"
	Jeremia do	10	Male	"		"	"	"
	Emanuel do	2	"	"		"	"	"
	John do	6	"	"		"	"	"
	Cecil Aurancier	40	Female	"	Coloured Free Woman	"	"	"
Schooner Antelope	William McCormick	35	Male	Oct 26	Augustine	Shop Keeper	Britain	Charleston
Ship	James Turnbull	56	"	"	Greenock	House Carpenter	"	"
Roger Stewart	John Ballantyne	21	"	Nov 3	"	Mason	"	"
	Alexander Brown	29	"	"				

PASSENGERS ARRIVING AT THE PORT OF CHARLESTON 1820-1829

Name of Vessel	Passengers names	Age	Sex	Date of arrival	Where from	Occupation	Country-belong	Country-inhabit
Schooner Alexander	Elizabeth Taylor	45	Female	Nov 3 1820	Augustine	Spinster	Britain	Charleston
	James Hassell	45	Male	"	"	Marriner	US	"
	Pierre Perrie	18	"	"	"	"	France	"
Ship Robert Fulton	Brada Jerrissa	25	Female	"	"	Free Color'd Woman	Spain	"
	Robert McCully	23	Male	"	Belfast	Tutor	Britain	"
	John Longman	22	"	"	"	Farmer	"	"
	John Sinclair	28	"	"	"	"	"	"
	David Walker	33	"	"	"	"	"	"
	Mary do	33	Female	"	"	"	"	"
	Issabella do	11	"	"	"	"	"	"
	Hugh do	9	Male	"	"	"	"	"
	John do	7	"	"	"	"	"	"
	William Moore	50	"	"	"	"	"	"
	Janet do	45	Female	"	"	"	"	"
	Nathaniel do	17	Male	"	"	"	"	"
	Thomas do	13	"	"	"	"	"	"
	Robert do	8	"	"	"	"	"	"
	John do	3	"	"	"	"	"	"
	Elizabeth do	24	Female	"	"	"	"	"
	Janet do	3	"	"	"	"	"	"
	Isaac Walker	26	Male	"	"	"	"	"
	Hugh Taylor	40	"	"	"	"	"	"
	Eleanor do	35	Female	"	"	"	"	"
	John do	10	Male	"	"	"	"	"
	Robert do	7	"	"	"	"	"	"
	William do	3	"	"	"	"	"	"
	Robert Wilson	21	Female	"	"	"	"	"
	Alexander McCallister	24	"	"	"	"	"	"
	Samuel Woodburn	21	"	"	"	"	"	"
	William Beatie	24	"	"	"	"	"	"
	Alexander McDowell	40	Female	"	"	"	"	"
	Mary do	40	"	"	"	"	"	"
	William do	20	Male	"	"	"	"	"
	Catherine do	18	Female	"	"	"	"	"
	Alexander do	17	Male	"	"	"	"	"
	Mary Ann do	15	Female	"	"	"	"	"
	James do	7	Male	"	"	"	"	"
Ship Robert Foulton	Samuel McDowell	4	Male	"	"	"	"	"
	John do	14	"	"	"	"	"	"
	Anthony do	25	"	"	"	"	"	"
	John Marks	25	"	"	"	"	"	"
	James Graham	44	"	"	"	"	"	"
	Elizabeth do	40	Female	"	"	"	"	"

PASSENGERS ARRIVING AT THE PORT OF CHARLESTON 1820-1829

Name of Vessel	Passengers names	Age	Sex	Date of arrival	Where from	Occupation	Country- belong	Country- inhabit
	James do	10	Male	Nov 3rd 1820	Belfast	Farmers & their children	Britain	Charleston
	Elizabeth do	13	Female	"	"	"	"	"
	Jane do	10	"	"	"	"	"	"
	Jane Gregg	25		"	"	"	"	"
	William do	8	Male	"	"	"	"	"
	Elizabeth Belliout	25	Female	"	"	"	"	"
	James Gray	23	Male	"	"	"	"	"
	Hugh McGraidy	30	"	"	"	"	"	"
	Robert do	20	"	"	"	"	"	"
	Alexander do	27	"	"	"	"	"	"
	Thomas do	12	"	"	"	"	"	"
	Elizabeth do	60	"	"	"	"	"	"
	Elizabeth do	22	"	"	"	"	"	"
	John Keyland	22	Male	"	"	"	"	"
	Martha do	22	Female	"	"	"	"	"
	Ellen do	1	do	"	"	"	"	"
	Susan Mallelet	40	"	"	"	"	"	"
	Allice do	5	"	"	"	"	"	"
	Richard do	4	Male	"	"	"	"	"
	Betty do	3	Female	"	"	"	"	"
	Thomas do	1	Male	"	"	"	"	"
	Joseph Davidson	49	"	"	"	"	"	"
	James do	15	"	"	"	"	"	"
	Margaret Bryson	25	Female	"	"	"	"	"
Ship James Bailey	Joseph Smith	65	Male	"	"	"	"	US
	Thomas do	24	"	"	"	"	"	"
	Moore do	21	"	"	"	"	"	"
	William do	17	"	"	"	"	"	"
	Martha do	24	Female	"	"	"	"	"
	Mary do	20	"	"	"	"	"	"
	Mary Alexander	26	"	"	"	"	"	"
	John do	5	Male	"	"	"	"	"
	Ellen do	3	Female	"	"	"	"	"
	Barnard McCaffrey	21	Male	"	"	"	"	"
	James Browley	26	"	"	"	"	"	"
	James Burns	19	"	"	"	"	"	"
Ship James Bailey	Joseph Gorley	46	Male	"	"	"	"	"
	Eliza do	40	Female	"	"	"	"	"
	Mary do	21	"	"	"	"	"	"
	Sarah do	24	"	"	"	"	"	"
	Margaret do	11	"	"	"	"	"	"
	Eliza do	24	"	"	"	"	"	"
	Robert do	21	Male	"	"	"	"	"

12

PASSENGERS ARRIVING AT THE PORT OF CHARLESTON 1820-1829

Name of vessel	Passengers names	Age	Sex	Date of arrival	Occupation	Where from	Country- belong	Country- inhabit
	Thomas do	4	"	Nove'r 3d 1820	Farmer	Belfast	Britain	U States
	Sally Murry	17	Female	"	"	"	"	"
	Anthony Reford	22	Male	"	"	"	"	"
	Alexander Harper	40	"	"	"	"	"	"
	Jane do	45	Female	"	"	"	"	"
	John do	21	Male	"	"	"	"	"
	James do	15	"	"	"	"	"	"
	Joseph do	10	"	"	"	"	"	"
	Alexander do	8	"	"	"	"	"	"
	Martha do	5	Female	"	"	"	"	"
	Jane do	1	"	"	"	"	"	"
	Betsy McCullock	26	"	"	"	"	"	"
	Samuel Bowman	21	Male	"	"	"	"	"
	Mary Murry	20	Female	"	"	"	"	"
	John Oneale	20	Male	"	"	"	"	"
	Catherine Oneal	13	Female	"	"	"	"	"
	William Crothers	18	Male	"	"	"	"	"
	Francis Wilson	24	"	"	"	"	"	"
Ship Portia	George Lorent	38	"	6	Merchant	Breeman	Germany	"
	C. F. Hugo	25	"	"	Book Binder	"	"	"
Schooner Hookee	Francis P. Sanchez	22	"	10	Merchant	Augustin	Spain	"
	J. Martinelli	36	"	"	Marriner	"	"	"
	R. Fontene	28	"	"	None	"	"	"
	W. Cornmstock	32	"	"	Merchant	"	US	"
	Joseph Sanchez	23	"	"	Planter	"	Spain	"
	William Gray	23	"	"	Sadler	"	US	"
Schooner Virginia	Samuel Cook	37	"	"	Shop Keeper	do	"	"
	James Mathews	43	"		"			
	John Grassett	30	"					
Brig Jane	John Rogers	24	"		Merchant	Liverpool	Britain	"
Schooner Jn Willis	Perry Rennue	13	"		None			
Brig	Mary Orr	36	Female	Novr 11	Merchant	"	"	"
Prince	William McDonald	26	Male	"	Farmer	"	"	"
Leopold	Ann do	23	Female	"	"	"	"	"
	Hugh do	3	Male	"	"	"	"	"
	William Baxter	25	"	"	"	"	"	"
	Charles Laughlin	26	"	"	"	"	"	"
	Samuel Pennel	15	"	"	"	"	"	"
	William Smith	18	"	"	"	"	"	"
	Adam Lauflin	19	"	"	"	"	"	"
	Anthony Sloane	28	"	"	"	"	"	"
	Nathaniel Hunter	22	"	"	"	"	"	"
	William McDowell	30	"	"	"	"	"	"

13

PASSENGERS ARRIVING AT THE PORT OF CHARLESTON 1820-1829

Name of vessel	Passengers names	Age	Sex	Date of arrival	Occupation	Where from	Country- belong	Country- inhabit
	Mary McDowell	25	Female	Novr 11 1820	Spinster	Belfast	Britain	U States
	Ephraim do	8	Male	"		"	"	"
	Margaret do	2	Female	"		"	"	"
	John Baggs	25	Male	"		"	"	"
	Thomas Johnson	38	"	"		"	"	"
	Elizabeth do & child	36	Female	"		"	"	"
	John do	4	Male	"		"	"	"
	James McCullie	42	"	"		"	"	"
	John McGummey	40	"	"		"	"	"
	James do	10	"	"		"	"	"
	Campbell Madden	26	"	"		"	"	"
	James Miller	30	"	"		"	"	"
	Matty do & child	26	Female	"		"	"	"
	Rose do	6	"	"		"	"	"
	Martha do	3	"	"		"	"	"
	Margarett McCulla	20	"	"		"	"	"
	Hugh McDowell	33	Male	"		"	"	"
	John do	14	"	"		"	"	"
	Thomas do	7	"	"		"	"	"
	Mary do	5	Female	"		"	"	"
	Ann do	3	"	"		"	"	"
	Elizabeth Brown	30	"	"		"	"	"
	Can'r McClennigan	24	Male	"		"	"	"
	Robert Pepper	34	"	"		"	"	"
	Jane McDowell	1	Female	"		"	"	"
	Thomas Johnson	2	Male	"		"	"	"
Ship Issabella	William Whiteman	60	Male	Nov 16	Silver Smith	London	U S	Charleston
	Sarah Valk	35	Female	"	None	"	"	"
	Maria do	5	"	"		"	"	"
	Sarah Ann do	3	"	"		"	"	"
	William W do	14	Male	"	Servant	"	"	"
	Sarah Mills	25	Female	"	None	"	"	"
	Pringle	20	Male	"		"	"	"
	do	18	"	"	Merchant	"	"	"
	William Hall	45	"	"		"	Britain	England
	Isaac Lewis	50	"	"		"	"	"
	Niel McNiel	41	"	"		"	U S	Charleston
	Whitfield	18	"	"	None	"	"	"
	S'r James Wright	20	"	"	Servant	"	"	"
	Williams	30	"	"	None	"	Britain	"
	Thomas Vanderherst	50	"	"	Servant	"	"	"
	Alphonzo	30	"	"		"	"	"
	William Aiken	50	"	"	Merchant	"	"	"

PASSENGERS ARRIVING AT THE PORT OF CHARLESTON 1820-1829

Name of vessel	Passengers names	Age	Sex	Date of arrival	Occupation	Where from	Country- belong	Country- inhabit
	Sarah do	40	"	[sic] Nov 16 1820	None	London	U S	Charleston
	William do	15	"	"		"	"	"
	James do	10	"	"		"	"	"
	Nicholas Boilston	48	"	[sic]	Attorney	"	"	"
	Sarah Randall	40	"		Spinster	"	"	"
	William Tennant	50	"		Labourer	"	Britain	"
	Robert West	30	"		"	"	"	"
	Merdicai Simons	20	"		"	"	"	"
	John Cunnigham	60	"		"	"	"	"
	Sarah do	55	"		"	"	"	"
	John Wood	21	"		"	"	"	"
Brig Proteus	Blaise Huber	25	"		Farmer	Havre	Germany	U S
Ship Laburnum	Michael Runa	27	"		"	Liverpool	Britain	"
	John Sweeny	23	"		"	"	"	"
	Richard Collin	24	"		"	"	"	"
Brig Perserverance	George W. Smith	20	"	Nov 18	Merchant	Havanna	U S	Rhode Island
Brig Martha	Dunbar Paul	28	"		"	Liverpool	Britain	Charleston
	William Landsden	30	"		"	"	"	"
	William Matchwing	19	"		"	"	"	"
	George Brown	14	"		"	"	"	"
	William Blair	15	"		"	"	"	"
	Jervis Indle	20	"		"	"	"	"

Name of vessel	Passengers names	Date of arrival	Age	Sex	Occupation	Where from	Country- belong	Country- inhabit
Ship Monarch	Neal McFacran	Novr 20th 1820	40	Male	Farmer	Greenock	Britain	U. States
	John McKinley		60	"	"	"	"	"
	Donald do		18	"	"	"	"	"
	John McNinch		20	"	"	"	"	"
	Dugald McBride		26	"	"	"	"	"
	Malcom Do		28	"	"	"	"	"
	Edward McNier		58	"	"	"	"	"
	Archibald Do		28	"	"	"	"	"
	Edward do		19	"	"	"	"	"
	Niel McNier		17	"	"	"	"	"
	John McGill		55	"	"	"	"	"
	Niel McGill		19	"	"	"	"	"
	Donald do		17	"	"	"	"	"
	Donald McDougald		30	"	"	"	"	"
	John do		18	"	"	"	"	"
	David Mitchell		55	"	"	"	"	"
	John McEckran		30	"	"	"	"	"
	Archibald Brown		28	"	"	"	"	"

PASSENGERS ARRIVING AT THE PORT OF CHARLESTON 1820-1829

Name of vessel	Date of arrival	Passengers names	Age	Sex	Occupation	Where from	Country- belong	Country- inhabit
Ship Monarch	Novr 20th 1820	Malcomb McPhail	47	Male	Farmer	Greenock	Britain	U. States
	"	Archibald McNair	34	"	"	"	"	"
	"	Archibald do	12	"	"	"	"	"
	"	Euphaim McEckran	35	Female	"	"	"	"
	"	Catherine McKinlay	50	"	"	"	"	"
	"	Margaret McBride	25	"	"	"	"	"
	"	Agnes McNair	54	"	"	"	"	"
	"	Elizabeth do	22	"	"	"	"	"
	"	Euphaim McGill	45	"	"	"	"	"
	"	Janet Mitchell	40	"	"	"	"	"
	"	Mary McKinley	18	"	"	"	"	"
	"	Janet McKinron	60	"	"	"	"	"
	"	Catherine do	50	"	"	"	"	"
	"	Mary McNair	15	"	"	"	"	"
	"	Mary McMillan	36	"	"	"	"	"
	"	Mary do Jun	20	"	"	"	"	"
	"	Euphaim Shaw	35	"	"	"	"	"
	"	Mary do	29	"	"	"	"	"
	"	Marion McKeckron	2	"	"	"	"	"
	"	Janet McKinley	9	"	"	"	"	"
	"	Mary McMillan	8	"	"	"	"	"
	"	Marion McMillan	5	"	"	"	"	"
	"	Catherine McMillan	4	"	None	"	"	"
	"	Margarett H. Mitchell	14	"	"	"	"	"
	"	Martha do	3	"		"	"	"
Ship Monarch	"	Mary McGill	9	Female	None	Greenock	Britain	U. States
	"	Donald McEckran	7	Male	"	"	"	"
	"	Duncan McKinley	11	"	"	"	"	"
	"	Duncan McEckran	9	"	"	"	"	"
	"	Niel McKinley	5	"	"	"	"	"
	"	Peter McMillan	10	"	"	"	"	"
	"	James Mitchell	10	"	"	"	"	"
	"	Robert do	8	"	"	"	"	"
	"	David do	6	"	"	"	"	"
	"	Archibald McGill	4	"	"	"	"	"
	"	Jannet McBride	1	"	"	"	"	"
	"	Margaret McBride	1 month	"	"	"	"	"
Schooner Louisa	"	Mrs. Mary Pratt	50	Female		Gibraltar	U. States	Charleston
	"	" Ann do	14	"		"	"	"
	"	Mr. John do	21	Male	Merchant	"	"	"
	"	Mrs. Shields	35	Female	None	"	"	"
Schooner Hiram	"	Daniel Oliver	26	Male	Merchant	Honduras	"	"
	"	John Smith	28	"		"	"	"

16

PASSENGERS ARRIVING AT THE PORT OF CHARLESTON 1820-1829

Name of vessel	Date of arrival	Passengers names	Age	Sex	Occupation	Where from	Country- belong	Country- inhabit
Schooner Hiram	Novr 20th 1820	Francis Tores	40	"	"	"	"	"
Schooner Opposition	"	James Wood	38	"	Marriner	Cuba	"	"
		Peter do	8	"	"	"	"	"
		Thomas White	20	"	"	"	"	"
Sloop Ann	"	Robert Ramsay	30	"	"	"	"	"
		Lancelot Billerly	40		Merchant	Havanna	"	"
		Rebecca Anthony	40	Female	Spinster	"	"	"
		James C. Coher	19	Male	Marriner	"	"	"
Brig Parragon		David Hassoan	22	"	Shoemaker	St. Thomas	Britain	"
		Moses do	25	"	"	"	"	"
Sloop Invincible		Phoenicus Pierce	25	"	Carpenter		U. S.	"
		Andrew Milne	33	"	Merchant	Havanna	Britain	"
		M. E. Levy	47	"	"	"	"	"
		Thomas Chartran	33	"	"	"	France	"
		R. G. Mitchell	30	"	"	"	"	"
Ship John Bainbridge		Thomas Y. Simons	23	Male	Doctor	Liverpool	Charleston	Charleston
		Margaret Do & Child	17	Female	none	"	Britain	"
		Arthur Buist	21	Mal	clergyman	"	Charleston	"
		Susan do	19	Female	none	"	Britain	"
		Jane Ballantine	45	"		"	"	"
		Charles Mayberry	56	Male	Merchant	"	"	"
		Edward Wilkins	36	"	none	"	"	"
		James Brett	66	"	Farmer	"	"	"
		Elijah Tourney	12	Female	None	"	"	"
		Mary Brett	46	"		"	"	"
Ship John Bainbridge		Patrichell Brett	25	Male	Bookkeeper	"	"	"
		William M. do	19	"	Farmer	"	"	"
		Mary do	20	Female	none	"	"	"
		Ellen do	10	"		"	"	"
		Ann do	11	"		"	"	"
		Joakim do	7	"	"	"	"	"
		Thomas do	21	Male	Farmer	"	"	"
		Patrick Ryan	22	"	"	"	"	"
		Thomas Purcell	25	"	"	"	"	"
		Pierce Choel	23	"		"	"	"
		Patrick Heartly	29	"	Mason	"	"	"
		Julia Heartly	22	Female	none	"	"	"
		Mary Heartly	6 months	"		"	"	"
		William do	23	Male	Farmer	"	"	"
		Daniel Flin	23	"		"	"	"
		Francis Russell	21	"	Mason	"	"	"
		Thomas Long	24	"	Mason		"	"
		Michael Maham	21	"	Grocer	"	"	"

17

PASSENGERS ARRIVING AT THE PORT OF CHARLESTON 1820-1829

Name of vessel	Date of arrival	Passengers names	Age	Sex	Occupation	Where from	Country- belong	Country- inhabit
Ship John Bainbridge	Novr 20th 1820	Donie Ryan	25	Male	Diaper	Liverpool	Britain	Charleston
	"	Chartom do	21	Female	Spinster	"	"	"
	"	John do	3	Male	None	"	"	"
	"	Ann do	6 months	Female		"	"	"
	"	Julia do	14	Female		"	"	"
	"	Patrick Walsh	32	Male	School master	"	"	"
	"	Elizabeth do	30	Female	None	"	"	"
	"	Johanny do	8	Male	"	"	"	"
	"	Thomas do	6	Male	"	"	"	"
	"	John do	5	"	"	"	"	"
	"	Edward do	3	"	"	"	"	"
Ship Jane	"	James Brett	7	Male	Farmers & family	Belfast	Britain	U. States
	"	James Young	48	Male	"	"	"	"
	"	Ann do & son & daughter	46	Female	"	"	"	"
	"	Susan Ferres	48	Female	"	"	"	"
	"	John Moore	50	Male	"	"	"	"
	"	Janet do	50	Female		"	"	"
	"	Martha do	28	Female		"	"	"
	"	Agnes do	16	"		"	"	"
	"	Jane do	14	"		"	"	"
	"	John do	20	Male		"	"	"
	"	David do	11	"		"	"	"
	"	Thomas do	8	"		"	"	"
	"	Janet Moore	5	Female		"	"	"
Ship Jane	"	Robert Coleman	24	Male		"	"	"
	"	Sarah do	24	Female		"	"	"
	"	Samuel do	4	Male		"	"	"
	"	Issabella do	1	Female		"	"	"
	"	William Moore	28	Male		"	"	"
	"	Ester do & 2 children	24	Female		"	"	"
	"	William Junkin	45	Male		"	"	"
	"	Elizabeth do	43	Female		"	"	"
	"	Margarett do	24	Female		"	"	"
	"	William do	22	Male		"	"	"
	"	Samuel do	16	do		"	"	"
	"	Robert do	14	do		"	"	"
	"	Rachael Cambrian	20	Female		"	"	"
	"	Alexander Stewart	24	Male		"	"	"
	"	David Robinson	24	Male		"	"	"
	"	Rachael do & child	23	Female		"	"	"
	"	William Young	15	Male		"	"	"
	"	Richard Coulthard	30	"		"	"	"
	"	Alexander Mawhinney	40	"		"	"	"

PASSENGERS ARRIVING AT THE PORT OF CHARLESTON 1820-1829

Name of vessel	Date of arrival	Passengers names	Age	Sex	Occupation	Where from	Country- belong	Country- inhabit
Ship Jane	Novr 20th 1820	Jane do & 8 children	40	Female	Farmers & family	Belfast	Britain	U. States
	"	James Dunn	24	Male	"	"	"	"
	"	Bella do & child	23	Female	"	"	"	"
	"	Daniel McMullin	70	Male	"	"	"	"
	"	Mary do	70	Female	"	"	"	"
	"	Charles Hay	40	Male	"	"	"	"
	"	James McMullin	34	"	"	"	"	"
	"	Ann do & 3 children	30	Female	"	"	"	"
	"	John McClacklan	20	Male	Farmer	"	"	"
	"	Francis Tolins	27	"	"	"	"	"
	"	Alexander Campbell	35	"	"	"	"	"
	"	Ann do & 3 children	28	Female	"	"	"	"
Schooner Eudora	Decr 1	P. Micalati	40	Male	Merchant	Havanna	U S	New York
	"	William McCleod	30	"	"	"	"	Charleston
	"	David Goria	25	"	"	"	"	"
	"	A. Mores	26	"	"	"	"	"
	"	John Matanis	40	"	"	"	"	"
	"	John Rodrigues	40	"	"	"	"	Havanna
	"	S. Morrisson	30	"	"	"	"	"
	"	Caroline Manuel	30	Female	"	"	Spain	"
Schooner Alexander	Decr 6	Elizabeth Taylor	40	Female	Trader	Augustine	U S	Charleston
	"	Sarah Phillips	64	"	"	"	"	"
	"	Jane Lindsay	14	"	"	"	"	"
	"	John Laguira	35	Male	"	"	"	"
	"	Mrs do	30	Female	"	"	"	"
Schooner Alexander	Decr 6	John Pepperer	21	Male	"	"	"	"
	"	Clarissa Edinborough	25	Female	"	"	"	"
Ship Arethusa	Decr 7	Robert Turnbull	17	Male	None	None	U S	Charleston
	"	James Green	24	"	Merchant	Merchant	Britain	U S
	"	Mary Ann do	19	Female	None	None	U S	Charleston
Ship So Boston	Decr 17	Robert Maxwell	45	Male	Merchant	Liverpool	U S	Charleston
	"	Mary do	45	Female	None	"	"	"
	"	Eliza Huxham	50	"	"	"	"	"
	"	Robert E. Ludlow	29	Male	"	"	"	"
	"	Mary ditto	29	Female	"	"	"	"
	"	A. E. Williman	45	"	"	"	"	"
	"	Mary Betthune	16	"	"	"	"	"
	"	George Hervey	33	Male	Merchant	Britain	"	"
	"	Charles Clark	35	"	"	"	"	"
	"	Thomas A. Hindlay	40	"	"	"	"	"
	"	Alexander Grant	41	"	"	"	"	"
	"	Alexander Denniston	26	"	"	"	"	"
	"	William Christie	35	"	"	"	"	"

19

PASSENGERS ARRIVING AT THE PORT OF CHARLESTON 1820-1829

Name of vessel	Date of arrival	Passengers names	Age	Sex	Occupation	Where from	Country- belong	Country- inhabit
	Decr 17 1820	William Jenner	36	"	Merchant	Britain	U S	Charleston
	"	William Drummond	13	"	"	"	"	"
	"	William Huldsworth	22	"	"	"	"	"
	"	John Irwing	20	"	"	"	"	"
	"	John White	52	"	"	"	"	"
Brig Julia	Decr 18	Frederick Trevanus	33	Male	Merchant	Havanna	Germany	U States
Steam Ship	Decr 20	William Fayest	25	"	"	"	U States	"
Robt Foulton	"	James McCouen	35	"	"	"	"	"
	"	Madaza	40	"	"	"	"	"
	"	Pedal Parceval	15	"	"	"	"	"
	"	Simon Claudier	16	"	"	"	"	"
Brig Cervantes	Decr 26	Robert Taylor	21	"	Marriner	Gibraltar	"	"
	"	John Lohman	27	"	Merchant	"	Germany	"
Brig Hiram	Decr 27	Francis Morea	24	"	Clergyman	Porto Prince	France	"
	"	Dominica Sherbur	25	"	"	"	"	"
Ship Thomas Gibson	Decr 27	George Sherry	22	Male	Farmer & wifes	Belfast	Britain	U States
	"	Margarett do	22	Female	"	"	"	"
	"	Sarah do	22	child	"	"	"	"
	"	Mary Dorrah	27	Female	"	"	"	"
	"	Sarah Walsh	22	Male [sic]	"	"	"	"
	"	Thomas McCleland	47	"	"	"	"	"
	"	Sarah do	46	Female	"	"	"	"
	"	Ann do	60	"	"	"	"	"
	"	Robert do	21	Male	"	"	"	"
	"	David do	17	"	"	"	"	"
	"	John do	12	Male	"	"	"	"
	"	Mary do	1	Female	"	"	"	"
	"	James Falconer	44	Male	"	"	"	"
	"	Mary do	50	Female	"	"	"	"
	"	William do	25	Male	"	"	"	"
	"	Sarah do	60	Female	"	"	"	"
	"	Elder do	28	Male	"	"	"	"
	"	Nancy Wallace	36	Female	"	"	"	"
	"	Martha	12	"	"	"	"	"
	"	Eliza	10	"	"	"	"	"
	"	Ann	7	"	"	"	"	"
	"	William	5	Male	"	"	"	"
	"	Margaret	1	Female	"	"	"	"
	"	William Elliott	24	Male	"	"	"	"
	"	Alexander Ferguson	50	Male	"	"	"	"
	"	Catherine do	50	Female	"	"	"	"
	"	John do	24	Male	"	"	"	"
	"	Alexander do Jun	22	"	"	"	"	"

20

PASSENGERS ARRIVING AT THE PORT OF CHARLESTON 1820-1829

Name of vessel	Date of arrival	Passengers names	Age	Sex	Occupation	Where from	Country- belong	Country- inhabit
Ship Thomas Gibson	Decr 27 1820	Jane do	19	Female	Farmer & wifes	Belfast	Britain	U States
	"	William do	14	Male	"	"		"
	"	Eliza do	10	Female	"	"		"
	"	Bell do	6			"		"
	"	Thomas Lyle	55	Male		"		"
	"	Rose do	60	Female		"		"
	"	Mary do	22	"		"		"
	"	Rose do Jun	20	"		"		"
	"	William do	14	Male		"		"
	"	John Kelso	22	"		"		"
	"	Jane do	21	Female		"		"
	"	Rachael do child	2			"		"
	"	James Sherry	56	Male		"		"
	"	Jane do	59	Female		"		"
	"	William McGakin	22	Male		"		"
	"	John Boyle	26	"		"		"
	"	James Murrin	48	"		"		"
	"	John Spence	40	"		"		"
	"	R. Hamilton	23	Male		"		"
	"	John do	20	"		"		"
	"	William Young	22	"		"		"
	"	Sarah Falconer	26	Female		"		"
	"	John Graham	53	Male		"		"
	December	Ann do	52	Female		"		"
	"	Martha McConnell	50			"		"
	"	Doctor England	40	Male	Clergyman	"		"
	"	Judah do	20	Female	None	"		"
	"	Henry Aukin	20	Male		"		"
Schooner Washington	"	Abraham Green	32	Male	Marriner	Matanzes	U States	"
	"	James Sargeant	26	"	Merchant	"		"
	"	Timothy White	17		Farmer	"		"
Schooner Mary	"	Miss Kinsburry	30	Female	Schoolmistress	"		"
	"	Amelia Cockerin	40	"		"		"
Brig Catherine	"	John Lopez	40	Male	Trader	Havana	France	"
	"	Joseph Mathews	50	"		"	Spain	"
	"	David Black	27	"		"		"
	"	George Munro	33	"	Marriner	"	U S	"
Ship Jane	"	Merde McKenzie	20	Male	Merchant	Liverpool		Died on the Passage
	"	William McMullin	24	"	Bookkeeper	"	Britain	U States
	"	George McLehose	22	"		"		"
	"	Christpher Mathews	24	"		"		"
	"	Robert Powers	20	"		"		"
	"	John McRae	20	"		"		"

PASSENGERS ARRIVING AT THE PORT OF CHARLESTON 1820-1829

Name of vessel	Date of arrival	Passengers names	Age	Sex	Occupation	Where from	Country- belong	Country- inhabit
Ship Jane	December 1820	John McDougald	22	Male	Cordwinder	Liverpool	Britain	U States
	"	Thomas McMillan	16	"	Shopkeeper	"	"	"
	"	John Dixon	47	"	"	"	"	"
	"	Thomas Thompson	17	"	None	"	"	"
	"	Archibald Hetcher	20	"	Merchant	"	"	"
	"	John Dixon	41	"	do	"	"	"
	"	Mary do	38	Female	None	"	"	"
	"	Ann do	6	"	"	"	"	"
	"	Agnes do	3	"	"	"	"	"
	"	Sarah Douthwait	36	"	"	"	"	"
	"	Donald Furguson	25	Male	"	"	"	"
	"	Robert Crawford	24	"	Labourer	"	"	"
	"	Eliza do	20	Female	"	"	"	"
	"	James Crawford	2 1/2	Male	"	"	"	"
	"	Thomas do infant	6 mos	"	"	"	"	"
	"	Ninian Thompson	30	"	"	"	"	"
	"	Mary do	27	Female	"	"	"	"
	"	Jane Gilchrist	20	"	"	"	"	"

PASSENGERS ARRIVING AT THE PORT OF CHARLESTON 1820-1829

Name of vessel	Passengers' names	Date of arrival	Age	Sex	Occupation	Where from	Country- belong	Country- inhabit
Ship Corsair	John Lowden & Lady	November 1821 34	33	man & wife	Merchant	Liverpool	Britain	U S
	Don Diago Carran	"	47	Male	None	"	Spain	So America
	Mrs. Elizabeth do	"	30	Female	do	"	Britain	"
	Andrew McDowall	"	31	Male	Merchant	"	do	U S
	Mrs. P. do	"	24	Female	none	"	U S	"
	Andrew Henderson	"	25	Male	Merchant	"	Britain	"
	Joseph Harrison	"	21	"	do	"	do	do
	Stephen Watson	"	24	"	do	"	do	do
	Geo Grairsson	"	22	"	do	"	do	do
	Mathewson	"	24		Teacher	"	do	"
Sloop Ann	Silvesto Domingo	"	35	Male	Trader	Matanzes	Portuguese	U S
	Louisa Venzey	"	33	Female	None	"	Spain	"
	Caroline do	"	16	"		"	"	"
Schooner	B. Gonsalves	"	38	Male	Trader	Havana	"	"
Mary Ann	J. P. Barre [Burre?]	"	28	"	do	"	France	"
	E. Chisolm	"	16	"	Marriner	"	U S	"
	Samuel Corman	"	22	"		"		"
	Adam free man	"	28	"	Trader	"	Africa	"
	Laura do woman	"	24	Female	do	"		"
— Eudora	Edward Buckler	"	24	Male	Merchant	"	France	"
	J. Slanter	"	35	"	Clerk	"	U S	"
Schoo'r Betsy & Peggy	Manuel Fernandez	"	39	"	Trader	"	Portugal	"
Ship Homer	George Welden	"	23	"	Labourer	Greenock	Britain	"
	Niel McDuffee	"	24	"	"	"	"	"
	John Patterson	"	22	"	"	"	"	"
	Niel McPhail	"	26	"		"	"	"
	Janet do	"	40	Female	None	"	"	"
Brig Phoeby	Bell McPherson	"	15	"	"	"	"	"
	Janet McNair	"	40	"	"	"	"	"
	Barbara do	"	2	"	"	"	"	"
	Jane do	"	11	"	"	"	"	"
	Janet do	"	5	"	"	"	"	"
	Eliza do	"	3 1/2	"	"	"	"	"
	James McDowall	"	17	Male	Labourer	"	"	"
	John do	"	13	"	"	"	"	"
	Marian Douglass	"	23	Female	None	"	"	"
	Wm Wilkie	"	18	Male	"	"	"	"
	James Wilson	"	25	"		"	"	"
	Elizabeth Marshall	"	28	Female	"	"	"	"
	Ann V. do	"	8	"	"	"	"	"
	Elizabeth & Amelia	"	75	"		"	"	"
	William Shields	"	35	Male		"	"	"

PASSENGERS ARRIVING AT THE PORT OF CHARLESTON 1820-1829

Name of vessel	Passengers' names	Date of arrival	Age	Sex	Occupation	Where from	Country- belong	Country- inhabit
Ship Adriana	Ramin Cheves	November 1821	34	Male	Taylor	France	France	U S
	H. N. Vest	"	35		Architect	do	do	"
Schoo'r Decatur	Jonathan Cooper	"	20		Planter	Porto Prince	U S	U S
	John Noga	"	26		Marriner	"	"	"
Brig Galen	John Salter	"	35		"	Turks Isle	"	"
Sloop	James L. Brown	"	35	Male	Merchant	Havana	Holland	U S
Gen Washington	Mrs. H. do	"	38	Female	None	"	Hambourgh	"
	William Welsh	"	35	Male	Taylor	"	Britain	"
	William do Ju'r	"	6		None	"	"	"
Schooner	Joseph Delamore	"	22	Male	Planter	"	"	"
Comet	Thomas Mara	"	19		"	"	Cuba	"
	C. M. Dumoulin	"	22		Merchant	"	France	"
	J. Ross	"	27		Mariner	"	"	"
Ship	Dr. Richardson, Lady & daughter	50 35 15	Man & Wife & dau	Physician	Liverpool	U S	"
So Carolina	Mrs. Campbell & daughter	50 18	Mother & dau	None	"	"	"
	Miss Coffin	"	19	Female	"	"	"	"
	" Field	"	30	"	"	"	"	"
	Dr. Hannah	"	24	Male	Physician	"	Britain	"
	John Paul	"	37	"	Merchant	"	"	"
Schooner Eliza	John McKenzie	"	41	"	None	"	"	"
	Charles Goodshee	"	21	"	Shoemaker	Matanzes	"	"
Ship	Edward Phillips	"	21	"	Farmer	Belfast	"	"
James Bailey	Samuel Adams	"	36	"	"	"	"	"
	Robert Wilson	"	30	"	"	"	"	"
	John Adams & Wife	"	24 & 25	Man & wife		"	"	"
	Isaac Walker	"	4			"	"	"
	Samuel Ewart	"	23			"	"	"
	Margaret Rennedy	"	45	Female		"	"	"
	William Kennedy	"	20	Male		"	"	"
	Betty do	"	22	Female		"	"	"
	Samuel McCohet	"	21	Male		"	"	"
	William Dunlop	"	19			"	"	"
	Thomas & Martha Bogs	"	32 32	Man & wife		"	"	"
	James, Willm, Thomas & David	"	from 11 to 1	boys		"	"	"
	Betty do	"	4	Female		"	"	"
	James & Agnes McClure	"	60 60	Man & Wife	Apothecary	"	"	"
	Martha, Eliza, Sarah & Nancy	"	girls	daughters	"	"	"	"
	Robert & Andrew	"	boys	sons		"	"	"
	Alexander Hunter	"	15	Male	None	"	"	"
	Jane Harper	"	45	Female		"	"	"
	Sarah, Ann, Margaret & Martha	"	girls	daughters		"	"	"
	Robert & John	"	boys	sons		"	"	"
	Betty McFee	"	24	Female		"	"	"

PASSENGERS ARRIVING AT THE PORT OF CHARLESTON 1820-1829

Name of vessel	Passengers' names	Date of arrival	Age	Sex	Occupation	Where from	Country- belong	Country- inhabit
Ship	Robert Irwin	November 1821	47	Male	None	Belfast	Britain	U S
James Bailey	James Irwin	"	22	Male	"	"	"	"
	Agnes do	"	20	"[sic]	"	"	"	"
	Daniel McClowell	"	24	"	"	"	"	"
	William Charles	"	23	Male	"	"	Britain	"
	John Heretain	"	25	"	"	"	"	"
	Martha Harper	"	22	Female	Spinster	"	"	"
	Margaret do	"	22	"	"	"	"	"
Ship Jane	Mary Kennedy	"	50	"	None	Liverpool	"	"
	Thomas & Richard do	"	27 21	sons	Labourer	"	"	"
	Henry McGahagan	"	22	Male	"	"	"	"
	James Haslett	"	20	"	"	"	"	"
	Mary Millegan	"	13	Female	"	"	"	"
	James Haslett	"	20	Male	"	"	"	"
	Mary Milligan	"	13	Female	"	"	"	"
	Maria Walker	"	10	"	"	"	"	"
	Margaret Davidson	"	44	Female	None	"	"	"
	Moses & Joseph do	"	12 10	Males	----	"	"	"
	Margaret Ann do	"	8	Female	daughter	"	"	"
	James & Mary Carslile	"	56 53	Man & Wife	labourer	"	"	"
	James & John do	"	26 21	Males	sons	"	"	"
	Alexander do	"	18	"	"	"	"	"
	Mary do	"	16	Female	daughter	"	"	"
	Thomas Henry	"	13	Male	none	"	"	"
	William & Susanna Martin	"	25 23	Man & Wife	Labourer	"	"	"
	H. McSurnigham	"	13	Male	"	"	"	"
	Andrew Dool	"	42	"	"	"	"	"
	Phillip McClery	"	25	"	"	"	"	"
	Alexander Henderson	"	21	"	"	"	"	"
	Philip Raney	"	20	"	"	"	"	"
	Mary Burns	"	42	Female	"	"	"	"
	Edwd John Saml & James Do	"	16 14 12	sons	"	"	"	"
	Mary do	"	50	Female	"	"	"	"
	Robert McMaster	"	26	Male	"	"	"	"
	William Owens	"	25	"	"	"	"	"
	William Dunn	"	30	"	"	"	"	"
	Ann & Ann Jane do	"	11 9	Females	"	"	"	"
	William James	"	7	Male	"	"	"	"
	William Fullerton	"	21	"	"	"	"	"
	Henry Caulfield	"	20	"	"	"	"	"
	Robert Dobbin	"	20	"	"	"	"	"
	Jane do	"	16	Female	"	"	"	"
	John & Jane Blair	"	55	Man & Wife	"	"	"	"

PASSENGERS ARRIVING AT THE PORT OF CHARLESTON 1820-1829

Name of vessel	Passengers' names	Date of arrival	Age Sex	Occupation	Where from	Country- belong	Country- inhabit
Ship Jane	James & Jane do	November 1821	27 19 children	Labourer	Liverpool	Britain	U S
	Pat Mannock & wife	"	49 45	"	"	"	"
	James & William & David do		16 13 6 sons	"	"	"	"
	Nancy & Jane do		12 10 daughters	"	"	"	"
	James McNeilly	"	20 Male	"	"	"	"
	William Riddon	"	26 "	"	"	"	"
	William White	"	18 Male	"	"	"	"
	William & Ellen Scott	"	24 26 Man & wife	"	"	"	"
	William McGowan	"	20 Male	"	"	"	"
	Mrs. Rogers	"	30 Female	"	"	"	"
	Susanna Kelly	"	20 "	"	"	"	"
	Charles Fitzsimmons	"	15 Male	"	"	"	"
	John McKissick	"	25 "	"	"	"	"
	Sarah Martin	"	20 "	"	"	"	"
	Robert & Margret Lawrey	"	67 53 Man & Wife	"	"	"	"
	Margaret & Mary do	"	15 12 daughters	"	"	"	"
	David McCallish	"	18 Male	"	"	"	"
	William Hugh	"	26 Male	"	"	"	"
	James Kirkpatrick	"	47 "	"	"	"	"
	William Do	"	29 "	"	"	"	"
	Mary Do	"	25 Female	"	"	"	"
	Mary Do	"	19 "	"	"	"	"
	Jane Do	"	16 "	"	"	"	"
	Issabella Do	"	14 "	"	"	"	"
	Agnes Do	"	12 Male	"	"	"	"
	Charles Johnson	"	12 "	"	"	"	"
Ship Issabella	Mrs. Dalton	"	21 Female	None	London	Britain	U S
	Miss Moore	"	18 do	"	"	"	"
	Campbell Douglass	"	40 Male	Grocer	"	"	"
	Henry Middleton	"	19 "	None	"	U S	"
	R. O. Anderson	"	26 "		"	Britain	"
	Robert Whitfield	"	25 "	Trader[?]	"	"	"
	Thomas Jones	"	23 "		"	"	"
	Thomas Simmons	"	20 "		"	"	"
	John Torrington	"	25 "	Turner	"	"	"
	William Cox	"	20 "	Carpenter	"	"	"
	John & Eliza Rose[?]	"	50 40	None	"	"	"
	Mrs. Topham	"	40 Female	None	"	"	"
	Caroline, Mary & Lucy do	"	25 11 9 daughters	None	"	"	"
	John & Robert do	"	14 5 children		"	"	"

26

PASSENGERS ARRIVING AT THE PORT OF CHARLESTON 1820-1829

Name of vessel	Passengers' names	Date of arrival	Age	Sex	Occupation	Where from	Country-belong	Country-inhabit
Ship Hunter	Edwd & Eliza Honeywell	Nov 1821	33 28	man & wife		Stockholm	U S	U S
	Eliza & Louisa do	"	8 6	daughters "		"	"	"
	David Meyer	"	21		Musician	"	Denmark	"
	Wevill	"	35		Merchant	"	"	"
Scho'r Louisa	George Pritchard	December	24	Male		Trinidad	U S	U S
Ship Mary & Susan	Joseph Veason	"	26	"		"	"	"
	T. H. Hindley	"	40	"		Liverpool	Britain	"
	T. B. Clough	"	33	"		"	"	"
	P. Fitzsimons	"	21	"		"	"	"
	Lieut Moffat	"	32	"	British Navy[?]	"	"	"
Ship Roger Stewart	John H. Reid	"				Greenoc	Britain	U S
	John Purvis	"				"	U S	"
Ship Roger Stewart	Mary Seabrook	"				"	Britain	"
	John Cocker	"				"	"	"
	James Wood	"				"	"	"
Brig Catherine	George White	December				Havana	U S	U S
	Alfred Huger	"	33		Planter	"	"	"
	Mrs. M. Meuece	"	33		minature	"	Italy	"
	Miss Meuece	"	14		do	"	"	"
	Louis Preiro	"	30		Servant	"	France	"
	Mr. Richard	"	40		Watch m[aker?]	"	"	"
	Mrs. Richard & son	"	40		none	"	"	"
	Mr. Sosie	"	45		Tenne---	"	"	"
	Mrs. Sosie	"	45		none	"	"	"
	Six daughters from	"	17 to 4		none	"	"	"
	Mrs. M. E. Levy	"	45		Trader	"	"	"
	Mr. Rutaut	"	45		Mech---	"	"	"
	James Miller	"	27		do	"	U S	"
	Mr Brurl	"	26		Trader[?]	"	"	"
	Adel	"	20		-----	"	"	"
	Paul	"	6			"	"	"
Schooner Ceres	Willink	"	30		Merchant	"	Holland	"
Brig George	Andrew McMillan & Wife	December	67 67	Man & Wife	Farmer	Belfast	Britain	"
	Betsy & Nancy do	"	24 20	daughters	"		"	"	"
	William McMullin	"	18	Male	"		"	"	"
	John Adams	"	3	Male	none		"	"	"
	Mary McMullen	"	20	Female	none		"	"	"
	Jane do	"	30	"			"	"	"
	Nancy do	"	25	"			"	"	"
	James Adams	"	3	Male			"	"	"
	Margaret McCoy	"	33	Female			"	"	"
	Elizabeth & Issabella do	"	8 & 4	daughters			"	"	"

PASSENGERS ARRIVING AT THE PORT OF CHARLESTON 1820-1829

Name of vessel	Passengers' names	Date of arrival	Age	Sex	Occupation	Where from	Country- belong	Country- inhabit
Brig George	Alexander do	December 1821	6	Male		Belfast	Britain	U S
	Aneas[?]	"	16	Male		"	"	"
	John Lipper[?]	"	21	"		"	"	"
	John & Mary Oniel	"	25 30	Man & Wife		"	"	"
	Catherine, Sally & Mary do		15 13 11	daughters		"	"	"
	Edward & Patrick	"	9 1	sons		"	"	"
	Cornelius McKeegan	"	24	Male		"	"	"
	Peter & Jane Sharp	"	24 26	Man & Wife		"	"	"
	Andrew & John do	"	6 4	sons		"	"	"
	Wm McWhier[?]	"	60	Male		"	"	"
	James Shannon	"	22			"	"	"
	John Printer	"	60			"	"	"
	John Cunningham	"	15			"	"	"
Sloop Cherub	Stephen Miller	December 1821	20	Male	Merchant	Porto Prince	Britain	U S
Schooner Emilly	John Cattell	"	24	"	Confectioner	Matances	France	"
Schooner Liberty	Townson More		30	"	Merchant	Aquin	U S	"
Ship Thos Gelston	Mrs. Crawford		40	Female	Free dealer	Liverpool	Britain	U S
	Archibald Watson		20	Male	clerk	"	"	"
Schooner	Lewis Flemming		26	Male	Merchant	Matanzes	U S	"
Col Ramsey	Mrs. do		20	Female	none	"	"	"
	Thomas Donathan		28	Male	merchant		Britain	"
Brig	Joseph Hogson		35	Male	Taylor	Liverpool	"	"
Harmony	Margaret do		30	Female	none	"	"	"
	Henry do		10	Male	"	"	"	"
	Elizabeth do		7	Female	"	"	"	"
	Mary do			Female	"	"	"	"
Schooner	James Ross		31	Male	Marriner	Havanna	"	"
Jane	Anthony Armar		33	"	Trader	"	"	"
Ship	Alfred Woodhouse		24	"	Merchant	Liverpool	"	"
So Boston	John Mahle		36	"	do	"	"	"
Sloop Ann	Joseph Urban	January 1822	30	Male	Merchant	Havanna	France	"
	Peter Monqued	"	32	"	"	"	Britain	"
	Henry Goldsmith	"	16	"	"	"	U S	"
	John Dash	"	20	"	"			"
	Geo. Phillips	"	18	"	"			"
Mary Ann	John Damon	"	40	"	Marriner	Havanna	Britain	"
Schooner	John Shegog	"	28	"	Merchant	Havanna	Spain	"
Cornet[?]	B. Gonsally	"	30	"			U S	"
Sarah Ann	John Howard	"	25	"	Cabinet maker	Havanna		"
Brig	John F. Ohl	"	30	"		Havanna	Hamburgh	"
Philadel'a	William Phillpot	"	30	"	Merchant		Britain	"
	William C. Kausler	"	40	"			Germany	"
	Mary Ann Magnan	"	35	Female	none		West indies	"

28

PASSENGERS ARRIVING AT THE PORT OF CHARLESTON 1820-1829

Name of vessel	Passengers' names	Date of arrival	Age	Sex	Occupation	Where from	Country- belong	Country- inhabit
Brig	Adel Segars	January 1822	30	Male	Trader	Havanna	U S	U S
Philadel'a	L. C. Gross	"	40	"	"	"	Germany	"
--- Ann	Charles Meyo	"	30	"	Marriner	Porto Rico	U S	"
--- Brooks	E. C. Brire[?]	"	28	"	Merchant	Amsterdam	Holland	"
--ooner	John Oaks	"	25	"	------	Havanna	U S	"
--mpson	William Hall	"	24	"	Marriner	"	"	"
--- Larch	Baldwin M. Halsey	"	24	"	Merchant	Turks Island	"	"
--hooner	Thomas Barnett	"	28	"	Engineer	Havanna	Britain	"
& Polly	Henry Brookins	"	50	"	Mariner	"	U S	"
	John Anthony	"	25	"	"	"	"	"
Schooner	Roger Harriett	"	58	"	Merchant	Matanzes	"	"
---- Smith	George do	"	20	"	Marriner	"	"	"
	William do	"	9	"	none	"	"	"
	Daniel Allen	"	30	"	Physician	"	"	"
	S. C. Potter	"	26	"	Merchant	"	"	"
Brig	J. Mathews	February 1822	50	Male	Merchant	Havanna	Portugal	U S
Catherine[?]	Assa Forsyth	"	52	"	Marriner	Greenock	U S	"
Ship Jane	Adam McClaren	"	45	"	Merchant	"	Britain	"
	Agnes McClaren	"	45	Female	none	Greenock	"	U S
	Margaret McClaren	"	22	Female	none	"	Britain	"
	Janet do	"	21	"	"	"	"	"
	Jane do	"	19	"	"	"	"	"
	Adam do	"	14	Male	"	"	"	"
	John do	"	12	"	"	"	"	"
	Agnes do	"	9	Female	"	"	"	"
	Susanna do	"	7	"	"	"	"	"
	Elizabeth do	"	4	"	"	"	"	"
Bark	George Shaw	"	28	Male	Butcher	Liverpool	"	"
Esther	James Phillips	"	35	"	do	"	"	"
	Thomas Hemmingsway	"	21	"	Baker	"	"	"
Ship	Patrick McBreet	"	27	Male	Lawyer	Liverpool	"	"
Bayard	Mary do	"	22	Female	none	"	"	"
	Thomas Latu	"	24	Male	Farmer	"	"	"
	James Carroll	"	28	"	"	"	"	"
	Edmund Dyer	"	44	"	"	"	"	"
	Ann Do	"	36	Female	"	"	"	"
	John, Richard, Patrick & Edmund		13 to 2	Males	sons of the above			
	Mary do		6 months	Female	daughter			
	Michael Dwyer		8	Male	none			
	William Do		34	"	"			
	John Duffy		45	"	"			
	Ellen Do		38	Female	"			
	Mathew, Dennis, John & William Do		19 to 6	Males	sons of the above			

PASSENGERS ARRIVING AT THE PORT OF CHARLESTON 1820-1829

Name of vessel	Passengers' names	Date of arrival	Age	Sex	Occupation	Where from	Country- belong	Country- inhabit
Ship	Allice, Mary, Ellen & Margaret do		15 to 1	Females	daughter do	Liverpool		
Bayard	William Lamb		24	Male	none	"		
	Bryan Sweeny		20	Male	Farmer	"		
	Michael Smith		22	"	"	"		
	Patrick Naughton		27	"	"	"		
	James Phaelan		22	"	"	"		
	Patrick Lahy		30	"	"	"		
	Michael Carroll		13	"	"	"		
	Charles Green		21	"	"	"		
Brig Mary	Charles Freebody		23	"	Merchant	Havanna	U S	U S
Ship Johanna	Stephen Singleton		36	"	Marriner	St. Ubes	"	"
Scho'r Content	David Canter		42	"	do	St. Jago	"	"
do Philander	Nathan Bacon		43	"	Trader	Matanzes	"	"
Brig Leopold	Hugh Graham		30	"	none	London	Britain	"
	Mary do		25	Female	none	"	"	"
	Edward Bacon		28	Male	Grocer	"	"	"
	Alexander Holstrum		19	"	Clerk	"	"	"
Brig Leopold	James Logan	February 1822	30	Male	Baker	London	Britain	U S
	Mrs Margarett Larmour		28	Female	none	"	"	"
	Two children		4 & 2			"	"	"
Brig	Pesquette Macalette		55	Male	Marriner	Havanna	Portugal	"
Neptunes Barge	Lewis do		28	"		"	"	"
Ship Lucies	Doctor Bolston		25	Male	Physician	Havana	U S	U S
	Francis DeCastro		44	"	Planter	"	Spain	"
	G. W. DeRoche		40	"	Merchant	"	France	"
	Mr. Gouve		19	"	do	"	do	"
	John Oats		60	"	Publican	"	U S	U S
Schooner Bee	John Urban		28	"	Taylor	Porto Prince	France	"
	Frederick Monquet		35	"	do	"	"	"
Scho'r Roxby	Abel Harris		60	"	Merchant	Hayti	U S	"
Schooner Grace	Samuel Snody		20	"	Labourer	Larne	Britain	"
	Jane McIrish		35	Female	Spinster	"	"	"
	Martha McIrish		29	"	do	"	"	"
Schooner Comet	M. Montandon		32	Male	none	Havanna	France	"
	M. Prandt		40	"			"	"
Schooner	John Dunscomb	March	40	Male	Merchant	Bermuda	Britain	U S
Industry	Cap. S. Baker		50	"	Mariner	"	U S	"
	Joseph Hammond		24	"	Merchant	"	"	"
Ship Portia	Thomas Williams		26	"	Broker	Bourdeaux	Britain	"
Schooner	Louis Monsieur		50	"	Trader	Havanna	France	"
Mary Ann	Lyebodiere		28	"	Merchant	"	"	"	died 13 March

PASSENGERS ARRIVING AT THE PORT OF CHARLESTON 1820-1829

Name of vessel	Passengers' names	Date of arrival	Age	Sex	Occupation	Where from	Country- belong	Country- inhabit
Ship Je-- Flora	Robert Wallace & Lady	March 1822	63 45	Man & Wife	Farmer	Belfast	Britain	U S
	Willm, Danl, Robt, John & Archy	do	21 to 3	Males	"	"	"	"
	Jane & Mary	do	8 1	Females	"	"	"	"
	Mary, Jane, Margaret & Mary Roane	do	30 to 4	Females	"	"	"	"
	John & Mary Robinson	do	30 26	do	"	"	"	"
	Alexander do		28	male	"	"	"	"
	Mary do		65	Female	"	"	"	"
	Alexander McPhaul		18	Male	"	"	"	"
	David Brown		25	Male	"	"	"	"
	---- [obliterated]		68 62	man & wife	"	"	"	"
	Jane -----		26		"	"	"	"
	John McKeown		23	Male	"	"	"	"
	John Shaw & Lady		35 30	man & wife	"	"	"	"
	Margaret do		4	Female	"	"	"	"
	Adam Wallace		24	Male	"	"	"	"
	John & Ann McCormick		36 35	man & wife	"	"	"	"
	Jannet & Ann do		16 & 14	females	"	"	"	"
	William, John & David do		12 8 2	males	"	"	"	"
	Thomas & Biddy McCoy		50 48	man & wife	"	"	"	"
	James, Isbell & Biddy A. McCoy		30 28 2	females	"	"	"	"
Tragan	Thomas Hart		27	Male	Merchant	St. Thomas	U S	U S
	Simeon Barthe		66	Male	Merchant	Hayte	"	"
	James Lawson		20	"	do	"	"	"
Col. Ramsay	Wm R. Faber		27	"	Marriner	"	"	"
	Capt. Anthony Geraldo		30	"	"	"	Spain	"
	John Langenette		27	"	"	"	U S	"
--- Jane	William Eckel		28	Male	Merchant	Havanna	Italy	"
Sarah Ann	John Dominique		40	"	do	Matanzes	Britain	"
Brig Ann	Robert McTannen		24	"	Farmer	Britain	"	"
	James Kinsey		25	"	"	Belfast	"	"
	Ann do		22	Female	"	"	"	"
	James McCann		30	Male	"	"	"	"
	Issabella do		21	Female	"	"	"	"
	James do		1	Male	"	"	"	"
	Samuel McKey		20	"	"	"	"	"
	Robert Harrit		30	"	"	"	"	"
Ship Orion	Mrs. Batker		42	Female	none	Lisbon	Germany	"
	Frederick do		8	Male	"	"	"	"
	Henry Dreffren		35	"	Taylor	"	"	"
	Maria do 1 child		20	Female	"	"	"	"

PASSENGERS ARRIVING AT THE PORT OF CHARLESTON 1820-1829

Name of vessel	Passengers' names	Date of arrival	Age	Sex	Occupation	Where from	Country- belong	Country- inhabit
Sloop Emilly	Samuel M. Smith	March 1822	36		Trader	Havanna	U S	U S
	Peter do		24		"	"	"	"
	Charles Hankives [sic]		28		Carpenter	"	"	"
	Barnard Hawkins		26		"	"	"	"
	George Beale		25		"	"		"
Ship Perfect	Otho Laurence		38	Male	none	Liverpool	U S	U S
	Charles Maxwell		25	"	School master	"	Britain	"
Brig Deux Freres	Bernard Chenee		28	"	Secretary of ____	Porto Prince	France	"
Brig Standard	John James Appleton		30	"	Merchant	Rio Jineiro	U S	"
	Nicholas Aquitar		26	"	"	"		"
	St. Jago Tabara		29	"	"	"	Spain	"
	Herman H. Green		23	"		"	U S	"
	Thomas Munroe		27			"	"	"
	Peter Barrett		37		Marriner		"	"
	Samuel Stimson		30		do			"
	John Nolan		27		Servant to ____			"
	Josia Calliona		35				Spain	"
	Michael Praya		29		Mariner		U S	"
	R. Pease		25		"		"	"
	Wm Fox		30					"
Brig Catherine	Charles Gedding		19					"
	Dr. Huger		30		Physician	Havanna		"
	Messr Siminton		34		Merchant	"		"
	Keith		24		"	"		"
	Deprass		25			"		"
	Alexander		28		Dr. H. Servant			"
Schooner Eliza & Polly	W. R. Smith	April 1822	28	Male	Merchant	Havanna	U S	U S
Schooner Col.	John Halden		35	"	do	Trinidad	"	"
Geo. Armstead	Miller Stevenson		38	"			Germany	"
	Jacob Gilbert		25	Female	Carpenter		U S	U S
	Sarah do		20	do	none			"
Schooner Betsy & Peggy	Amelia Torrigard		17	Female	none			"
	John W. Trott		40	Male	Merchant	Barracoa	France	U S
	Henry Goldsmith		17	"			Britain	"
	John Noga		45	"	Marriner		Portuguese	"
	Antonio Pannell		15	"			Spaniard	"
Schooner Comet	H. Eymar		30	"	Shopkeeper	Havanna	Spain	"
	H. Debal		21	"				"
Schooner Neptune	Augustus Linguart		30	Male	Merchant	Porto Platt	Austrian	"
	Francis Prioye		32	"	do		do	"
	Mary Redrigues		29	Female	none		Dane	"
	Enes Emenes		60	Male	"		"	"

PASSENGERS ARRIVING AT THE PORT OF CHARLESTON 1820-1829

Name of vessel	Passengers' names	Date of arrival	Age	Sex	Occupation	Where from	Country- belong	Country- inhabit
Schooner	John Wurner	April 1822	23	Male	Merchant	Havanna	U S	U S
Emeline	Mrs do		21	Female	none		"	"
	Piene		30	Male	Merchant		"	"
	Dr. Montgomery		40	"	Planter		"	"
	G. W. Geddes		22	"	Lawyer		"	"
	John Gill		25	"	Planter		Spain	"
	Manuel Piera		38	"	Marriner	Havanna		"
	M. Walker		17	Male	Mariner		U S	"
	Frederick Polles		27	"	"		"	"
Brig Commerce	P. Reynal		46	Male	Merchant	Bourdeaux	France	"
Schooner Mary	John Chartran		35	Male	Planter	Matanzes	U S	"
	Louisa do & child		20	Female	none		France	"
	Monquoit		38	Male	"		Britain	"
	Willm Sullivan		26	"	"		Spain	"
	Louisa col'd woman		38	Female	"		U S	"
Sch'r Louisa	C. E. Tate	May	19	Female	none	Trinidad	Spain	"
	Jose A. Iswaga		26	Male	Merchant			"
Sch'r Jane	Florance Delahanka		25	"	"		Britain	"
	Benjamin Buckhannan		45	"	"	Havanna	Britain	"
Ship	P. J. Lorent		60	"	"	Liverpool	Germany	"
So Boston	H. T. Faber		23	"	none		U S	"
Brig Catherine	Henry Rolando		28	"	Merchant	Havanna		U S
Ship	Joseph Mathews						Portugal	"
	Mary Dechamp		40	Female	None	Havre	France	"
Jas Bailey	William Barton		12	Male	"	Bristol	Britain	"
Brig Experiment	Charles Mugridge		20	Male	Blacksmith	London	Britain	"
Ship Issabella	John Androne		21	Male	Sugar Baker			U S
Ship Issabella	Claud Rache	May 1822	20	Male	Sugar Baker	London	Britain	"
	Cokon Vigue		18	"	"			"
	Henry Sheretts		24	"	"			"
	John Loconro		22	"	"			"
Ship Saley	William Callender		38	"	Merchant	Greenock	U S	U S
Sloop Liberty	Townsend Moore		36	"	"	Hayti	"	"
Schooner Fama	John Coleman	May 1822	24	Male	Watchmaker	Matanzes	Britain	U S
	Patrick McCleventy		34	"	Shoemaker		"	"
Ship Triton	David Michell		32	"	Farmer	Liverpool		"
Ship Roger	Janet Nelson		27	Female	none	Greenock		"
Steward								
Schooner	James J. Lawson		20	Male	Merchant	Hayti	U S	U S
Sally	Morgan Jones		52	"	do		"	"
Sch Eliza & Polly	B. Gonsales		29	"	"	Havanna	Spain	"
Sch. Eudora	J. Cardoza		35	"	Trader		"	"

33

PASSENGERS ARRIVING AT THE PORT OF CHARLESTON 1820-1829

Name of vessel	Passengers' names	Date of arrival	Age	Sex	Occupation	Where from	Country- belong	Country- inhabit
Ship Bayard	James Todd	June 1822	40	Male	Farmer	Liverpool	Britain	U S
Schooner	William Stewart		45	"	Marriner	Havanna	U S	"
Comet	Francis Falio		35	"	Merchant		Spain	"
	Patrick Gilmore		28	"	do		Britain	"
	J. A. Barrelli		21	"	do		Italy	"
	Lewis Pilaluguer		35	"	do		Britain	"
	Nass Rutal	June	40	Female	none	Havanna	France	U S
	Miss Rutal		20	"	"		"	"
	Merton Rutal		10	Male	"		"	"
	John Barrelli		40	"	Trader		Italy	"
Schooner Bee	C. H. Riley		40	"	Merchant	Barracoa	U S	"
Schooner	D. Cantor		40	"	Marriner	Havanna	Cuba	"
Mechanic	P. Munoz		30	"	Traveller		U S	"
	John DEll		35	Female	Shoemaker		"	"
	Mrs. DEll		18	Male	none		"	"
	Antonio Free		14	"	"		"	"
	Servant							
Schooner	Timothy White		19	Male	Planter	St John	Spain	"
Joseph	Cetaro Pevaso		35	"	Merchant	Cuba	"	"
	John Chaves		22	"	"		"	"
	Francisco Fernandez		28	"	"		"	"
	Francis Mearandez		25	"	"		"	"

34

PASSENGERS ARRIVING AT THE PORT OF CHARLESTON 1820-1829

Name of vessel	Passengers' names	Date of arrival	Age	Sex	Occupation	Where from	Country- belong	Country- inhabit
Brig Mary	Gilhome DelRoches	July 1822	37	Male	Farmer	France	France	U S
Schooner	Urban		30	"	Trader	Matanzes	"	"
Sally & Polly	Madam Toumassen		31	Female	None	None	"	"
	John Routledge		27	Male	Marriner	U S	U S	"
Sloop Victory	J. H. Magwood		27	"	Merchant	Hayte	"	"
Brig Catherine	Mrs. Hamilton		30	Female	none	Havanna	Britain	"
	William Hamilton		6	Male	"		"	"
Schooner Felix	John Rodrigues		30	"	Trader	Porto Rico	U S	"
do F	Samuel Withington		30	"	Merchant	Matanzes	"	"
Schooner	David Tirundale		31	"	"		"	"
FAMA	Charles Delorme		18	"	none		"	"
	Joseph John Vollee		13	"			"	"
Ship	Isaac Wolf		38	"	Trader	Liverpool	"	"
	Mrs. Wolf		28	Female	none		"	"
So Carolina	Sarah, Eliza & Mary do	10 8 4					"	"
	Charles & Henry	6 2	Males				"	"
	Sarah Wolf		60	Female			"	"
Scho'r Louisa	E. Morris		25	Male	Merchant	Trinidad	Spain	Spain
	J. Tate		14	"	none		"	U S
	Antonio Ramerez	August	35	"	Planter		"	"
Schooner	Thomas Legium		30	"	Trader	Matanzes	France	"
Eliza & Polly	Louis Vegin		29	"	Carpenter	Havanna	Spain	"
Brig Neptunes	Anthony Bragas		30	"	Merchant		do	"
Barge	Joaquim Savater		33	"	do		U S	"
	Thomas Swain		35	"	Marriner	Greenock	Britain	"
Ship	Archibald McFarlane		54	Male	Farmer		"	"
Jane	Mary McFarlane		54	Female	none		U S	"
	Mary ditto		17	Female			"	"
	George ditto		29	Male			"	"
Sloop Fitideavour	John Watson		27	Male	Cooper	Florida	"	"
Sch'r Sarah Ann	John Naga		40	"	Marriner[?]	Barracoa	Spain	"
Ship Ceres	John Lomis		22	"	Millener[?]	Liverpool	Britain	"
	John Davis		41	"	Shop Keeper		"	"
Ship Perfect	John C. Beale		46	"	[obliterated]		U S	"
	Henry Noyes		32	"			"	"
Schooner	Genl John Geddes		50	"	Lawyer	Havanna	"	"
Betsy & Peggy	G. H. Geddes		17	"	none		"	"
	Miss H. Geddes		19	Female			"	"
	Mr. Montgomery		40	Male	Planter		"	"
	Henry Goldsmith		19	"	Trader		"	"
Scho'r Sally	John B. Rogers		28	"	Merchant		Britain	"
Schooner	Hugh Shannon		36	"	"	"	"	"
Mechanic	John Arthur		32	"	Mechanic[?]	"	"	"

35

PASSENGERS ARRIVING AT THE PORT OF CHARLESTON 1820-1829

Name of vessel	Passengers' names	Date of arrival	Age	Sex	Occupation	Where from	Country- belong	Country- inhabit
Ship	Robert Holbertin	September 1822	30	Male	Hozier[?]	Liverpool	Britain	U S
Fana	Christopher McDonald		19	"	Farmer		"	"
	Gallagher		32	"	Trader		"	"
	Mrs. Gallagher		58	Female	None		"	"
	Miss Gallagher		14	do	"		"	"
	" Gallagher		12	do	"		"	"
	John C. Ross		27	Male	Merchant		"	"
	Mrs. Ross		20	Female	None		"	"
	R. R. Ross		13	Male	"		"	"
	L. Y. Abrahams		45	"	Trader[?]	Amsterdam	Holland	"
	H. J. Janke		22	"	None		"	"
Ship Charles & Henry	Jennet DeWolf		30	Female	"		"	"
Schooner Felix	James Ross		36	Male	Marriner	Havanna	Britain	"
Schooner Fame	James Green		25	"	Merchant		"	"
Brig Catherine	J. Flint		40	"	do		U S	"
Ship James Bailey	Thomas McCreedy	October	24	"	"	Belfast	Britain	"
	James Moore & child		50 1	"	Farmer		"	"
	John Glass		22	"	"		"	"
	Archibald McGinnis		24	"	"		"	"
	Thomas Hawthorn		27	"	"		"	"
	John McGowan		19	"	"		"	"
	Sarah McDonald		40	Female	none		"	"
	Mary McDonald		30	"	"		"	"
	Robert Carlisle		10	Male	"		"	"
	Benjamin Hill		18	"	Farmer		"	"
Bayard	William McKenzie		55	"	Farmer	Liverpool	"	"
	Robert Horry		24	"	none		"	"
	George Horry		14	"	"		"	"
	Daniel Nicholson		20	"	Farmer		"	"
Sch. Col. G. Armistead	John Nevell		45	"	Merchant	Trinidad	"	"
Brig Leopold	Joseph Sampson		28	"	"	London	"	"
	N. Cohen		15	"	"		"	"
	J. Lee		10	"	"		"	"
Ship Corsair	John Lowden		35	"	"	Liverpool	"	"
	Ann Lowden		35	Female	none		"	"
	Alexander Black		33	Male	"		"	"
	Eliza Black		30	Female	none		U S	"
	Seth Watson		25	Male	"		Britain	"
	J. S. Vaughn		18	"	"		U S	"
	J. Howe		20	"	"		"	"
Schooner	Elisha Larnerd		25	"	Mechanic	Havanna	"	"
Eliza & Polly	J. D. Hamilton		24	"	Merchant		Britain	"

36

PASSENGERS ARRIVING AT THE PORT OF CHARLESTON 1820-1829

Name of vessel	Passengers' names	Date of arrival	Age	Sex	Occupation	Where from	Country- belong	Country- inhabit
Ship Roger Stewart	James Brown	October 1822	21	Male	None	Greenock	Britain	U S
	James Smith		22	"	clerk		"	"
	William Anderson		22	"	Lawyer		"	"
	William Kennedy		19	"	clerk		"	"
	John Blair Thompson		23	"	do			"
	Alexander Campbell		30	Male	Farmer			"
Ship Plantaganet	Dougald McIntyre		28	Male	Farmer	Greenock	Britain	U S
	Letty McIntyre		28	Female	none		"	"
	Betty & John do children		3 5	children "			"	"
	Dougald McIntyre		63	Male	Farmer		"	"
	Christiana McIntyre		60	Female	none		"	"
	Archibald do		13	Male			"	"
	Geo W. Frost		25	"	Merchant		"	"
	Hugh & Jannet Wilson		45 45	Man & Wife	Farmer		"	"
	John & Hugh & William		11 1	20 sons of above	none		"	"
	James McGregor		26		"		"	"
Schooner Louisa	Y. Isnaga		18	Male	Planter	Trinidad	Spain	Spain
Schooner Comet	M. Menici		30	Male	Painter	Havanna	Italy	U S
	Mr. Theodore		30	"	Marriner		France	"
Schooner Mary	Catharine Pritchard		25	Female	none	Matanzes	U S	"
	John Smith		30	Male	Marriner		Portugal	"
	James Emelly		28	"	Planter		U S	"
	Urban Graen		28	"	Marriner		France	"
	J. P. Lavencendue		32	"	Merchant			"
Schooner Felix	P. Cassen		45	Male	Merchant	Havanna	Britain	"
	Cork		33	"	"		"	"
	Kesler		30	"	"			"
Ship Portea	S. B. Benoist	November	54	Male	Trader	Bourdeaux	France	"
	S. B. Acho Benoist		22	Female			"	"
	Tehe[?] Benoist		20[?]	"	none		"	"
	Mr. Peter		24	Male	Merchant		"	"
	Mrs. Petit		23	Female	"		"	"
Ship Newberryport	James Tenmouth		38	Male	"	Belfast	Britain	"
	Mary Tenmouth		38	Female	none		"	"
	Jane Tenmouth		13	Female	"		"	"
	Henry Tenmouth		0	Male	"			"
Schooner Swift	John George		25	Male	Marriner	Nassau		"

37

PASSENGERS ARRIVING AT THE PORT OF CHARLESTON 1820-1829

Name of vessel	Passengers' names	Date of arrival	Age	Sex	Occupation	Where from	Country- belong	Country- inhabit
Ship	Margaret McKalister & two Sons		30 9 & 6		Spinster	Belfast	Britain	U S
James Bailey	Hans McKalister	November 1822	25	Male	Farmer		"	"
	Elizabeth Elliott		28	Female	Spinster		"	"
	James Reid		27	Male	Farmer		"	"
	Agnes Habeson		60	Female	Spinster		"	"
	Robert Kidd		22	Male	"		"	"
	Mary Dunseith		19	Female	Spinster		"	"
	Mary Mull		30	"	"		"	"
	John Callwell		24	Male	Farmer		"	"
	Nancy Blair		25	Female	none		"	"
	Thomas Palmer		22	Male	Farmer		"	"
	Hugh Kelly		30	"	do		"	"
	George Ferguson		19	"	"		"	"
	Margaret McGill		60	Female	Spinster		"	"
	Jane McGill		20	"	"		"	"
	Andrew & Agnes McGill	36	25	Man & Wife			"	"
	John, Margaret, Eliz., Thomas & James do	9 to 1		children of the above			"	"
	Margaret McGill		24	Female	Spinster		"	"
	Mathew Petticrue		10	"	"		"	"
Schooner	M. Sarrazen		70	Female	None	Havanna	U S	U S
Eudora	J. Sarrazin		20	do	"		"	"
	Patrick Packet		40	Male	Taylor	Belfast	Britain	
	Mrs. Packet		40	Female	none			
Ship	Mr. Fernandez		45	Male	Marriner	Havre	Portugal	
Brig Bowen	John M. Hopkins		55	Male	Merchant		U S	
	William Timmond		50	Male	"			
	A. Dubois		68	"	Shopkeeper		France	
	Andrew Jacque		30	"	Locksmith		"	
	Piere Tuiller		57	"	Baker		"	
	Buffe Chois Blanche Elenee[?]		35	"	Carpenter		"	
Schooner	Joseph Espree		21	"	Trader	Havanna	Spain	
Sarah Ann	Marion Viller		21	"	"		"	
Brig	Henry Thatcher		22	"	Merchant	Cape Francois	U S	
Bellvedere	William Jerry		24	"	Carpenter		"	
Schooner	N. Brown		25	"	Merchant	Nassau	"	
Trio	Mrs. Brown		60	Female	none		"	
	Mrs. Gardener		25	"	"		"	
Brig	William S. Dewer		24	Male	Merchant	Dundee	Britain	
Traveller	William Duncan		24	"	"		"	
	William Bernie		38	"	"		"	
	James Hay		22	"	Farmer		"	
	David Anderson		24	"	"		"	

38

PASSENGERS ARRIVING AT THE PORT OF CHARLESTON 1820-1829

Name of vessel	Passengers' names	Date of arrival	Age	Sex	Occupation	Where from	Country- belong	Country- inhabit
Schooner Eudora	Jacque D Nezale	November 1822	46	Male	Mariner	Matanzes	Portugal	U S
Scho Eliza & Polly	Jos Ramize		35	"	"		Italy	"
	William Labetine		21	"	Barber	Havanna		"
Brig Leod	William Kerr		34	"	Merchant	St. Thomas	Britain	"
Ship Issabella	John Mill		38	"	U S Navy	London	"	"
	R. S. Pinckney		21	"	Merchant		U S	"
	James Thomas		52	"	none		Britain	"
	R. M. Allen		18	"	Merchant		U S	"
	Alexander Grant		44	Female	none		Britain	"
	Dina Williman		24	Female	none			"
Ship Issabella	Christiana Davis & 6 children	Dec 1822	46	Female	none		Britain	U S
	Benjamin Cromwell & 3 do		35	Male	Mason		"	"
	Clara Cromwell		34	Female	Seamstress			
	Rebecca Moses & 2 children		35	Female	none			
	Sampson Sampson		30	Male	Shopkeeper		U S	"
	Jane Sampson & 5 children		30	Female	none		Britain	"
	James Brown		19	Male	"			
	James Beit[?]		12	"	"			
Slo New York Packet	William Hathway		27	"	Merchant	Turks Isle	U S	U S
Brig Catherine	James Green	December	25	"	"	Havanna	"	"
	Robert McCartney		35	"	none		"	"
	Hugh McMurron		35	"	"	Belfast		"
Brig Finchett	Margaret Henry		42	Female	"		Britain	"
	Margaret Henry		16	"	"		"	"
	William Henry		10	"	"		"	"
	Hugh Henry		12	"	"		"	"
	James Ford		63	Male	Farmer		Britain	U S
	Jane Ford		23	Female	none		"	"
	William Ford		21	Male	"		"	"
	Sarah Ford		11	Female	"		"	"
	John Craig		25	Male	Farmer		"	"
	George McNiel		16	"	Shoemaker		"	"
	Issabella McGarl		25	Female	none		"	"
	Thomas Douthurst		22	Male	Farmer		"	"
	Samuel Kirkpatrick		48	"	none		"	"
	Margaret Kirkpatrick		47	Female	Spinster		"	"
	John & David	23 13		sons	Farmers		"	"
	Eliza, Jane, Peggy & Sally	21 17 18 15		daughters	none		"	"
	George McCormick		25	Male	Joiner		"	"
	David Milling		24	"	clerk		"	"
	William Lowan		40	"	Weaver		"	"

PASSENGERS ARRIVING AT THE PORT OF CHARLESTON 1820-1829

Name of vessel	Passengers' names	Date of arrival	Age	Sex	Occupation	Where from	Country-belong	Country-inhabit
Brig Finchett	James Hamilton	December 1822	51	Male	Wheelwright	Belfast	Britain	U S
	Jane ditto		50	Female	none		"	"
	William & Robert do		23 20	sons	Joiner & Farmer		"	"
	Mary		18	daughter	none		"	"
	Mary Hamilton		25	Female	"		"	"
	Jane & Ann do		20 3	do			"	"
	John Johnson		32	Male	Blacksmith		"	"
	Margaret do		30	Female	none		"	"
	Eliza, Mary, Margaret & Sarah		6 5 3 1	daughters	"		"	"
	Margaret Baird		60	Female			"	"
	William Rowan		14	Male	clerk		"	"
	James Welsh		28	"	Weaver		"	"
	Issabella Welsh		25	Female	none		"	"
Brig Finchett	John & James do		6 4	sons	none		"	"
	John Hunter		32	Male	Surgeon		"	"
	James Boyd		21	"	clerk		"	"
	John German		40	"	Farmer		"	"
Schooner Swift	Thomas Carman		25	"	Marriner	Nassau	U S	U S
	John Antonio		26	"			"	"
	James Baldwin		14	"			"	"
Schooner Delight	W. H. Trott		26	"	Marriner	Jamaica	Britain	Britain
Brig Centurion	James Gracia	January 1823	30	Male	Marriner	St. Bartholomews	Spain	Spain
Schooner	Edward Goware [Goivare?]		35	Male	Merchant	Aquadilla	"	
Horatio	John Rodriguez		32	Male	Mariner		"	United States
Ship	Eliene Bordier		35	Male	Merchant	Havre	Geneva	United States
Bingham	Jean Babtist		22	Male	Painter		Swiss	
	Joseph Markilola		23	Mal			ditto	
Brig Rachael	Gardner		35	Male	Marriner	Havanna	United States	"
& Sally	Urban		28	Male	Trader		France	
	Wm Holebear		22	Male	ditto		ditto	
Ship Corsair	John Brown		30	Male	None	Liverpool	Britain	
Schr Maid of the	Col. B. Young		30	Male	Military	St. Thomas	Columbia	Columbia
Mill								
Ship Perfect	James B. Clough		38	Male	Merchant	Liverpool	Britain	Britain
	Mrs. Ann Clough		28	Female	None			
	Charles B. Clough		6	Male	"			
	Arthur A. Clough		4	Male	"			
	George A. Clough		4	Male	"			
	Ann J. Clough		3	Female	"			
	Mary Marshall		39	Female	Servant			
	Ann Bennett		19	Female	"			
	Thos H. Hindley		43	Male	Merchant			
	Alexander Adam		21	Male	"			

PASSENGERS ARRIVING AT THE PORT OF CHARLESTON 1820-1829

Name of vessel	Passengers' names	Date of arrival	Age	Sex	Occupation	Where from	Country-belong	Country-inhabit
Ship Perfect	Capt. Isaac Silliman	January 1823	32	Male	Marriner	Liverpool	United States	United States
	Willis Silliman		11	Male	None		"	"
Schoo Abigail & Darmacy[?]	Henry Goldsmith		18	Male	Trader	Baracoa	United States	United States
Schoo Col. Armstead	Henry Brown		35	Male	Merchant	Havanna	Germany	United States
	Issabella Brown		38	Female	None		Portugal	
	Joseph Lopez		35	Male	Merchant		Spain	
	Joseph Mathews		40	Male			United States	
	Nathaniel Lopyez[?]		32	Male	Planter		Spain	
	Thos Marld		45	Male	Merchant			
	Joagin Gonsales		35	Male	Lawyer			
Schoo Eliza & Polly	Hester Forester		20	Female	Millener	Havanna	United States	United States
Schoo Belona	Ann Wilson		25	"	"		"	"
Schoo Serah Ann	Diego Marso		27	Male	Military	ditto	Chili	Chili
Ship Mary	John Hersepool	February 1823	30	Male	Merchant	ditto	United States	United States
	I. H. F. S. Chanquion		22	"	Merchant	Rotterdam	Netherlands	Britain
	Le Bretton		5	"	None	Britain	Britain	"
Ship Hannah	John Crosbere		55	"	Farmer	Liverpool	Britain	United States
	John Pierce		28	"	"		"	"
	Samuel McCullough		50	"	"			
	John G. Beale		26	"	Mariner		United States	United States
	John Thompson		22	"	Farmer		Britain	
Bark Jane	William Rowland		21	"	Surveyor		"	
	James Maloney		35	"	Farmer		"	
	John Williams		19	"	Clerk			
Schoo Mechanic	Charles Maghim		43	"	Merchant	Havanna	France	United States
	Mitchel Lorent		30	"	"		"	
	Francis Caura		30	"	"		Spain	
	John Calabra		30	"	"		"	
	John Caladara		20	"	"		"	
Schoo Nancy & Felix	Geo Lowe		33	Male	Columbian officer	Curacoa	Columbia	Columbia
Ship Le Neptune	Dartigues		22	Male	None	Havre	France	United States
Brig Rosina	John Finlay		21	Male	Merchant	Dundee	Britain	
	Jane McMoran		45	Female	None			
	Robert McMoran		3	Male	"			
Brig Charles	Wm. B. Hall		32	Male	Merchant	Matanzas	United States	
Sloop Lively	J. S. Russell		25	Male	"	Nassau	"	

41

PASSENGERS ARRIVING AT THE PORT OF CHARLESTON 1820-1829

Name of vessel	Passengers' names	Date of arrival	Age	Sex	Occupation	Where from	Country- belong	Country- inhabit
Schoo Midas	Sally Vincent	March 1823	40	Female	None	Gauduloupe	United States	
	Fred Vincent		19	Male	Carpenter		"	
Brig Ann	Lerwick Sproll		20	Male	Farmer	Liverpool	Britain	Britain
	Moses Sproll		21	Male	"			
	Thomas Sproll		3	Male	None			
	Jane Sproll		1	Female	"			
	Robert Quigley		17	Male	Farmer			
	McColum		40	Male	"			
Brig Sall & Hipe	Ben Chapman		43	Male	Merchant	Martinique	United States	
Schoo Felix	David Canter		40	Male	Merchant	Jamaica	Britain	
	A. Henrey		24	"	"	"	"	
	Captn. J. Ross		33	"	Marriner		"	
Brig Francis	William Humble		22	Male	None	Dundee	"	
Schoo: Phoenix	Martin Long		45	Male	Merchant	Grenada	"	
Brig Pelgrim	John McGowan		45	Male	Merchant	Liverpool	"	
Schoo Marion	Doctor Monet		44	Male	Dr. Medicine	Havanna	United States	
	Mrs. Monet		16	Female	None		"	
	R. Fontanroie		24	Male	Planter			
	J. Denaco		24	"	Merchant		Italy	
	J. Sperow		20	"	Trader		Spain	
Schoo Eliza &	Francis Joseph		30	Male	Trader		Portugal	
Polly	Ann Lopez		24	Female	None		United States	
Schoo Swift	Charles Lowrey		50	Male	Taylor	Nassau	United States	
Ship St. Peter	Henry Austin		41	Male	Merchant	St. Thomas	United States	
	A. Puttman		41	"	"	"	"	
	Le bothe		70	"	"		France	
Schoo Louisa	Peta Mitchell	April	19	"	Servant	Trinidad	United States	
Ship Mary	Mrs. Ann Daughty		58	Female	None		United States	
Catharine	John Ward		32	Male	Merchant	Liverpool	Britain	
Ship Fama	Mrs. Berry		26	Female	none	ditto	U S	"
Brig Clarissa Ann	John Donaughan		45	Male	Merchant	Havana	Britain	"
Ship Thalia	John Routiers		25	Male	none	Antwerp	Holland	Holland
	Doctor McGinn		36	"	Doctor Me.	Matanzes	Britain	U S
	Mrs. McGinn (two children)		24	Female	none		U S	"
	Christopher Castino		32	Male	Merchant		Spain	"
	Antonio Aimar		28	"	Trader		Portugal	"
	Madam Lelnoise[?]		45	Female	none		Spain	"
	Peter Dordelay		23	Male	"		Germany	"
Schooner	Damus Smith		30	"			Britain	Britain
Favorite	L. J. Smith		20	Female		St. Thomas	"	"
	Caroline Smith		18 months	"			"	"
	Kollrain		2 do	"			"	"

PASSENGERS ARRIVING AT THE PORT OF CHARLESTON 1820-1829

Name of vessel	Passengers' names	Date of arrival	Age	Sex	Occupation	Where from	Country-belong	Country-inhabit
Brig Caroline Ann	M. Samporac	April 1823	30	Male	Merchant	Bourdeaux	France	France
Schooner Leopardo	Mariana Pala		22	Male	None	Neuivitas	Spain	Spain
	Josse Harrizle		22	"	"			
Brig Minerva	Ann Anderson		30	Female	none	Liverpool	Britain	Britain
Brig Columbia	John Ross		20	Male	Labourer	London	do	U S
Brig Alexander le Grande	Antonio Cabal		48	Male	None	Porto Prince	France	Hayti
	F. Samiento		32	"	"		"	"
	J. Couffon		30	"	Merchant			
	H. Danviers		24	"	Merchant			
Schooner Swift	Henderson Furgoson		60	Male	Planter	Nassau		
	Mrs. Furgoson		50	Female	none		U S	U S
	Theodore Gaillard		50	Male	Factor		Britain	Nassau
	Sextus Gaillard		26	"	do		U S	Charleston
	L. Watkins		28	"	do			
Schooner Jane	John Warner		50	Male	Commercial Agent	Havanna		
	Charles Starr		23	"	U S Navy			
	Doctor Bell [Bett?]		28	"	do			
Schooner Harriet	Francis Marshall		52	Male	Planter	Matanzes		
Schooner Wicker	Thomas D. Loughany				Merchant	Turks Isle		
Sloop Providence	Isaac Suthram	April 1823	44	Male	Manufacturer	Jamaica	U S	Charleston
	John Murphy		22	"	Merchant			
	L. R. Strong		27	"	ditto			
	Mary Ann			Female	none			
Brig Catherine	Mrs. Jeve & child		39	Female	none	Havana		
	Mr. Galuchat		35	Male	MD			
	A. Schutt		27	"	Planter		France	
	LeMaetre		25	"	Merchant		Italy	
	Urban		30	"	"		U S	
	Gaillard		35	"	"		U S	U S
Schooner Harret	Peter Maccaletti		45	Male	Marriner	Havanna		
	Walter Wilkie		33	"	Trader			
	John Shuburk		27	"	Marriner			
Brig Phoeby	Henry Little	May	48	Male	Farmer	Greenock	Britain	Britain
	Jean Little		30	Female	None			
	Brian, Robert, William		15, 13, 12 Males		Sons of the above			
	John George, David & Thos		10, 9, 8 "		ditto			
	Mary & an infant		5, 1 Females		Daughters of the above			
Brig Rachael & Sally	Joseph Esprina		50	Male	Merchant	Havana	Spain	Spain
	Stephen Anderson		25	"	"		U S	U S
	Anthony Purdy		35	"	"			
	Stephen Aurrows		32	"	"			
	John Morriston		27	"	"			
	Mr. Aiken		50	"	"			

43

PASSENGERS ARRIVING AT THE PORT OF CHARLESTON 1820-1829

Name of vessel	Passengers' names	Date of arrival	Age	Sex	Occupation	Where from	Country- belong	Country- inhabit
Sloop Norfolk	T. Tomaison	May 1823	38	Male	Mariner	Barracou	France	U S
Brig	Charles O'Sullivan		32	Male	Painter	Matanzes	Britain	"
Charles Coffin	Mrs. O'Sullivan 3 children		23	Female	none	none	U S	"
	Anthony Aymar		30	Male	Trader		Italy	"
	Madame Delorme		53	Female	none		France	"
	Peter Dordilly		24	Male	"		Britain	"
	J. B. Zegmage		23	"	"		"	"
	John Stoddard		26	"	"		"	"
Sloop Venus	Capt. Martinelli		35	Male	Mariner	St. Thomas	Spain	"
	Miss Martinelli		5	Female	none		"	"
	Stanley		40	Male	"		"	"
Brig Leod	William Kerr		40	Female	Merchant	Turks Isle	Britain	British Isles
Ship	Jesse Levingston		32	Female	None	Greenock	do	U S
Roger Stewart	Ann ditto		4	"	"		"	"
Ship	John Black		11	Male	"	London		"
Issabella	Mrs. Lowe		35	Female	"			"
	Jessie Lowe		7	"	"			"
	Therissa Lowe		5	"	"			"
	Somerville		32	Male	Butcher			"
	Flalman		25	"	Sugar Baker		Germany	"
	Feckman		26	"	do		"	"
Ship Phacion	James Magile		22	Male	Farmer	Belfast	Britain	U S
	Ester Magile		21	Female	none		"	"
Brig Fanny	Francis LaRousellier		33	Male	Merchant	Havanna	France	"
	Joseph Barriele		32	"	"		"	"
	James Gordall		29	"	"		"	"
	M. Mendoza		35	"	"		"	"
	Mrs. Mendoza & three children		28	Female	none		"	"
	Mrs. Rosella		28	"	"		"	"
Schooner	Siles E. Lightbourn		37	Male	Merchant	Matanzes	Britain	Africa
Dolphin	James Greese		30	"	do		Charleston	U S
Schooner Return	H. W. Junge		22	"	do	St. Lucie	N. Carolina	"
Brig	Brown		48	"	Merchant	Havana	Britain	U S
Catharine	Cloth		35	"	do		Germany	"
	Joseph Tholesan		30	Male	do		France	"
	Robert) slaves of the			"	none		U S	"
	Alfred) Rev. Dr. Gahahas			"	"			"
Schooner Eliza	A. Forsyth		55	"	Marriner	Havana	France	"
Schooner Aurora	Robert F. Martin		28	"	Trader	Marseilles	"	"
	William S. Barton		34	"	"			"
Brig Phoeby	Alexander Brewington[?]	October	28	Male	Mariner	Greenock	Britain	"
	Tho's Thornton		27	do	do			"

44

PASSENGERS ARRIVING AT THE PORT OF CHARLESTON 1820-1829

Name of vessel	Passengers' names	Date of arrival	Age	Sex	Occupation	Where from	Country- belong	Country- inhabit
Ship	John Louden	October 1823	36	Male	Merchant	Liverpool		
Lola Rookh	Mary Ann Louden		36	Female	none			
	Geo Louden		25	Male	none			
	Joseph Watson		25	"	Clerk			
Ship Science	E. H. Ormond		22	"	Merchant	Greenock		
	Elizabeth ditto		26	Female	Merchant			
	James Agnes Russell		18	Female				
	J[?] Keller[?]		7	child				
	John McIver[?]		23	Male	Merchant			
	John Campbell		36	Male	Labourer			
	Mary Spencer		26	Female	Spinster			
Leoparde	Bedon[?] Ar---		22	Male	Merchant	Port Principe	K---	
	F. V. Orango		23	"	do			
Ship Majestic	William Hudson		22	"	Druggist	Liverpool	Britain	
Sch'r Mary Ann	P. M. Peeron[?]		35	"	Merchant	Matanzas	Spain	
	Joseph Percell[?]		20	"	do			
Schr Geo Armsted	Pascal Mccolloh		46	"	Trader	Havanna	Italy	
Ship James	John Richardson		26	"	Farmer	Belfast	Britain	
Bailey	John Haveron		24	"	Clerk			
	James Gray		25	"	Farmer			
	James Kennedy		22	"	do			
	John Kennedy		7	"	none			
	Howard Kennedy		13	"	do			
	Andrew Kennedy		40	"	Doctor			
	Ann Kennedy		40	"	none			
	Cunro[?], Isabella[?]		children to the above					
	William McCabe[?]		27	Male	Farmer			
	Joseph Hunter		17	"	Clerk			
	John Gilliland		17	"	do			
	James Brown		34	Male	Farmer			
	Precilla Steward		20	Female	Spinster			
	Eliza Steward		19	"	do			
	Nathan Todd		28	Male	Farmer			
Sch'r Marion	J. F. Tavel	November	25	Male	Merchant[?]	Havanna	Spain	
	Francis Aves		30	"	Planter			
	John Edme		34	"	Merchant			
Sch'r Eliza &	James Martin[?]		30	"	Marriner			
Polly	James Green		70	"	Trader			
	Antonio White[?]		27	"	do			
Brig	Dr. Mc---		35	"	Physician			
Catherine	S-----		24	"	Merchant			
	A. ----		21	"	carpenter			

PASSENGERS ARRIVING AT THE PORT OF CHARLESTON 1820-1829

Name of vessel	Passengers' names	Date of arrival	Age	Sex	Occupation	Where from	Country- belong	Country- inhabit
Ship	James ----	November 1823	35	Male	Merchant	Liverpool	Britain	
Mary	Edward ----		75	"	do		"	
Catherine	A. H. ----		78	"	Physician			So Carolina
	Henry ----		26	"	do			"
	Thomas P---		27	Male	Lawyer		Britain	
	Thomas Dixon		48	Male	-----		"	
	Thomas Dixon's children		children ----					
	Lemette						France	
Sh'r Mary & Eliza	William Lee		26	Male	Doctor		U S	
Ship Marmion	R. Steward		20	Male	Merchant	Turks Isle	U S	
	J. Weliby		30	"	do	Liverpool	"	
	John Man Taylor		24		Planter		"	
	William Broadfoot		28		Merchant		"	
	Niel McNeil		40		do		"	
	James Evans		45		Stone Cutter		"	
	D. McNichol		35		Merchant		"	
	Thomas Kirk		32		do		"	
	R. E. Brown		38		do		"	
	Hugh Smith		35		do		"	
Ship	J. L. Mulineau		31		Sailmaker		"	
Margarett	J. W. Roandell		32		do		"	
	A. Byrne[?]		27		do		"	
	James Mayberry		20		do		"	
	Edward Walker		20		do		"	
Brig	A. Weatherby		30		Merchant		"	
Caroline Ann	J. Rogers		18		Merchant	Havana	U S	
	J. Sullivan		24		do		"	
	A. Valeth & Lady		42		do		"	
Ship Portia	Abraham Dorliz[?]		25 & 18		Merchant	Bordeaux	U S	
	Wm. H. Potter		23		do		"	
	J. Lemont		25		Marriner		U S	
Bark	John Shaw		42		Merchant	Belfast	France	
Caledonia	William Hart		24	Male	Merchant		Britain	
	Rev. F. Rolando		21	"	do			
	Dr. McLarmore		43	"	Catholic			
	James Lowry		20	"	-----			
	Wm Loyd		20	"	Clerk			
	William Canson		28	"	do			
	Jane Carson & child		28	Female	Agriculture			
	D. McKinley		24	Male	"			
	John Dinney[?]		28	"	"			
	James Martin		24	"	"			
	Alexander Gilson		17	"	"			

46

PASSENGERS ARRIVING AT THE PORT OF CHARLESTON 1820-1829

Name of vessel	Passengers' names	Date of arrival	Age	Sex	Occupation	Where from	Country- belong	Country- inhabit
Bark Caledonia	William McDowell	November 1823	20	Male	Agriculture			
	John McConnell		50	"	"			
	Mary Ditto & seven children		48	Female	"			
	James McAnnell wife & child		24		"			
	James Rea		50	Male	"			
	Jane Rea & six children		46	Female	"			
	John Faulkner		44	Male	"			
	Martha ditto & children							
	Hugh McCarley[?]		25	Male	"			
	Ruth Wilson		38	Female	"			
	Jane Wilson		26		"			
	John Wilson & children		40	Male	"			
	Willm McConnell & 2 ditto		30	"	"			
	William Ba---		22	"	"			
	James Rogers[?]		20	"	"			
	John M----		30	"	"			
	Elinore & __ child		30	Female	"			
	Mary Ann Lecky		10	Female	"			
	William Lecky		13	Male	"			
	James McCarrol		13	"	"			
	Davis McCarrol[?]		32	"				
	Issabella Johnson & 7 children		42	Female				
	William Stewart		18	Male				
	William Kelso		12	"				
	John Scott & __ children		49	"				
	Robert [torn]		--					
	Robert Kirkpatrick[?]		--					
	Issabella do & __ children		54	Female				
	John Kelp		9	Male				
	John McNab & child		24	Male				
	Margaret ditto		20	Female				
	Margaret Black[?]		22	"				
	Patrick Grubb[?]		21	Male				
	Jane -----		20	Female				
	William ----		30	Male				
	John Kerr[?]		45	"				
	Mary ---- & child		24	Female				
	Patrick ----		32	Male				
	Roger Wilson[?]		24	"				
	Renard ----		30	"				
	Robert Connor[?]		24	"				
	Margaret Boyd & five[?] children		50	Female				
	Peter Taffey		12	Male				

47

PASSENGERS ARRIVING AT THE PORT OF CHARLESTON 1820-1829

Name of vessel	Passengers' names	Date of arrival	Age	Sex	Occupation	Where from	Country- belong	Country- inhabit
Bark								
Caledonia	John Fegan	November 1823	20	Male			So Carolina	
	Patrick Brady		22	"				
	Eliza Wilson		23	Female				
Ship								
South Carolina	Arnoldus Vanderhorst	December	60	Male	Planter	Liverpool	Britain	
Brig Union	James Mitchell		40	do	Mechanic			
	Nathan Reuben		40	"	Trader	Jamaica		
	Francis Illsby		21	"	Mechanic			
	Harting Cohen		35	"	Jew Priest			
Sch Cammilla	LeMaitre		16	"	Merchant	Havre	France	
Sch Susan	William Bond[?] [Bird?]		30	"	none	Gibraltar	U S	
	H. Hooker[?]		26	"				
Ship Alfred	Robert Wallace		23	"	Merchant	Greenock	Britain	
	Mrs. Wallace		30	Female	"			
	Miss Wallace		20	"				
	Mary McGovern		25	"	Servant			
	Min Douglas		16	"				
Ship Harriott	Alexander Lois[?]		37	Male	Marriner	Liverpool	"	
	John Reid		35	"	Farmer			
Ship Solon	John Barlow		55	"	"	"	"	
	Ann Barlow		15	Female	"			
	Henry Barlow		45	Male	"			
	Mary Barlow		47	Female	"			
	Mary Ann Barlow		7	"				
	Martha & James Archer		16 12	M & Female				
Ship Hercules	William Green		56	Male	Laborer	Belfast	Britain	
	Mary Green		56	Female	"			
	Sarah Green		13	do	"			
	William Whitecar, Lady & 2 children		24		Farmer			
	John ----		10	male				
	John McGovern		22	"				
	Robert Boyd		30					
	Jane Boyd		22	Female				
	Eliza Sincler[?]		24	"				
	James do		26	male				
	Alexander do		14	"				
	Mary do		28	Female				
	Robert Lowry		16	male				
	Ann McConnell[?]		60	Female				
	William do		30	male				
	Archie, Salley & _____		13 18 16					
	John do		10	male				
	Benjamin Catlett[?]		17	"				
	Thomas Henderson		21	"				

PASSENGERS ARRIVING AT THE PORT OF CHARLESTON 1820-1829

Name of vessel	Passengers' names	Date of arrival	Age	Sex	Occupation	Where from	Country-belong	Country-inhabit
Ship Hercules	Thomas L. Cobb[?]	December 1823	24	male				
	Charles McK---		30	"				
	Robert Kennedy		27	"				
	Charles do		33	"				
	Sarah & Ann Eliza		22 23	females				
	William & Samuel		70 60	males				
	Wm Mury[?] & Wm Henderson			children				
	Samuel English & children							
	James Bethel		68	male				
	Jane Livingston[?]		22	female				
	Joseph J------		24	male				
	John McG---		30	"				
	Henry Caulfield							
	Henry Fallow							
	Bella Gunl--							
	Henry ---		21	male				
	Sarah Coulter		20	female				
	William Hamilton							
	Mon Flack ----							
	James Parker		18	male	Merchant			
	Mary Patterson[?]		26	female	do			
	James -----		18	male	Cath ----			
	J. Johnson		29	do	Merchant			
	J. E. G---		27	do	do			
	William ----		22	do	do			
	Arthur Davis		24	do				
	William		32	do				
	William		30	do				
	Sally Todd		35	do				
	B-- Agnew		7					
	James		22					
	William		32					
Schooner Eliza & Polly	James Green		26		Merchant	Havanna	Spain	
	Jesse D---		41		do			
	John Lopez		35		do			
Brig Hero	R. P. Barien		45		Mariner	Greenock	Britain	
	Woodrow		36		Merchant	Liverpool	"	
Brig Genl Brown	Thos Hindley		46		"			
	Gardner		33		"			
	Dr. James Smith		27		Physician			
	George Oates		34		Merchant			
	L. Trapman		36		ditto	Havanna	Spain	

49

PASSENGERS ARRIVING AT THE PORT OF CHARLESTON 1820-1829

Name of vessel	Passengers' names	Date of arrival	Age	Sex	Occupation	Where from	Country- belong	Country- inhabit
Schooner Chase	Samuel Taylor	December 1823	48		Merchant			
	A. E----		23		do			
	P. O'Sullivant		50		do		Britain	
Brig Angeline	James ----		20		Marriner	Havanna		
	P. S. Sutton		40		Mason			
Brig Panther	Charles Bacon		32		Merchant	Havanna	U S	
	William S. Mason		33		Mariner			
	William Johnson		31		Planter			
	J. Gronnill		35		do			
Brig Brutus	William Hood		36		Merchant	Turks Isle	Britain	
Brig Charles	A. Aymar		40		"	Matanzas	Spain	
	James Harswell		23		"			
	J. O. Campos		30		"			
	Christopher		33		"			
	John Asparo		39		"			
	Antonio B---		35		"			
	Madam Campos		37	female	"			
	H. B. Crews		27	male	"			
Schooner Sallie & Polly	J. G. Thompson		30	male		Jamaica	France	
	Marquess[?]		25	"				
Brig Wave	Haracues[?]		36	male	Merchant	Rochelle	ditto	
	S. S. Davis[?]		26	"				

50

PASSENGERS ARRIVING AT THE PORT OF CHARLESTON 1820-1829

Name of vessel	Passengers' names	Date of arrival	Age	Sex	Occupation	Where from	Country- belong	Country- inhabit
Brig Catherine	Mr. & Mrs. Dally	January 1824	52	47	Merchant	Havanna	Britain	Britain
	Sullivan		32	Male	Trader	"	do	U S
Ship Fama	John Thomas		70	Male	ditto	Liverpool		"
Schooner Mars	R. Fitzpatrick		29	"	none	Havanna	U S	U S
Schooner	John Hussey		25	"	Merchant	"	Britain	"
Only Daughter	H. B. Hemmely		28	"	Planter	Matanzes	U S	"
Schooner	John Esnard		23	"	do		"	"
Lordy Kesiah	Willm Ripely		37	"	Merchant	Havanna	Britain	Britain
Schooner Mary	Antonio Belancourt		20	"	"		Spain	Spain
	V. B. Holmes		25	"	"		do	do
	P. M. Purniar[?]		30	"	"	Matanzas	do	do
	Antonio Mova		28	"	"		do	do
	Joseph Riles		27	"	"		U S	U S
Ship	Mrs. McGregor		32	Female		Glascow	Britain	U S
Margaret Bogle	Elizabeth & Jessie do	6 & 4	"	"		"	"
	Donald		3	Male				
	M. McKinlay		27	"	"		"	"
Schooner	John Roderique		35	"	"	Porto Rico	Spain	"
Horatio	A. G. White		25	"	"		"	"
Schooner	John Repito		39	"	Mariner		U S	U S
Martha	Antonio Visco		44	"	Merchant	Havanna	Italy	
	Pedro Gracia		35	"	Mariner		"	
	James Green		27	"	Merchant		Britain	"
Brig	James Hamilton		14	"	Marriner		U S	"
James Munroe	William Amassin		26	"	do	Marseilles	Britain	"
	John Vidall		32	"	Trader		U S	"
	Joseph Urban		25	"	do		France	"
	Edward Carmett		23	"	do		"	"
	Mrs. Carmett		22	[sic]	do		"	"
	Joseph Stubbs		36		none		"	"
Schooner	Mrs. P----		27	female	-----	Charleston	"	"
Genl Brewer	Mr. Tilmus		25	Male	-----	Havanna	Havana	"
	Mrs. Tilmus		20	female	none			"
	Lewis Cortea		19	Male	Trader			"
	John Rogers		27	do	do		N York	"
Schooner Trio	Alexander M. Edwards	February	41	do	Judge	Nassau	Britain	Britain
	Mrs. Edwards		40	female	none			"
	Miss Edwards		22	do	"			"
	Miss S. Edwards		7	do	"			"
	John Wm. ditto		5	female				"
	Mr. Longelipe		29	do	Merchant			"
	Miss Hewett		22	female	none			"

PASSENGERS ARRIVING AT THE PORT OF CHARLESTON 1820-1829

Name of vessel	Passengers' names	Date of arrival	Age	Sex	Occupation	Where from	Country-belong	Country-inhabit
Brig Toderson	Mr. Hewson	February 1824	35	Male	Marriner	Turks Isle	U S	U S
	Kerr		36	"	Merchant		"	"
Sloop Halcyon	Don Augustus Ayrias		51	Male	Planter	Havanna	Spain	U S
Brig Rachael & Sally	James McEwain		35	Male	Horse ----	Havanna	Spain	
Schooner Ann	Wm. H. Fowle		30	"	Merchant	St. Domingo	U S	U S
Ship Triton	Wm Stilley		55	"	Farmer	Liverpool	Britain	"
	James Stilley		19	"	"		"	"
	Juncus[?] Stilley		17	"	"		"	"
	G. Fitzpatrick		30	"	"		"	"
	Mary Fitzpatrick		25	"	"		"	"
	Charles Mooney		21	"	"		"	"
Schooner Amity	John DeNully	omitted	40	"	Merchant	St. Thomas	St. Thomas	"
	Sebastian Arzimo	in March	50	"	"		France	"
	Francisco Page		35	"	"			"
Schooner Mary	Don Carlos Rumos		26	"	"	Trinidad	Spain	"
	E. Blamenhugen		27	"				"
Brig Rachael & Sally	John D. Bowen		27	"	Lawyer	Havana	U S	"
	Mrs. M. Bowen		27	"	Lady			"
	Mr. E. L. Bowen		19	"	none			"
	E. Tashnach		30	"	Mariner		Britain	"
	John Lamoth		30	"	Merchant		Spain	"
	Miss C. Asavada		11	female	none			"
Schooner Swift	Wm. Martin	February	37	Male	Lawyer	Nassau	Britain	Britain
	H. McIntosh		21	Female	none		"	"
	Mrs. P. Young		41	do	none		"	"
Brig Hunter	Geo. Fraser		18	Male	Farmer	Belfast	Britain	U S
	James Bunten		40	"	"		"	"
	James McCance		25	"	"		"	"
	Sally McCance		53	Female	"		"	"
	John McCance		55	Male	"		"	"
	Rose McCance		54	Female	"		"	"
	John McCance Sr.		58	Male	"		"	"
	John McCance Jr.		16	"	"		"	"
	Hugh McCance		12	"	"		"	"
	William McCance		10	"	"		"	"
Brig Florida	Jacob Wiss		25	"	Trader	Trinidad	France	"
Brig Charles	Antonio Eymar		30	"	Merchant	Matanzas	U S	"
	D. P. Rogers		30	"	Planter			"
Schooner Chase	Stevenson Richards		35	"	"	Havana		"
	Antonio Boria		38	"	"		"	"
	Julen Drishe		27	"	"		"	"
	Lewis Tantee		24	"	"		"	"

PASSENGERS ARRIVING AT THE PORT OF CHARLESTON 1820-1829

Name of vessel	Passengers' names	Date of arrival	Age	Sex	Occupation	Where from	Country- belong	Country- inhabit
Sloop Mary Jane	F. Roye	February 1824	34	Male	Merchant	Baracca	Spain	U S
Brig Catharine	Col. Todd		35	"	U S --	Havana	U S	"
	Mr. Hanby		35	"	----		Britain	"
	" Conway		30	"	U S --		U S	"
Brig Catherine	Mr. Horsworth		28	Male	M---	Havana	U S	U S
Schooner Esther	Jeremiah ----n		35	Male			U S	U S
	Myers		40	"			"	"
	Alexander Anderson		45	"			"	"
	H. D. Cartwright		27	"			"	"
Schr Only Daughter	M. OBryan	March	35	"		Matanzes	"	"
Brig Caroline Ann	Thos Martin		26	"	School master[?]	St. Thomas	"	"
Schooner Chace	Stephen Richards		28	"	M--------	Havana	"	"
	Esteben S. Inclar		30	"			"	"
	Samuel Espry		27	"			"	"
	Isaac Minehull		40	"			"	"
	John R. Caldwell		38	"		Matanzes	"	"
Sloop Rising Sun	Henry Bigdon		30	"	Mun--	Havana	"	"
Sch'r Sally & Polly	Edward Delorme		25	"			"	"
	William Michelletto		25	"			"	"
	C. Belin		30	"			"	"
	S. Horspool		20	"			"	"
Brig Charles	Mr. Edan		29	"		Matanzes	"	"
	Wm. C. Gowen		45	"			"	"
	Edward Bruce		20[?]"				"	"
	Anthony Eymar		40	"			France	France
Ship Brandt	Miss E. Steinhawrn		16	Female		Havre	U S	U S
Ship Marmion	Mr. L. H. Himely		25	Male		Liverpool	"	"
	R. J. Scott		21	"			"	"
	A. Scott		18	"			"	"
	D. Hannah		20	"			"	"
Ship Mary Catherine	Rev. Wm. Hogan		35	"	Catholic minster	Liverpool	Britain	U S
	Job Tomlinson		20	"	Farmer[?]		Britain	"
Brig Catherine	Doctor Mayat	April	35	Male	Physician	Havanna	U S	U S
	C. Magnan		28	"	Planter		"	"
	Charles Winthop		25	"	Merchant		"	"
	Mr. Sampson		30	"	Trader		"	"
Schooner Esther	Madam Lachain		50	"	None	Matanzes	"	"
	A. Barbot & child		38	"	Merchant		France	France
	John Biscase		28	"	"		"	"
	James McElorne		32	"	"		"	"
Schooner Eudora	Antonio Buederot		35	"	Taylor	St. Jago	Britain	"
	Edward Baker		30	"	Mechanic		U S	U S

53

PASSENGERS ARRIVING AT THE PORT OF CHARLESTON 1820-1829

Name of vessel	Passengers' names	Date of arrival	Age	Sex	Occupation	Where from	Country- belong	Country- inhabit
Schooner Franklin	Lemartie	April 1824	22	Male	Merchant	Carthagena	France	U S
Schooner Only Daughter	Thomas Cooper		29	"	"	Matanzes	Britain	"
Brig Genl Brown	Robert King		82	"	none	Liverpool		
Brig Panther	A. Lambert		27	Male	Merchant	Havanna	U S	U S
	Phillip Young		40	"	"		"	"
	Henry Young		18	"			"	"
	Paul Thomasin		41	"	Mariner	Jamaica	"	"
Schooner Rabit	J. B. F. Fubachet		45	"	none		"	"
	James Ward		21	"	"		"	"
	Alphus Locur		52	"			"	"
	Samuel Kerr		30	"	Mariner		"	"
Ship Favorite	Mrs. Levy & Child		25	Female	none	London	Britain	Spain
Schooner Betsy	Brooks Pots		14	Male	Merchant		U S	U S
	Theodore Flotard		25	"	Merchant	Gaudaloupe	Britain	"
	Louis Burtell		24	"			"	"
	John Murrichen		24	"	Doctor		"	"
Schooner Lovely Kesiah	John Ross	May	45	"	Merchant	Havanna	U S	U S
	John Lopez		40	"	"		"	"
	B. Durban		35	"	"		"	"
	Valentine Sala		38	"	"		Spain	Spain
	Anthony Brayas		45	"			"	"
Ship Conova	George French		40	"	Farmer	Havre	Switzerland	U S
	Philip Hailfort		25	"	"		"	"
	John Schefer		23	"	"		"	"
	Frederick Miller		19	"	"		"	"
Brig Charles	A. Eymar		30	"	Merchant	France	France	
	Hatten		26	"			"	
	R. Perrot		19	"	Mechanic		"	
	J. Asparo		39	"	Merchant	Matanzes	U S	
Schooner Esther	Alexander McBeath		45	"	Planter	Matanzes	Britain	Britain
	Mrs. McBeath		22	Female	none		"	"
	2 children		13 9	Male	"			
	James Green		26	"	Merchant		"	
Schooner Chan	Negroe Lucy wench		25	Female	Domestic	Havanna	Spain	Spain
	John Scott		26	Male	Merchant		U S	U S
	Orr		28	"	"		"	"
Brig Orient	Geo DeRoche		45	"	"		Britain	
Ship Corsair	Josep Farnandez	June	25	"	Stone Cutter	Cadez	Spain	U S
	Jeremiah Connelly		30	"	Farmer	Liverpool	Britain	U S
	Thomas Conelly		17	"	"		"	"
	Andrew Crothy		41	"	"		"	"
	Joseph Cutting			"	"			

54

PASSENGERS ARRIVING AT THE PORT OF CHARLESTON 1820-1829

Name of vessel	Passengers' names	Date of arrival	Age	Sex	Occupation	Where from	Country- belong	Country- inhabit
Sloop Mercator	C. Milligut	June 1824	35	Male	Merchant	Porto Rico	France	U S
Brig James Munroe	Elizabeth Richards		32	"	none	Havanna	Britain	St. Domingo
	Jon Urban		35	"	merch		U S	U S
	Pedre Joseph F. Soltomayer		40	"	minister		St. Domingo	St. Domingo
	Jon Bouchet		32	"	cutler		U S	U S
	Richard Zimmerman		35	"	merchant		"	"
Brig James Munroe	Lewis Michallette		40	Male	merchant		U S	U S
	Houserman		42	"	mariner		"	"
Schooner Chase	S. C. Tennant		24	Male	Merchant	Havana	Britain	U S
	Morres ODonald		32	"	Tutor		Britain	U S
	M. C. Kelly		28	"	"		"	"
	J. M. Tuesky		31	"	Merchant		"	"
	A. R. Fernandez		40	"	Clerk		Holland	"
Ship Issabella	J. S. Cohen		24	"	merchant	Liverpool	Spain	"
	Miss A. Cohen		18	Female	none		Britain	"
	Martin Pendygrass		20	Male	clerk			"
Brig Panther	Charles Conyers		25	"	Merchant	Jamaica	U S	"
Brig Carolina Ann	Alexander Harang		50	"	Planter	Porto Rico	"	"
Brig Leod	Edward G. Lightbourn		19	"	"	Turks Isle	Britain	Cuba
Schooner Louisiana	James Magnian		33	"	Merchant	Havanna	U S	U S
Ship Marmion	J. C. Jenkins		28	"	none	Liverpool	Britain	Britain
Brig Atlas	Michael OReily		22	"	none	Liverpool		"
Ship Tarantula	Joseph Wompomero		40	"	Military Officer	Havanna	Spain	Spain
	Margaretta Wompomero & child		35	"	none			"
	Augustine Ordonera		35	"	do			"
	Francis Bravo		35	"	"			"
	Guaro Guezo & niece		65	"	Merchant			"
	Rouan Oliver		40	"	Priest			"
	John Meatas		35	"	Merchant			"
	Gregorus Lepez		33	"	Serjean			"
	Romaro Galegas		40	"	do			"
	Castatiner Lopez & child		27	Female	Soldiers Wife			"
	Cadigo Oliva		40	Male	soldier			"
	Pedro Orago		39	"	"			"
	Antonio Pena		37	"	"			"
	Manuel Gill		36	"	"			"
	Johan Vayoas		39	"	"			"
	Diego Toleno		40	"	"			"
	Manuel Martinez		37	"	"			"
	Antonio Herrira		40	"	"			"
	Felip Cartu		47	"	"			"

55

PASSENGERS ARRIVING AT THE PORT OF CHARLESTON 1820-1829

Name of vessel	Passengers' names	Date of arrival	Age	Sex	Occupation	Where from	Country- belong	Country- inhabit
Schooner Mars	Herman Follin	June 1824	35	Male	Merchant	Barracoa	U S	U S
	Willm. G. Lowry		22	"	Physician		"	"
	Ulins Romylae		22	"	Merchant		"	"
Brig Catherine	Don Juane Xene	July 1824	19	Male	None	Havanna	Spain	Spain
	" Dronido Mantilla		20	"	"	"	"	"
	" Joaquim Penalvers		22	"	"		"	"
	Miguel de Corderos		10	"	"		"	"
	J. P. Bane		29	"	Merchant		French	U S
	Mrs. Obegnaud		48	Female	none		do	Spain
	Olario servant		22	Male	Domestic		Spain	U S
Brig Charles	James Pepnot		31	"	Mechanic	Matanzes	France	"
	William G. Barney		31	"	Marriner		U S	"
	Barre		33	"	Merchant		France	"
Brig Trader	Durban		26	"	do	Havanna	do	"
Ship Charles & Henry	Nicholas Sergas		15	"	Schoolmaster		Spain	"
	Anthony Pelzer		45	"	Mechanic	Amsterdam	Holland	"
	Henry Cockroft		52	"	none		U S	"
	" Cockroft		14	"				
Ship Mary Catherine	James Downes		15	"	Mechanic	Liverpool	Britain	"
	Robert Warren		16	"	"			
	[two names obliterated]		30	"			U S	U S
			27	"				
	Baptist Goeres		57	"	Merchant		Spain	Spain
do Leopardo	Cutan		38	"	do	ditto	ditto	do
Brig Catharine	Ogelby	August	38	"	none	St. Johns Cuba	U S	U S
Ship Crierie	John W. Bradley		22	"	Merchant	Havanna	Britain	"
	G. A. Lowe		40	"	Sol----	Londonderry	Britain	Britain
Schooner Mary	John Albert		35	female	none	Honduras	"	"
	Mrs. Albert		13	"	"		"	"
	Miss Albert		23	"	Dom---			
	Servant		40	Male	Mar---			
	Isago Torrella		18	"	La----		Spain	Spain
	Nicholas Rey		27	"	Merchant		"	"
Schooner Sally & Polly	P. Sanchez		23	"	?	Matanzas	"	"
	Jesse Alvaraz		30	"	do		"	"
	Antoine Aymar		27	"	do		France	U S
	James Green						U S	"
Schooner Mary	James Himely		29	Male	Planter	Havanna	U S	"
do Eliza	John Lopez		35	"	Trader	"	Spain	Spain
do Eliza & Jane	Burgar		22	"	Merchant	Barracoa	U S	U S
	Thomas Davis		37	"	Marriner		"	"
	Johns		40	"	"		"	"
Ship Triton	Margaret Mitchell		30	Female	none	Havre	"	"

PASSENGERS ARRIVING AT THE PORT OF CHARLESTON 1820-1829

Name of vessel	Passengers' names	Date of arrival	Age	Sex	Occupation	Where from	Country- belong	Country- inhabit
Schooner --iza	Jose Olibe	September 1824	29	Male	Merchant	Nassau	Spain	Spain
	Melnono Laman		27	"	"		"	"
	Juan Alvez		22	"	"		"	"
	John Salduar		17	"	"		"	"
	Aldefenso de Pamdedar		39	"	"		"	"
Schooner --iza	Francis Reye		35	Male	Merchant	Barracoa	U S	U S
Schooner	John Parcle		21	Male	"		U S	U S
Madison	George Bell		36	"	"	Havanna	"	"
Trader	Nicholas Grand		30	"	"		"	"
Trader	James Robertson		20	"	"		"	"
Ship	Charles E. Miller		38	"	"	Liverpool	Liverpool	"
	George Relph		38	"	"		U S	"
--rfect	Thomas Walton		36	Female	none	Bordeaux	France	"
	Madam Bollinaire		16	"	"		"	U S
Catharine	Julianna Chereugh		--	--	----			
	Fra------							
Schooner Eagle	Robert Buiger	October	30	Male	Marriner	Havanna	U S	U S
	J. P. Bean		30	"	Merchant		"	"
Ship Ceres	Jacob Hyams		24	"	Trader	Havre	Poland	"
Brig Antelope	Catherine Appleton		17	Female	none	Havanna	Cuba	"
Ship Corsair	John Gemmell		22	Male	Farmer	Liverpool	Britain	"
	Jane Gemmell		21	Female	none		"	"
	Martin Moult		36	Male	Merchant		"	"
	W. C. Mollineau		30	"	"		"	"
	Edward Menlove		25	"	"		"	"
	Stephen Watson		26	"	"		U S	"
	Thomas Bridgewood		30	"	"		"	"
	James Brown		20	"	"		"	"
	Frederick Miller		24	"	"		"	"
	Charles Brenan		33	"	Teacher		Britain	"
	Joe Oneale		27	"	Merchant		"	"
	Thomas Faulkner		48	"	Comedian		"	"
	James Howard		28	"	do		"	"
	Charles Hood		25	"	Carpenter		"	"
	John Syle		28	"	do		"	"
	Edward Henry		21	"	Clerk		"	"
	Patrick Dixon		30	"	Farmer		"	"
	James Dixon		30	"	do		"	"
	Andrew Dixon		26	"	Taylor		"	"
	John Dixon		26	"	"		"	"
	Daniel Conely		20	"	Farmer		"	"
	Alexander Campbell		24	"	"		"	"
	John Flaherty		27	"	Artist		"	"

57

PASSENGERS ARRIVING AT THE PORT OF CHARLESTON 1820-1829

Name of vessel	Passengers' names	Date of arrival	Age	Sex	Occupation	Where from	Country- belong	Country- inhabit
Ship Corsair	John Kelly	October 1824	26	Male	Clerk	Liverpool	Britain	U S
	Mary Kelly child		26	Female	none		"	"
	Eliza Hughes		34	"	Spinster		"	"
	Catherine Hughes		10	"	"		"	"
	Frances Hughes		7	"	"		"	"
	Mary Hughes		6	"	"		"	"
Brig Catherine	Mary Ann Tardy	November 1824	22	Female	none		Spain	"
	John Missroon		19	Male	Marriner		U S	"
	Frances de Sylva		35	"	Trader	Havanna		"
	P. Roderigues		26	Male	none		U S	U S
	J. Martinelle		42	"	"		"	"
Schooner Eliza	Susan Nichols		31	Female			"	"
	Capt. Lawrence		35	Male	Marriner		"	"
Schooner Eudora	Carreased Gomales		38	"	"	St. Jago Cuba	Spain	"
			40	"	"		"	"
Schooner Issabella	J. C. Stewart		24	Male	Merchant	Matanzes	Britain	U S
Brig Traveller	John Clark		56	Male	Surgeon	Dundee	"	"
	Robert Featherington		24	"	merchant		"	Britain
	Wm. B. Yates		18	"	none		"	"
	John Longmer		21	"	"		"	"
	John Lowden		40	"	Merchant		"	"
	Mrs. Lowden		38	Female	none		"	"
	George Lowden		18	Male	"		"	"
	Mrs. Martin		60	Female	"		U S	U S
Ship Ganges	Miss Campbell		19	"	Merchant	Liverpool	Britain	"
	Mr. Isaac		40	Male	Merchant		Britain	"
	" Higginbottom		50	"	"		"	"
	" Smith		23	"	"		"	"
Ship Minerva	Mrs. Carvin		45	Female	Trader		France	"
	A. LaBarbeire		24	Male	Merchant		U S	"
	J. LeMartre		16	"	do		U S	"
	J. Antonio Moore		25	"	"		Spain	"
Scho'r Thos Washington	Peter Poria		55	"	"	Havanna	"	"
	Henery Newman		40	Female	British Consul		Britain	Britain
	Mrs. Newman		35	Female	Lady		"	"
	3 children		11 9 3		children		"	"
	Three servants			Females	Servants		"	"
Ship Robt. Edwards	McClure		33	Male	Marriner	London	U S	"
	Mrs. McClure & Infant		27	Female	none		"	"
	Mrs. Morrison		31	"	Servant		Britain	Britain
	Miss Giles		29	"	none		"	"
	Mr. Fistre		40	Male	"		"	"
	Mrs. Reily & two children		33	Female	"		"	"

PASSENGERS ARRIVING AT THE PORT OF CHARLESTON 1820-1829

Name of vessel	Passengers' names	Date of arrival	Age	Sex	Occupation	Where from	Country- belong	Country- inhabit
Ship Robt. Edwards	Mrs. Clark & child	November 1824	35	Female	none	London	Britain	Britain
	J. J. Middleton		22	Male	none		U S	U S
	Mrs. Cullen		34	"	"		Britain	"
	John Coop		24	"	"		"	"
	John Brown		16	"	"		"	"
Ship Eagle	Don Roque Quintan		27	Male	Planter	Havanna	Spain	Spain
	" Josse Elsuarde		28	"	"			"
	" Manuel Arcaya		21	"	Military Officer			"
	Jon Gabriel Arcaya		21	"	"			"
Brig Dougy Trouen	Dr. Rauol		40	"	Physician	Havre	France	U S
	William Longsdon		45	"	Merchant		Britain	Britain
	Col. H. H. Bacot		47	"	Lawyer		U S	U S
Ship Majestic	T. H. Hindley		45	"	Merchant	Liverpool	Britain	"
	Dr. Wittr. Hume		25	"	Physician		"	"
	Alex. Mazyck		24	"	Lawyer		"	"
Ship Margaret Bogle	Wm. G. Scott		30	Male	Agriculturists	Greenock	Britain	U S
	Robt. McIntosh		45	"	"		"	"
	James Porter		23	"	"		"	"
	John Miller		40	"			"	"
	Mary Brown		34	Female	none		"	"
	Elizabeth Hazard		16	"	"		"	"
	Elizabeth Patterson		35	"	"		"	"
	Mary Tshudy		34	"	"		"	U S
Ship Mary Catherine	Mrs. Finn	December	45	Male	Planter	Liverpool	Britain	"
	John Rodgers		52	"	none		"	"
	James Gafney		18	"	merchant		"	"
	Mr. Hatton		28	"	none		"	"
	Mrs. Hatton		56	Female	Merchant		"	"
Scho'r Marion	Juan Baptist Cousa		60	Male	Baker	Havanna	Spain	"
	Thomas Ferath		40	"	Merchant	Belfast	Britain	U S
	Samuel Reed		30	"	none		"	"
Ship Caledonia	Samuel Singer		11	"	Merchant		"	"
	John J. Cassidy		23	Female	none		"	"
	Fannie[?] C. Cassidy		19	Male	Merchant		"	"
	William Logan		18	"	Farmer		"	"
	Preston Charters		21	"	"		"	"
	John Walker		34	"	"		"	"
	James Aiken		36	"	"		"	"
	Joseph Biggart		67	"	"[sic]		"	"
	Alex'r Biggart		40	"	"		"	"
	Mary Biggart		38					
	James, Joseph & John do 3 sons 20 19 17							
	Archy, Alexr, W. W. 3 do younger 12 9 3							

59

PASSENGERS ARRIVING AT THE PORT OF CHARLESTON 1820-1829

Name of vessel	Passengers' names	Date of arrival	Age	Sex	Occupation	Where from	Country- belong	Country- inhabit
Ship	Betty & Peggy daughters	20 13		Females		Belfast	Britain	U S
Caledonia	Daniel Stewart		45	Male	Farmer		"	"
	Robert Stewart		20	"	"		"	"
	James Stewart		18	"			"	"
	Martha, Jane & Mary, Eliza do 4 Females sisters		15		13 10 6		"	"
	Mary Collins & Infant		25	Female			"	"
	Mary Adams		34	Female			"	"
	Roseann, John & Esther children	13	6 3				"	"
	William Wylee		35	Male	Farmer		"	"
	David Happer		30	"	"		"	"
	Samuel Rath		20	"	"		"	"
	Bernard Henny		30	"	"		"	"
	Samuel Keenan		30	"	"		"	"
	Elizabeth Keenan		30		none		"	"
	Mary, Michael, John & George do	9, 8, 7, 4					"	"
	Natty Boulton		20	Male	Farmer		"	"
	Thomas Boyd		26	"	"		"	"
	Mary Boyd & two children		26	Female ages 3 & 1			"	"
	Alexander Henry		21	Male			"	"
	Maybella Henry & Infant		20	Female	3 months		"	"
	Ellen Harper		20	do	"		"	"
	William Thompson		24	Male	"		"	"
	Margaret Thompson		24	Female	"		"	"
	George Craig		26	Male	"		"	"
	Ann Craig & two children		24	Female 3 & 2 months			"	"
	John Marks		26	Male	"		"	"
	Margaret Marks		20	Female	"		"	"
	John Morran		24	Male	"		"	"
	Margaret Moran		22	Female	"		"	"
	Esther Gribben		22	do	"		"	"
	Catherine Murray		34	do	"		"	"
	James Murray		16	Male	"		"	"
	Pat & Robert Murray sons	12	2	do	"		"	"
	Ellen Murray daughter		9	Female	"		"	"
	William McCord		28	Male	"		"	"
	Robert Martin		6	"	"		"	"
	Sally Mooney		18	Female	"		"	"
	James Barbour		2	Male	"		"	"
	William McCand		28	"	"		"	"
	William Taylor		24	"	"		"	"
	John Elder		32	"	"		"	"
	William McRee		30	"	"		"	"
	Eleanor McRee & 2 children	1 & 2 months			"		"	"

60

PASSENGERS ARRIVING AT THE PORT OF CHARLESTON 1820-1829

Name of vessel	Passengers' names	Date of arrival	Age	Sex	Occupation	Where from	Country- belong	Country- inhabit
Ship Georgiana	James Barnett	December 1824	27	Male	Merchant	Belfast	Britain	U S
	Jane Eccles		18	Female	none		"	"
	John Rowand		35	Male	Farmer		"	"
	Eliza Jane Rowand		9	Female	"		"	"
	Sarah Rowand		32	Female	"		"	"
	James Rowand		7	Male	"		"	"
	Margaret Rowand		4	Female	"		"	"
	Edward Lathers		14	Male	"		"	"
	Richard Lathers		9	Male	Farmer		"	"
	Betty Mitchell		19	Female	"		"	"
	Timothy Dodd		38	Male	"		"	"
	Issabella Dodd		36	Female	"		"	"
	John & Samuel Dodd sons 14		4	Males	"		"	"
	Eliza, Maria, Jane & Isabella daughters 12, 9, 6, 2							
	Thomas Orr		18	Male	Farmer		"	"
	Betty McCoy		18	Female	"		"	"
	James McClane		22	Male	"		"	"
	Elizabeth McClane		19	Female	"		"	"
	James Johnson		21	Male	"		"	"
	William Walker		21	"	"		"	"
	William Smith		23	"	"		"	"
	Robert Boyd		21	"	"		"	"
	Samuel May		40	"	"		"	"
	Dennis ODonnald		28	"	"		"	"
	Thomas McCarven		28	"	"		"	"
	John McCormick		16	"	"		"	"
	Joseph Davis		18	"	"		"	"
	Jane Haskell		53	Female	"		"	"
Brig Charles Coffin	Henry M. Watson	January 1825	35	Male	Lawyer	Havanna	U S	U S
	William Symes		30	"	Mechanick		"	"
	Anthony Aymar		39	"	Trader		"	"
	Matheu Dustass		35	"	"		"	"
	John Hone Jr.		30	"	"		"	"
Scho'r Eagle	R. G. Wallace		30	"	Inspector		"	"
	William Foster		28	"	Pilot		"	"
	Alexander Harran		32	"	Trader		France	"
Scho'r Susan	Joab Blackman		30	"	Carpenter		U S	"
	Mrs. Blackman & 2 children		25	Female	none		"	"

PASSENGERS ARRIVING AT THE PORT OF CHARLESTON 1820-1829

Name of vessel	Passengers' names	Date of arrival	Age	Sex	Occupation	Where from	Country-belong	Country-inhabit
Ship Sarah &	O. H. Middleton	December 1824	25	Male	Factor	Liverpool	U S	U S
Caroline	C. J. Manigault		29	"	none		"	"
	J. C. Vanderhorst		43	"	"		"	"
	M. Gray		26	"			"	"
	G. Dates [Dales?]		35				"	"
	Ann Peak		25	Female			"	"
Ship Thornton	William Bunney		20	Male	Clerk		"	"
	P. O. Reilley		30	"		Greenock	Britain	"
Brig Ariel	Major Williside		30	"	Farmer		"	"
	Mary Williside		35	Female			"	"
Ship Lucies	A. Richardson		30	Male	Slater	Havre	France	"
Schooner Eliza	John Fiteau		30	"	Tailor	Havanna	"	"
Sch. Endeavour	Robert Hunter		26	"	Merchant	Chargres	Britain	"
Brig Emeline	Augustus Certenger		35	"	Mariner	St. Jago	Spain	"
Brig Pomona	Rev. Charles Isham	February 1825	35	Male	Minister	Matanzes	U S	U S
	Mr. Victor		35	"	Mechanic		France	
Schooner	Mrs. Moss & 2 children		30	Female	none	Jamaica	U S	
Col. Armstead	Mr. Gilmore		28	Male	"		Britain	
Brig Azores	James Minot		22	"	none	Madeira	U S	
Brig Commerce	Richard Goldsmith		35	"	Cabinet maker	Havre	"	
Sch'r Wicker	Dr. B. Tickner		40	"	N. Officer	Havana	"	
	Dr. G. Weems		22	"	"		"	
	A. Wood		29	"	Trader		"	
	Anget Roberts		35	"				
	P. Ficardo		35	"				
Brig Leod	William Kerr		37	"	Merchant	Turks Isle	Britain	
	James E. Durrell		15	"	Marriner		"	
Sch. Marion	Godfrey Schutt		25	"	Planter	Havanna	U S	
	James Reynolds		40	"	merchant		"	
	J. L. Peizant		45	"	do		"	
Brig Miller	William Harper		47	"	Planter	Hayti	U S	
Ship Hannah	Mr. McCarty		30	"	Priest	Liverpool	Britain	
	" Lewis		46	"	Merchant		"	
Brig Silvester	J. B. LeMartre		24	"	do	the Cargena	U S	U S
Healey	Peter Norman		24	"	Mariner		"	
Scho'r Eagle	Joseph Elzurde		28	"	Merchant	Havanna	Spain	
Brig Amiable	Lalemand Lamont		45	"	Gardener	Havre	France	
Victoire								
Sloop Venus	S. Chatran	March	35	"	Trader	Matanzas	U S	
	Aimar		35	"	do		"	
	E. Graham		31	"	Carpenter		"	
	J. Atland		22	"	Trader		Spain	

PASSENGERS ARRIVING AT THE PORT OF CHARLESTON 1820-1829

Name of vessel	Passengers' names	Date of arrival	Age	Sex	Occupation	Where from	Country- belong	Country- inhabit
Schooner Albion	D. S. Anderson	March 1824	22	Male	Merchant	Bermuda	U S	U S
	N. Swift		41	"	do		"	"
Ship Robin Hood	Joseph Ingersoll		45	"	do	Antwerp		"
Brig Catharine	A. Buria		28		do	Havanna	Spain	"
	A. Jove		17		do		U S	"
	J. Lopez		40		do			"
Ship Perfect	Alwin Ball		17		Students	Liverpool		"
	Elias Ball		15		do		"	"
Ship Mary Cathar.	Mathew Coates		23		Farmers	Liverpool	Britain	"
	Patrick Hearty		37				"	"
	Mary Hearty 7 Children		37				"	"
	William Jany[?]		28				"	"
	Willm. C. Adams		8				"	"
	Bridget Adams		33				"	"
	William O. Adams		40				"	"
	R. Maxwell		32				"	"
	John Hearty		11				"	"
Ship Mary Cathar.	Edward Hearty	March 1825	13		Farmers	Liverpool	Britain	U S
	Mary Hearty		4				"	"
	Nancy Hearty		8				"	"
	Ellen Hearty		5				"	"
	Kitty Hearty		3				"	"
	Johanna Hearty		1 6/12				"	"
Brig Elizabeth	Edward Dwight		45		Merchant	St. Thomas	U S	"
	Mrs. Dwight		32	Female	none		"	"
	N. Kennedy		25	Male	Servant		"	"
Schooner Waterloo	Mozes Mapora		45	"	Teacher	St. Kitts	Britain	"
	Mrs. Mapora & 6 children		40	Female			"	"
Schooner Col. Armstead	Mr. Mensh		29	Male	Merchant	Havanna	Germany	"
	Edward Tennant		26	"	"		do	"
Brig Carolina Ann	Isaac Young		36	"	Mechanick		Spain	"
	Michael Fronteneau		58	"	Merchant	Havanna	France	"
	Mr. Chanson		66	"	do		U S	"
	Mr. Crouchois		19	"	"		"	"
	Mr. Fernandez		40	"	Teacher		Portugal	"
	Mr. Almeida		40	"	Mariner		U S	"
	Mr. Roberts		40	"	do		"	"
	Mr. Pink		30	"	do		"	"
Schooner Marion	J. Fennick		55	"	Minister	Havanna	"	"
	J. H. Lewis		35	"	Trader		"	"
	Thomas Hill		40	"	"		"	"
	Sidney Brooks		26	"	"		"	"
	J. P. Barr		28	"	"		"	"

63

PASSENGERS ARRIVING AT THE PORT OF CHARLESTON 1820-1829

Name of vessel	Passengers' names	Date of arrival	Age	Sex	Occupation	Where from	Country-belong	Country-inhabit
Ship Dunlop	James Moor	March 1824	26	Male	Farmer	Belfast	Britain	U S
	Margaret Moor		26	"	"		"	"
	Margaret Moor		24	"	"		"	"
	Mathew Crawford		19	"	"		"	"
	William Crawford		25	"	"		"	"
	William Thompson		22	"	"		"	"
Schooner Ranger	Joseph Nooks[?]		23	"	Preacher			"
	Charles Delorme		34	"	Upholsterer	Matanzes	U S	"
	G. Dalini		42	"	Distiller		"	
	G. Untesed		40	"	none		Spain	
	C. Uspolele		50	Male	Mariner		France	
Brig Germania	J. A. Graser	January 1826	25	"	Merchant	Bremen	U S	
	C. A. Bieben		50	"			Prussia	
Ship Hannah	J. H. Hindley		16	"		Liverpool	Britain	
	J. H. Hindley Junr			"	"			
Ship Amelia	Thos Eswine		28	"	Doctor	Harva	United States	
Schooner	Ira Saville		26	"	Merchant	St. Thomas	"	
Washington								
Brig Jasper	Anseline Fromaget		34	"	Hatter	Amsterdam	France	
Brig Catharine	Capt. Kelly		47	"	Mariner	Havanna	United States	
	Daniel Don Calelo Blanco		18	"	Nun		Spain	
Sch: Perry	E. Power		30	"	Mariner	Matansas	United States	
Brig Scion	S. Eymar		40	"	Merchant	"		
	John Batist		35	"		"	Spain	
Sch: Eclipse	John Lopes		40	"	Trader		United States	
	Messner		24	"	Merchant	Havanna	Spain	
	Lorilla		43	"	Mariner			
	Papa		6	"		"		
Brig Mary	Emanuel Hurnandes		38	"	Merchant	"	Charleston	
	Francisco Romero		50	"	Sea Captain	"	Spain	
	Louis Chastean		30	"	Do	"	"	
Sloop Enterprise	George Thrasher	February	40	"	American Seaman	Nassau	United States	
	George Fitz		30	"	Gentleman			
Brig Atlantic	Chas Benick		20	"	Merchant	Burmuda	Britain	
	R. Boot		50	"	Gentleman			
Brig Deveron	Jacob Walker		40	"	Teacher of Languages	Greenock	Prussia	
Ship Roger Stuart	Benjamine Adair		23	"	Physician		Scotland	
Brig Charles	R. C. Geyer		25	"	Merchant	Matansas	United States	
Ship Sarah	Geo W. Johnson		62	"	"	Liverpool	New York	
& Caroline	A. M. Williams		48	"	"		Charleston	

64

PASSENGERS ARRIVING AT THE PORT OF CHARLESTON 1820-1829

Name of vessel	Passengers' names	Date of arrival	Age	Sex	Occupation	Where from	Country- belong	Country- inhabit
Ship Langdon Chevis	E. Morris	February 1826	25	Male	Merchant	Havanna	Charleston	
	Efner		35	"	"	"	New York	
	Christie		35	"	"		Jamaica	
	Toia		46	"	"		Spain	
Brig Somoset	David Couan		20	"	Farmers	Belfast	Britain	
	Jane do		26	"	"	"	"	
	Patrick McVeagh		30	"	"	"	"	
	James McMullan		32	"	"	"	"	
	Mary & Ann do children	5	10	Female	"	"	"	
	William Elliot		60	Male	"	"	"	
	Agnes do		60	Female	"	"	"	
	do do		30	"	"	"	"	
	Richard do		28	Male	"	"	"	
	Matilda do		26	Female	"	"	"	
	William do		6	Male	"	"	"	
	William Sumionson		20	"	"	"	"	
Brig Somoset	Robt Davis		18	Male	"	"	"	
	Margaret Buchanan		40	Female	"	"	"	
	Mary do		16	"	"	"	"	
	Jane do		11	"	"	"	"	
	William Allen		30	Male	"	"	"	
	Randal Stuart		20	"	"	"	"	
	William do		22	"	"	"	"	
	William Davis		21	"	"	"	"	
	Jane McClure		32	Female	"	"	"	
	Ellen Maguire		28	"	"	"	"	
	James Mullan		25	Male	"	"	"	
	Lawrance Hoey		21	"	"	"	"	
	James Conner		26	"	"	"	"	
	James McDermont		22	"	"	"	"	
	Mary Collin &		26	Female	"	"	"	
	3 Children	5 3	8	"	"	"	"	
	Thos Campbell		19	Male	"	"	"	
	James Maguire		65	"	"	"	"	
	Catharine do		55	Female	"	"	"	
	John do		28	Male	"	"	"	
	Margaret do		30	Female	"	"	"	
	Eliza Scott		19	"	"	"	"	
	Ann McClain		22	"	"	"	"	
	Mary Rutledge		25	"	"	"	"	
	Ann do		4	"	"	"	"	
	Jane Allen		21	"	"	"	"	
	Mary McVeigh		24	"	"	"	"	

PASSENGERS ARRIVING AT THE PORT OF CHARLESTON 1820-1829

Name of vessel	Passengers' names	Date of arrival	Age	Sex	Occupation	Where from	Country- belong	Country- inhabit
Ship Xenophon	Ruliard Askew	March 1826	40	Male	Shoemaker	London	England	
	Sophia do		38	Female		"	"	
Ship Dunlop	Robt Turner		25	Male	Farmer	Belfast	Ireland	
	John Johnson		22	"	"	"	"	
	James Carsinell		30	"	"	"	"	
Ship Pauline	Theodore Verslays		32	"	Super Cargo	Milford Haven	Holland	
Brig Catharine	Stevens S. Tardy		26	"	Painter	Havanna	Europe	
	Jane Roderigues		51	Female	"	"	Florida	
	William Williamson		26	Male	"	"	Europe	
	Francisco De Suere		30	"	Trader	"	Havanna	
	Antoinica do do		40	"	Marriner	"	"	
Brig Marcia	Robert Ross		35	"	Merchant	Surinam	Scotland	
	William Wilkinson		40	"	"	"	Jemeca	
Schooner Susan	Peter Leland		25	"	Trader	Havanna	East Indeas	
Schooner Jane	Edward Delorme		25	"	Musick Master	Matanzas	Charleston	
Brig Step'n Gerard	John Seigling	July	32	Male	Merchant	Havanna	United States	U S
	Levi Hart		25	do	do	do	do	do
Ship Isabella	Edward Darrell		26	Male	Merchant	Havanna	United States	Charleston
Sch'r Josepa	George Tippehs		40	"	Mechanic	Carthagena	U S	U S
	John Clevenger		30	"	"	"	"	"
	William Hall		20	"	"	"	"	"
	Levery Woodrow		26	"	"	"	"	"
	John Jackson		27	"	"	"	"	"
	John Samuel		21	"	"	"	"	"
	Richard Forrest		42	"	"	"	"	"
	Francis Leverick		25	"	"	"	"	"
	Henry Clark		30	"	"	"	"	"
	Lewis Newton		32	"	"	"	"	"
	John Morris		28	"	"	"	"	"
	George Gosley		23	"	"	"	"	"
	Richard Adams		22	"	"	"	"	"
Brig Wade	A. Louis Stiner		45	"	Shoemaker	Havre de Grace	Germany	Germany
	Jos Evolt		22	"	Clockmaker	do	"	"
	Ferdinand Miscker		22	"		"	"	
	John Tourner		40	"		"	"	
Sch Eliza Ann	Wm Young		30	"	Farmer	Bahamas	United States	U S
Sch Lucinda	John Berre		40	"	Merchant	Matanzas	Spain	
	James P. Wood		25	"	Carpenter	"	United States	U S
	Louis Faver		19	"	Planter	"	"	"
Brig James Munroe	P. C. Verger	August	45	"	Merchant	Madeira	France	U S
Ship Perfect	G. E. King		18	"	"	Havre De Grace	United States	U S

PASSENGERS ARRIVING AT THE PORT OF CHARLESTON 1820-1829

Name of vessel	Passengers' names	Date of arrival	Age	Sex	Occupation	Where from	Country- belong	Country- inhabit
Brig Catharine	Carlo Delle	August 1826	54	Male	Merchant	Matanzas	Paris	Paris
	Romero Carell		32	"	"	"	Spain	"
	A. R. Drayton		18	"	"	"	United States	U S
	Lamero Sanchez		20	"	"	"	Florida	Florida
	Francisco Peaza		18	"	"	"	Cuba	Cuba
	Faustins Pereno		30	"	Mariner	"	Spain	Spain
	Deonicio Clar		55	"	Merchant	"	France	France
Brig Steph'n Gerard	F. P. Sanches		27	"	do	"	U States	U S
	A. Eymar		32	"	"	"	do	do
Sch. Bolina	Charles Deloram		60	"	"	Havana	Spain	Spain
	Mary do		21	"	"	"	"	"
Sch'r Marion	E. Verdery	September	21	Male	Painter	Jamaica	Augusta, Geo.	Augusta, Geo.
Ship Majestic	George Relph		25	"	Merchant	Liverpool	Charleston	Charleston
	Mrs. Relph		30	"		"	do	do
	William Tebedeau		28	"	Gentleman	"	France	France
	Thomas Maw		40	"	Merchant	"	England	England
	Alex'r Grant		40	"	"	"	U S	U S
	Edward Nelson		30	"	"	"	do	do
Ship Chilsea	Conrad Parker	October 1826	30	Male	Lock Smith	Havre	Germany	United States
	Charles Scott		42	do	Mariner	do	United States	do
Sch'r Lucinda	Peter Esnard		30	Male	Planter	Matanzas	United States	Cuba
do Lancer[?]	Elias Boston		32	do	Mariner	Nassau	United States	U S
Brig Catharine	Edmd Getarson		58	do	do	Havana	do	U S
Brig William	James Smith		33	do	Farmer	Belfast	Ireland	U S
	Elizabeth do		35	do	do	do	do	U S
	John do		30	do	do	do	do	U S
	John Reece[?]		40	do	do	do	do	U S
	William Kane		40	do	do	do	do	U S
	Margaret do		41	female		do	do	U S
	Hugh do		12	Male		do	do	U S
	Rebecca do		7	female		do	do	U S
	Mary do		2	do		do	do	U S
	Danl McCrean		36	Male		do	do	U S
	William Asherhurst		30	do		do	do	U S
	Thos do		12	do		do	do	U S
	John McClough		22	do		do	do	U S
	James McClough		22	do		do	do	U S
	William do		18	do		do	do	U S
	Arthur Star[?]		29	do		do	do	U S
	Ann Ranoles		21	do		do	do	U S
	James Gill		25	female		do	do	U S
	Henry Harper & Lady		40 30	M & F	Gentleman	do	do	U S
	John Fraser		30	Male	do	do	do	U S

PASSENGERS ARRIVING AT THE PORT OF CHARLESTON 1820-1829

Name of vessel	Passengers' names	Date of arrival	Age	Sex	Occupation	Where from	Country-belong	Country-inhabit
Barque Herald	Mary Reddoch	October 1826	35	female	None	Dundee	Scotland	U S
	Margaret do		12	do	do	do	do	U S
	Jesse do		10	do	do	do	do	U S
	Harriet Waters		18	do	do	do	do	U S
	John McCulloch		26	Male	Merchant	do	do	U S
	Mathew Ogilvie		17	do	do	do	do	U S
	Alexr Collie		43	do	Laborer	do	do	U S
Ship Saml Robertson	William Stewart		40	do	Merchant	Liverpool	United States	U S
	M. Moult		38	do	do	do	do	U S
	Dr. Dickson		33	do	Physician	do	do	U S
	Wm. McWhirter[?]		28	do	Merchant	do	do	U S
	D. McWhirter		26	do	do	do	do	U S
	Mr. & Mrs. Hamilton		25 30	m & f	do	do	do	U S
	Miss Kiddle		17	female	None	do	do	U S
Barque Oxford	Mr. Crosby		30	Male	Gentleman	do	do	U S
	James Hamilton[?]		31	do	Painter	do	Ireland	U S
	John Hamilton		25	do	do	do	do	U S
	William Wilkie		20	do	Gentleman	do	Scotland	U S
	N. S. Goodrich[?]		35	do	do	do	Virginia	U S
	Joseph Aiken		35	do	Wheelwright	do	Ireland	U S
	Mary do		22	female	None	do	do	U S
	Andrew Thetford[?]		33	Male	Carpenter	do	do	U S
Brig Mary	William Foster	October 1826	28	Male	Mariner	Havana	United States	U S
Schr Lov. Keziah	A. Durban	November	35	Male	Merchant	Havana	United States	U S
	Ann Graves		17	Female	None	do	do	U S
Brig Emeline	Mary Ellis		31	female	None	Nassau	United States	"
	Benjamin Ellis		15	Male	do	do	do	"
	Mary Ranger		33	female	do	do	do	"
	Sarah Ledder		15	do	do	do	do	"
	Matilda do		7	do	do	do	do	"
	Emma Calvo		25	do	do	do	do	"
	John Calvo		5	Male	Merchant	do	do	"
	Charles do		3	"	"	do	do	"
	Catharine Douglas		32	female	None	do	do	"
	Jane do		7	do	do	do	do	"
	Mary do		3	do	do	do	do	"
Ship Sar'h Caro'e	John McKinzie		45	Male	Merchant	Liverpool	do	"
	Mrs. McKinzie		30	female	do	do	do	"
	Mrs. Oats & 2 Children		35	do	do	do	do	"
	J. B. Clough		40	Male	Merchant	do	do	"
	John Fant		40	do	do	do	do	"
	Wm. Young		52	do	do	do	do	"
	John Bird		40	do	do	do	do	"

PASSENGERS ARRIVING AT THE PORT OF CHARLESTON 1820-1829

Name of vessel	Passengers' names	Date of arrival	Age	Sex	Occupation	Where from	Country- belong	Country- inhabit
Ship Sar'h Caro'e	William Mitchel	November 1826	32	Male	Merchant	Liverpool	United States	U S
	Wm. Broadfoot		14	do		do	do	"
	Miss L. B. Broadfoot		12	female		do	do	"
Ship Robt. Edwa's	Henry Newman		35	Male	British Consul	London	England	"
	Charles Baring & Lady		55	Male	Merchant	do	do	"
	Jane Hughs		25	female	Servant	do	do	"
	George Jackson		30	Male	do	do	do	"
	Mrs. Mary Cordes		40	female	Lady	do	do	"
	Miss L. Cordes		15	do	do	do	do	"
	Margaret Jackson		20	do	Servant	do	do	"
	Robt. Pringle		30	Male	Gentleman	do	do	"
	Benjn Lards		21	"	do	do	do	"
	John Mill		45	"	Merchant	do	do	"
	Joseph Mill		35	"	Gentleman	do	do	"
	William W. Ball		30	"	do	do	do	"
	Christr. Schroder		22	"	Merchant	do	do	"
	Wm. Schroder		25	"	"	do	do	"
	Chas Foygie[?]		23	"	None	do	do	"
	John H. Hammond		28	"	"	do	do	"
	John H. Hinman		20	"	None	do	do	"
	J. M. Sulcher		24	"	"	do	do	"
	Betsy do		21	female	"	do	do	"
Brig Soldie	A. P. R. Grandeu		28	Male	"	Havre	France	"
Brig Andromeda	Kenneth Macrae	November 1826	24	Male	Planter	Glasgow	Scotland	Florida
	S. Jones		40	do	Surgeon	do	do	United States
	R. M. Laren		43	do	Taylor	do	do	do
Ship Bolivar	J. Mulholland		15	Male	Gentleman	Belfast	Ireland	United States
	Chas Scott		15	do	Merchant	do	do	"
	James Thompson		22	do	Portrait Painter	do	do	"
	Robt Moor		30	do	Gentleman	do	do	"
	Wife & Two Children			females	None	do	do	"
	William Todd		45	Male	Weaver	do	do	"
	John Clarke		30	do	Farmer	do	do	"
	Robt White		25	do	do	do	do	"
Ship Jupiter	M. DePougers	November	50	Male	French Consul	Havre	France	United States
	John Parker Junr		45	do	Planter	do	Charleston	"
	Lady & Six Children			females		do	do	"
	J. Bignou		50	Male	Merchant	do	France	"
	Miss Bignou		15	female	none	do	do	"
	Fran's Duboc		50	Male	Merchant	do	do	"
	Lady & Daughter			females		do	do	"
	C. G. A. Lacoste		49	Male	Merchant	do	do	"
	A. Ladevere		16	do	do	do	do	"

Name of vessel	Passengers' names	Date of arrival	Age	Sex	Occupation	Where from	Country- belong	Country- inhabit
Ship Jupiter	N. Ragnal	November 1826	52	Male	Merchant	Havre	France	United States
	T. Bourdon		45	do	do	do	do	"
	T. Roger		27	do	do	do	do	"
Brig ClarrissaAnn	Elisha Arnold		48	do	Mariner	Liverpool	United States	
Brig Catharine	J. Lausand[?]	December	37	do	Merchant	Havana	France	Cuba
	John Woodrup Ju'r		19	do		do	United States	United States
	James Parker		50	do	Merchant	do	do	do
	L. M. Woodberry		30	do	Mariner	do	"	
Brig Ocean	John Coskary		19	do	Farmer	Belfast	Ireland	"
	William Wiley		40	do	do	do	do	"
	Molly Wiley		40	female		do	do	"
	William Samuel		30	Male	do	do	do	"
	& Three Children			females		do	do	"
	Cornelius Guffigan		45	Male	do	do	do	"
	Marg't do & Six children			females		do	do	"
	Jas Carr		30	Male	do	do	do	"
	John Campbell		20	do	do	do	do	"
	Jane Campbell		21	female	do	do	do	"
	Pat Corrie		20	Male	do	do	do	"
	Hugh McClerlon		22	do	do	do	do	"
	Pat Ryan		21	do	do	do	do	"
	John Canavah		20	do	do	do	do	"
	Frank Corrie		25	do	do	do	do	"
	Elizabeth do		21	female	do	do	do	"
	Mary do child		3	do	do	do	do	"
Brig Ocean	Francis Connoly	December 1826	30	Male	Farmer	Belfast	Ireland	United States
	Danl Welch & 3 Children		45	M & F	do	do	do	"
	James McIver		30	Male	do	do	do	"
	Mary & Pat McIver		20 15	M & F	do	do	do	"
	Saml Lamburn		13	Male	do	do	do	"
Ship Mary Catharine	W. C. Molyneau		28	do	Merchant	Liverpool	Great Britain	G B
	E. Moyleaux		27	do	do	do	do	"
	E. Menlove		28	do	do	do	do	"
	James Robertson		29	do	do	do	United States	United States
	Edward Hughes		45	do	do	do	Great Britain	"
	James Nicholson		60	do	do	do	"	"
	R. C. Cunningham		32	do	do	do	"	"
	Thomas Gates		27	do	do	do	"	"
	S. Woodward		40	do	do	do	"	"
	Mary Cameron		16	female	do	do	"	"

PASSENGERS ARRIVING AT THE PORT OF CHARLESTON 1820-1829

Name of vessel	Passengers' names	Date of arrival	Age	Sex	Occupation	Where from	Country- belong	Country- inhabit
Ship Lydia	James Hall	December 1826	25	Male	Mariner	London	United States	United States
	Warren Crawford		26	do	do	do	"	"
	John L. Hubbard		42	do	do	do	"	"
	William Johnson		32	do	do	do		
Brig Retrench	B. F. McDonald		25	Male	Clerk	Liverpool	Ireland	United States
	A. W. Wiley		26	do	Gentleman	do	do	"
Ship Commerce	James Gordon		27	do	Merchant	Portsmouth	Great Britain	Great Britain
Brig Step'n Gerard	Richd Gray		40	do	Mariner	Trinidad	United States	United States
Sch'r Lucinda	Geo. E. Carter		25	do	Merchant	Matanzas	"	"
	Rich'd Norton		21	do	Clerk	do	"	"
	Ann M. Burk		18	female	none	do	"	"
Ship Eliza Grant	Jacob Eggart		50	Male	Merchant	Havre		
Ship Lycurgus	P. R. Yonge		50	do	do	Liverpool	Florida	"
	P. R. Younge, Jun'r		18	do	do	do	do	"
	Francisco Yonge		49	do	None	do	do	"
	Eliza do		19	female		do	do	"
	J. A. Barretie		26	Male	Merchant	do	do	"
Sch'r Alfred	Capt'n Henry Bates		29	do	Maroner	United States	United States	United States
	Capt'n Nathan Foster		21	do	do	do	do	do
	Danl Richardson		31	do	do	do	do	do
	Tilson Ney		20	do	do	do	do	do
	Joseph Class		21	do	do	do	do	do
Sch Bolivar	Henry Brackenbridge		50	do	Judge	Havana	do	E. Florida
	Henry Nelson		35	do	Planter	do	do	do
Ship Huntley	Thaddeus Chambers		18	do	Mariner	London	do	United States

71

PASSENGERS ARRIVING AT THE PORT OF CHARLESTON 1820-1829

Name of vessel	Passengers' names	Date of arrival	Age	Sex	Occupation	Where from	Country- belong	Country- inhabit
Sch'r Sally & Polly	F. Dupont	[blank] 1827	28	Male	Merchant	Matanzas	United States	United States
Ship Home	J. P. Gardner		30	do	Gentleman	Liverpool	do	
	E. Mazy		40	do	do	do	England	England
Sch'r Arrozana	Francis Geram		40	do	do	Matanzas	United States	United States
	Saml. Pedrick		35	do	do	do	do	do
Brig Sall & Hope	T. Morris		25	do	Merchant	Havana	do	do
	J. Bonhonom		25	do	do	do	do	do
	Mrs. Bonhonom		38	female		do	do	do
Brig Hesper	Ezra Field		26	Male	Merchant	Matanzas	do	do
	T. Powell		28	do	Planter	do	Cuba	Cuba
	Daniel McLaughlin		19	do	Merchant	do	Ireland	United States
Ship Wm Dawson	Rich'd Morgan		58	do	Gentleman	Liverpool	do	do
	Sarah Morgan		50	female		do	do	do
	Eliza Sawyer		54	do		do	do	do
Brig Atlantic	John Lafon		55	Male	Cooper	Bordeaux	United States	United States
	E. Gergand		55	do		do	Bordeaux	Bordeaux
	E. Gergand		45	Female		do	do	do
	E. Fayolle		30	Male	Merchant	do	United States	United States
	S. Buran		24	do	Ship carpenter	do	do	do
	J. Cherry		24	do	Block Maker	do	Bordeaux	Bordeaux
	Felix Gerand		14	do	do	do	do	do
	Lucas Fredrick		32	do	Lock Smith	do	do	do
	James Fowler		28	do	Bricklayer	do	do	do
Brig Rose Bank	Wm. McKessick		40	do	Farmer	Belfast	United States	United States
	Martin McKessick		30	do	do	do	Ireland	do
	David Cowan		25	do	do	do	do	do
	Isabella Cowan		20	Female		do	do	do
	Jane Cowan		16	do		do	do	do
	Sarah Cowan		15	do		do	do	do
	Mary Cowan		13	do		do	do	do
	John Cowan		21	Male	do	do	do	do
	Thos Maxwell		35	Male	do	do	do	do
	Thos Kerrion		30	do	do	do	do	do
	Agnes Kerrion		31	Female	do	do	do	do
	Robt Kervion		46	Male	do	do	do	do
	Ann Beattie		20	Female	do	do	do	do
	James Richardson		23	Male	do	do	do	do
	Ralph Bamford		22	do	do	do	do	do
	Eliza Coulter		25	Female	do	do	do	do
	Susannah Coulter		19	do	do	do	do	do
	Saml Sporlt		18	Male	do	do	do	do
	David Caron		20	do	do	do	do	do

PASSENGERS ARRIVING AT THE PORT OF CHARLESTON 1820-1829

Name of vessel	Passengers' names	Date of arrival	Age	Sex	Occupation	Where from	Country- belong	Country- inhabit
Brig Rose Bank	James Mooney	1827	16	Male	Farmer	Belfast	Ireland	United States
	James McKibber		28	do	do	do	do	do
	Edw'd Gillelan		30	do	do	Belfast	Ireland	United States
Sch'r Ranger	G. B. Claxton	1827	29	Male	Merchant	Nassau	United States	United States
Barque Aurora	James Dorman		23	Male	None	Liverpool	Scotland	United States
Brig Chas Forbes	Mrs. Beveridge		25	Female		Leith	United States	United States
Gen Brown	Mrs. Mugridge		30	do		Liverpool	England	United States
	Miss Mugridge		11	do		do	do	do
	Miss Mugridge		9	do		do	do	do
	Mr. Hindley		45	Male	Merchant	do	do	do
	Mr. Thos Hindley		18	do	do	do	do	do
	Mr. Watson		30	do	do	do	do	do
	A. Low		45	do	do	do	do	do
	Mr. Buckham		46	do	do	do	do	do
Sch'r Juno	Mr. Cunnigan		40	do	Merchant	Hallifax	United States	United States
	Richard Welch		23	do	Laborer	do	do	do
Brig Varonica	Andrew Mantand		40	do	Merchant	Belfast	Ireland	United States
	Wm. Close		22	do	do	do	do	do
Ship Perfect	James Hassett		14	do		Liverpool	United States	United States
	Michael Hassett		10	do		do	do	do
Ship Lucies	Mr. Hartley		40	do	Planter	Kingston	Ireland	United States
	Mrs. Cleland & Four children		30	Female		do	United States	do
	Mrs. Boyer		25	do		do	do	do
	John Kelly		18	Male		do	do	do
Sh'r Planter	Harriet Harper		50	Female	Servant	Matanzas	Matanzas	Matanzas
	T. Thompson		22	Male		do	United States	United States
	Lamothe		30	do	Clerk	do	do	do
Brig Mary	Wm. Campbell		35	do	Mariner	do	do	do
	C. G. Carbajet		25	do	Merchant	do	do	do
Sch'r Lucinda	Wm. Carter		30	do	do	Havana	Spain	United States
Sch'r Saluda	A. Roberts		25	do	do	Matanzas	United States	United States
	Joseph A. Darby		36	do	Merchant	Havana	do	do
	Vassa Velbassa		40	do	do	do	do	do
	James York		26	do	do	do	Havana	Havana
Ship Telegraph	James Easton		35	do	Merchant	do	United States	United States
	John Pleasant		23	do	do	Antwerp	do	do
	E. Small		29	do	Mariner	Nassau	do	do
Ranger	Geo: Robinson		21	do	do	do	do	do
	James Anderson		22	do	do	do	do	do
Brig Catharine	F. C. Blanco		28	do	Merchant	Havana	Cuba	Cuba
	Thos S. Danforth		23	do	do	do	United States	United States

PASSENGERS ARRIVING AT THE PORT OF CHARLESTON 1820-1829

Name of vessel	Passengers' names	Date of arrival	Age	Sex	Occupation	Where from	Country- belong	Country- inhabit
Brig Native	Jos Rivera	1827	25	Male	Segar Maker	Havana	Havana	Havana
	Miss M. Johnson		21	do	do	do	United States	United States
	S. Chappels		40	do	Merchant	Trinidad	do	do
Brig. Step'n Gerard	John S. Lynn		26	do	do	do	do	do
	Isaac M. Lord		21	do	Ship Wright	do	do	do
Brig Sophia	James Marsh Junr		26	Male	Merchant	Havana	do	do
Brig Marcia	Bartholomew Blanco		24	Male	Merchant	Havana	Spain	Havana
Brig Mary	Henry Catlin		31	do	do	do	France	United States
	Freeman Mont		44	do	Merchant	Spain	Spain	Spain
	Emanuel Lanch		18	do	Servant	do	do	do
Brig Apthorp	Jos Tomlinson		16	do	Clerk	Liverpool	England	United States
" Scion	James DeWolfe Junr		25	do	Merchant	Matanzas	United States	do
Sch'r Lov'y Kezia	Captn. Roberts		35	Male	Mariner	United States	United States	
Sch'r Ranger	Henry Yonge		25	do	Merchant	do	do	
	Alex'r Kindill		45	do	Physician	Ireland	do	
Brig Jean	Campbell D. Hight		18	do	Merchant	Scotland	United States	
Ship Francis	Sol'n Davis		34	do	Gentleman	United States	do	
	John W. Williams		18	do	do	England	United States	
Sch'r Juno	Wm. Raney		25	do	Mariner	United States	do	U S
Brig Shakespear	John Philip		20	do	Laborer	Britain	do	"
Ship Mary	G. Relph	April	40	Male	Merchant	Liverpool	U S	"
Catherine	John Jones		67	do	do	"	"	"
	Robert Brunnel		71	do	do	"	"	"
Brig Catherine	C. A. Stolt		30	do	None	Havanna	Germany	Mexico
Brig Sophia	Petit		48	do	Merchant	do	U S	U S
	Silva		35	do	none	do	"	"
Brig Katherine	Bonhommie		26	do	Trader	Havanna	"	"
	OReilley & 2 children		32	female	none	Havanna	"	"
Ship Jupiter	Henry Von Glahn		23	male	Sugar baker	London	Hanover, G. B.	U S
	John Muller		20	"	"	"	"	"
	J. Meyer		23	"	"	"	"	"
	Henry Buie		22	"	"	"	"	"
Brig Scion	James Usher		38	"	Merchant	Matanzas	U S	"
	A. Barrelle		25	"	"	"	"	"
	D. Thompson		30	"	"	Havanna	"	"
Sch'r Lovely Kezia	E. Murford		43	"	"	"	"	"
	D. Montere		27	"	"	"	"	"
Schooner	J. Chartrand	May	40	"	Planter	Matanzas	"	"
Sally & Polly	N. Burrell		35	"	Merchant	"	"	"
	S. S. Rice		25	"	"	"	"	"
Scho'r Lucinda	T. Dupont		30	"	"	"	"	"
	A. Barbot		40	"	"	"	"	"

PASSENGERS ARRIVING AT THE PORT OF CHARLESTON 1820-1829

Name of vessel	Passengers' names	Date of arrival	Age	Sex	Occupation	Where from	Country-belong	Country-inhabit
Brig Mary	Mrs. Gardere	May 1827	55	female	none	Havanna	U S	U S
	Miss Gardere		30	"	"	"	"	"
	Delorme		60	Male	Planter	"	"	"
Brig Genl.Brown	Capt. Lafette		40	Male	Mariner	Liverpool	Britain	"
Brig Catherine	Mrs. Morrisson		28	Female	none	Havanna	U S	"
Brig Retrench	A. P. Jive		22	Male	none	Greenock	U S	U S
	Margaret McNab		50	female	Plantress	"	"	"
Ship Roger	Archibald Campbell		30	male	Clerk	Greenock	Britain	"
Stewart	William White		25	male	Clerk	"	Britain	U S
Brig Andromac	Dr. Robertson		50	"	Physician	Liverpool	"	"
	Arthur Connell	June	26	"	Farmer	"	"	"
	John FitzPatrick		23	"	Merchant	"	"	"
Brig Katherine	Tore McValdre		20	"	Planter	Havanna	Spain	"
	Juan Valdez		49	"	do	"	"	"
	Manuel		37	"	do	"	"	"
	Augusta de Salva		35	"	do	"	"	"
	Delene Valdez		54	female	do	"	"	"
	Luganda Valdez & three children		24	"	do	"	"	"
			27	"	do	"	"	"
Brig Sophia	Le Suge		65	Male	Merchant	Havanna	France	U S
	Berlin		22	"	Mariner	"	U S	"
Schooner	E. Hogskin		27	"	Merchant	Matanzas	"	"
Planter	A. Eymar		45	"	Mechanic	"	"	"
	Anton Faymel[?]		30	"	Merchant	"	"	"
Bark Agnes & Ann	Jervis[?]		27	"	Mechanic	"	"	"
Sch. Lovely	Don Ramond Perez		33	"	Planter	Glascow	Britain	"
Kezia	Benj. W. Barden		33	"	Merchant	Matanzas	U S	"
Sch'r Lucinda	George T. Carter		25	"	do	"	"	"
	Francis Ylurrian		30	"	do	"	"	"
Brig Emeline	J. W. Mitchell		30	"	do	Havanna	Spain	"
	C. M. Ploney[?]		35	"	do	"	Britain	"
	M. Fernandez		30	"	do	"	U S	"
Brig Mary	H. H. Martins	July	22	Male	Merchant	Havana	Spain	"
Sch'r Marion	Aymar		42	do	do	Matanzas	Germany	United States
	Blanchet		28	do	do	do	France	do
Sch'r Sally & Polly	Francis Dupont		30	do	Supercargo	Trinidad	Charleston	Charleston
Brig	James Richardson	August	40	do	Gentleman	Havana	England	England
	N. Grant		35	do	Merchant	Bonacoua	Cuba	Cuba
	Joseph Howland Jur		40	do	do	Havana	United States	United States
	John H. Lorance[?]		25	do	do	do	do	do
Brig Sophia	Wagner		28	do	do	do	Hamburg	Havana

75

PASSENGERS ARRIVING AT THE PORT OF CHARLESTON 1820-1829

Name of vessel	Passengers' names	Date of arrival	Age	Sex	Occupation	Where from	Country- belong	Country- inhabit
Sch'r Jane	Fredk Bowman	August 1827	40	Male	Merchant	Havana	Germany	Germany
	Patrick Kelly		30	do	do	do	Ireland	United States
Sch'r Johanna	Thos Lesesne		20	do	do	do	United States	United States
	John Collins		35	do	None	do	Ireland	do
Brig Mary	George Brown		27	do	Merchant	do	United States	do
	Bonhomme		32	do	do	do	France	Havana
Brig Orient	J. H. Debloist	September	17	do	Marriner	Havre	do	United States
Brig Wade	William Smiellie		30	do	Mason	Liverpool	Scotland	do
Sch'r Jane	J. P. Beaufelt		30	do	Watchmaker	Matanzas	United States	do
Sch'r Pilgrim	A. McKinsie	October	36	Male	Mechanic	Havana	United States	United States
Mary & Susan	Thomas Mair		48	Male	Merchant	Liverpool	Scotland	United States
	William Flinn		32	do	do	do	Ireland	do
Ship South Boston	Capt'n J. D. Brower		25	do	Marriner	Havana	United States	do
Brig Mary	James Morgan		30	do	Merchant	do	do	do
Brig Retrench	Alex'r Campbell		21	do	Clerk	Greenock	Scotland	do
Sch'r Marion	Wm McMillen		40	do	Carpenter	Havana	United States	do
Brig Emeline	A. Aimar		38	do	Merchant	Matanzas	Cuba	Cuba
Brig Isabella	Wm. Dick		40	do	do	Liverpool	Scotland	United States
	Bridget Dempsey		30	do	do	England	England	do
Sch'r Johanna	Edw'd Morris		25	do	do	Trinidad	United States	United States
Ship Lathalie	Jacob Schoeler	November	39	do	Stone Cutter	Havre	Germany	do
	Theus Schoeler		40	female		do	do	do
	Catharine Schoeler		18	do		do	do	do
	Jacob Schoeler		17	male	Stone Cutter	do	do	do
	Theus Schoeler		15	female		do	do	do
	Joseph Schoeler		11	male		do	do	do
	Marienna Schoeler		4	female		do	do	do
	Rasoline Schoeler		18 mos	do		do	do	do
	Francis Xavier		23	male		do	do	do
Bark Herald	David Philp		22	Male	Carpenter	Dundee	United States	United States
Ship Majestic	Mrs. Stephens		45	female	None	Liverpool	do	do
	Miss Stephens		18	do		do	do	do
	Mrs. Lowden		42	do		do	do	do
	Miss Lowden		18	do		do	do	do
	William Longsdon		48	Male	Merchant	do	do	do
	R. Campbell		28	do	do	do	do	do
	Wm. C. Molyneau		35	do	do	do	do	do
	J. G. Moodie		27	do	do	do	do	do
	J. Lowden		22	do	do	do	do	do
	Thos Walton		30	do	do	do	do	do
	J. McDougald		25	do	do	do	do	do
	M. Cullinau		40	do	do	do	do	do
	G. J. Lowden		20	do	do	do	do	do

PASSENGERS ARRIVING AT THE PORT OF CHARLESTON 1820-1829

Name of vessel	Passengers' names	Date of arrival	Age	Sex	Occupation	Where from	Country- belong	Country- inhabit
Ship Majestic	John Keller	November 1827	37	Male	Merchant	Liverpool	United States	United States
	Wm. Reddish		22	do	do	do	do	do
	Elisha Sollimons		38	do		do	do	do
S Brig Czar	James Benny		45	Male	Mason	Grenock	Scotland	United States
	John Benny		30	do	Farmer	do	do	do
	James Adam		22	do	BlackSmith	do	do	do
	John Lennie		20	do	Mason	do	do	do
	Alexr Mackie		23	do	do	do	do	do
	Robt Taylor		22	do		do	do	do
	Isabella Taylor		18	female		do	do	do
	David McNell		55	Male	Farmer	do	do	do
	Archd McNell		21	do	do	do	do	do
	John Reston		35	Male	Farmer	do	do	do
	Peter McLean		18	do	do	do	do	do
Brig Dryas	Herbemont		19	do	Cabinet Maker	Havre	France	do
Sch'r Pilgrim	Charles Howe		27	do	Merchant	do	United States	do
	Moses Smith		35	do	do	do	do	do
	John Wall		44	do	do	do	do	do
Brig Catharine	A. R. Drayton		20	do	do	do	do	do
Ship Rob't Kerr	John Watson		36	do	do	do	do	do
	Jane Watson		30	female	Taylor	Belfast	Ireland	do
	Thos McCartney		20	Male		do	do	do
	William Rutherford		28	do	Gentleman	do	do	do
Brig Step Gerard	A. Robert	December	30	do	Taylor	do	do	do
	J. Vebaseca		28	do	Merchant	Havana	Spain	do
Brig William	William Hunter		30	do	do	Belfast	United States	do
	Joseph Bains		25	do	Accountant	do	Ireland	do
	Henry Lomy[?]		14	do	do	do	do	do
	Andrew Reed		17	do	do	do	do	do
	Mrs. Evans		25	female	do	do	do	do
	Nancy McFadden		42	female	Spinster	do	do	do
	Robt Evans		12	Male	do	do	do	do
	Mary McCrea		23	female	do	do	do	do
	Sarah Magee		20	do	do	do	do	do
	Jane Magee		21	do	do	do	do	do
	Lucinda McCrea		30	do	do	do	do	do
	Joseph McCrea		11	Male	None	do	do	do
	William Hunter		35	do	do	do	do	do
	Elizabeth Hunter		38	female		do	do	do
	James do		6	Male	None	Belfast	Ireland	United States
	William Hunter		4	Male		do	do	do
	Mary do		2	female		do	do	do
	Elizabeth do		1	do		do	do	do

77

PASSENGERS ARRIVING AT THE PORT OF CHARLESTON 1820-1829

Name of vessel	Passengers' names	Date of arrival	Age	Sex	Occupation	Where from	Country- belong	Country- inhabit
Brig William	Mary White	December 1827	14	Female		Belfast	Ireland	United States
	M-ther Caranchal		26	do		do	do	do
	----- McMurray		40	Male	Farmer	do	do	do
	Margt do		30	female		do	do	do
	Rebecca do		2	do		do	do	do
	Robert Arnold		22	Male	Farmer	do	do	do
	William Yelly		50	do	do	do	do	do
	Jane do		50	female		do	do	do
	Joseph Cameron		20	Male	do	do	do	do
	William Whitaker		35	do	do	do	do	do
	Mrs. do		30	female		do	do	do
	Daughter of the above		6	Male		do	do	do
	John Whitaker		4	Male		do	do	do
	C. Dickey		30	female		do	do	do
Brig William	----- Dickey	December 1827	14	Male		Belfast	Ireland	United States
	Martha do		12	female		do	do	do
	John do		8	Male		do	do	do
	Hugh do		6	do		do	do	do
	Jane do		4	female		do	do	do
	James do		2	Male		do	do	do
Bark Mary	Christopher Atkinson		20	do	Merchant	Liverpool	Great Britain	do
Sch'r Hope	Isaac Smith		35	do	do	Havana	United States	do
	Rich'd Hill		25	do	do	do	do	do
	Edm'd Hamilton		30	do	do	do	do	do
	Rich'd Bearns		28	do	do	do	do	do
Brig Jane Vilet	Thomas Meacher		35	do	do	do	do	do
	Peter Finland		40	do		do	do	do
	Mrs. McDonald		37	[female]		do	do	do
	Ellen Do		20	do		do	do	do
	Honora Do		18	do		do	do	do
	Maria Do		16	Male		do	do	do
	James Do		15	do		do	do	do
	Michael Do		12	Male		do	do	do
	Mary Polson		50	female		do	do	do
Ship Mary	James Evans		50	Male	Merchant	Liverpool	Scotland	United States
Bark Mary Ann	Robert Muir		16	do	do	do	England	do
	Mrs. Meacher		36	female	None	do	do	do
	& two children		5 9	do		do	do	do
	David Meacher		19	Male		do	do	do
	--- Blythe		40	do	Baker	do	do	do
	--- Blythe		38	female		do	Ireland	do
	John Daniel		45	Male	Tutor	do	do	do

78

PASSENGERS ARRIVING AT THE PORT OF CHARLESTON 1820-1829

Name of vessel	Passengers' names	Date of arrival	Age	Sex	Occupation	Where from	Country- belong	Country- inhabit
Brig Rose Bank	Trever Cowan	December 1827	20	Male	Watch Maker	Belfast	Ireland	United States
	Andrew Little		22	do	Gentleman	do	do	do
	Andrew Logan		19	do	Farmer	do	do	do
	Marshal Mooney		25	do	Mechanic	do	do	do
Ship Eucharis	Peter Swan		60	Male	Merchant	Bordeaux	France	United States
	Rose Swan		35	female		do	do	do
	Amanda Swan		15	do		do	do	do
	Felix Swan		12	Male		do	do	do
	Peter Swan		5	do		do	do	do
	Cecelia Swan		9	female		do	do	do
Ship Amelie	Lewis Marchand		50	Male	Merchant	Havre	United States	do
	Mrs. Marchand		35	female		do	do	do
	Miss Marchand		10	do		do	do	do
	J. Geneste		17	Male	Silver Smith	do	do	do
Ship Jubiter	Fred'k Baum		18	do	Clerk	Antwerp	Bremen	do
	Charles Smelger		18	do	do	do	do	do
Ship Science	James Nicholson		70	Male	Merchant	Liverpool	United States	United States
	Henry Wright		50	do	do	do	do	do
	John Bird		30	do	do	do	do	do
	Sarah Bird		45	female	do	do	do	do
	M. J. George		35	Male	do	do	do	do
Brig Catharine	Capt'n Myrick		35	do	Marriner	Havana	do	do
	James McDonald		30	do	do	do	do	do
Ship Sar'h	Abraham Wolfe		45	do	Merchant	London	do	do
Ralston	William M Ray		46	do	Dyer	do	France	do
	Mrs. do		25	female	do	do	do	do
Brig Henrietta	Leopold Barwith		27	Male	Accountant	Bremen	Germany	United States
Sch Lovely Kezia	Jos Mathea		36	do	Physician	Havana	United States	do
	John West		26	do	do	do	do	do
Brig Mary	J. G. Blois	January 1828	35	Male	Planter	Havanna	U S	Georgia
	M. Gibson		42	"	Merchant	do	"	So Carolina
Brig Scion	Antonio Eymar		34	"	do	Matanzes	Portugal	do
Brig	Alexander M. Edwards		50	"	Judge	G. Cavanna	Britain	Nassau
Philadelphia	John McEneroe		45	"	Priest	do	do	So Carolina
sloop	S. Auger Salaror		40	"	none	Portorico	Spain	Spain
Connecticut	Johannce Jones		30	"	Mariner	"	U S	U S
Scho'r Marion	William Rogers	February	20	"	Merchant	Havanna	U S	Kentucky
Ship Perfect	William Martin wife & Child		28	"	do	Liverpool	Britain	U S
Brig	Joehanias Thayer		42	"	do	Havana	U S	New York
Stephen Gerard	Mrs. Maxwell		20	female	None	"	"	So Carolina

PASSENGERS ARRIVING AT THE PORT OF CHARLESTON 1820-1829

Name of vessel	Passengers' names	Date of arrival	Age	Sex	Occupation	Where from	Country- belong	Country- inhabit
Brig	Mary Scannell	January 1828	36	do	Grocer	Havana	U S	U S
Miles Standish	Sophia Barker		38	do	none	"	Spain	Spain
	Josse Assard		22	Male	do	"	"	"
	Mathew Hunt		40	"	Engineer	"	U S	U S
	Phillip Sullivan		51	"	Drover	"	"	"
	E. W. Horton		35	"	"	"	"	"
	Nathaniel Rogers		20	"	"	"	"	"
Brig Shakespear	Dougald Mathewson	March	25	"	Merchant	Aberdeen	Britain	Britain
Ship	Thomas H. Hindley		50	"	"	Liverpool	do	do
Lady Rowena	Thos. H. Hindley Jr.		20	"	"	"	do	do
	John Duffield		40	"	"	"	do	do
	William Carlyon		20	"	Planter	Matanzes	Cuba	U S
Brig	John Ohartran		40	"	Merchant	"	U S	So Carolina
Stranger	Lewis Dubois		62	"	"	"	"	"
	Ambrose Dubois		30	"	Physician	"	"	"
	Mothly Gilson		30	"	Merchant	"	"	"
	James M. McKie		25	"	Labourer	"	"	"
	Charles Esward		25	"	None	"	"	U S
Bark	Dennis L. Kelly		24	"	Labourer	Belfast	Britain	"
William Booth	Mary Kelly		17	female	Labourer	"	"	"
Brig Step. Gerard	William Latham		25	Male	Merchant	Matanzes	Germany	U S
Brig Scion	John Shefner		25	Male	Merchant	Matanzes	Portugal	Charleston
	Antonio Eymar		33	do	do	Bordeaux	U S	"
Brig Atlantic	John Bass		39	"	"	"	"	
	Saventuer		24	"	none	"	"	
Ship Unicorn	Charles Newman		26	"	Merchant	Liverpool	Britain	Britain
Brig Sally Barker	Edward Morris		28	Male	Merchant	Trinidad	U S	U S
Sch'r Hope	Antonio F. Melan	April	41	do	do	Havana	Spain	Spain
	James R. Russell		31	do	do	do	do	do
Sch'r Isis	Josa Villepurte		28	do	do	Nenvetas	do	do
	Juan Forie		25	do	do	do	do	do
Sch'r Sar'h Francis	J. Davis		45	do	Mariner	Havana	United States	United States
Brig William	William Adamson		26	do	Planter	Belfast	Britain	do
	Ann Adamson		22	do[sic]	none	do	do	do
	Alex'r Glenner		21	do	Schoolmaster	do	do	do
Sch'r Superb	Henry Moore	May	36	do	Carpenter	Point Peter	United States	do
	M. G. Street		14	do	none	do	do	do
Ship Columbia	John Hadley		35	do		Hamburgh	do	do
	John Newman		40	do			do	do
Sch'r	Francis C. Black		30	do	Merchant	Havana	do	do
Lovely Keziah	Viclin Harrit		31	do	do	do	do	do

PASSENGERS ARRIVING AT THE PORT OF CHARLESTON 1820-1829

Name of vessel	Passengers' names	Date of arrival	Age	Sex	Occupation	Where from	Country- belong	Country- inhabit
Brig Sprightly	James McBeth	May 1828	23	Male	Cooper	Dundee	Britain	United States
	William Rosia		20	do	do		do	do
Brig Magnet	Alex'r Bonnacle		25	do		Leish[?]		do
Brig Catharine	Mrs. Jove & Child		45	female	Devine	Havana	United States	do
	Mr. Abbott		55	Male	do	do		do
	M. J. Miu[?]		28	do	Merchant	do		do
Ship Perfect	Grace Mead		23	female				do
Brig Gen Brown	M. Kelly	June	23	Male	Plasterer	Liverpool	Britain	do
	J Ross		24	do	do	do	do	do
Ship Chas & Henry	H. Mohr		40	do	Grocer	Amsterdam	Germany	do
	L. M. Watchterhouse		30	do	Shoemaker	do	do	do
	J. Bremar		32	do	Book Binder	do	do	do
	J. Kriderick		35	do	Weaver	do	do	do
	J. Izakece		40	do	do	do	do	do
Brig Meredian	J. Bristine		62	do	Shoemaker	Havre	do	do
	B. Bustin & 5 Children		60	Females		do	do	do
	G. Hetzel		30	Male	Taylor	do	do	do
	K. Hetzel & 5 Children		26	M & F	do	do	do	do
	P. Vill		45	Male	do	do	do	do
	S. Vill & 6 Children		40	Female		do	do	do
	J. Fluger		58	Male	Weaver	do	do	do
	K. Fluger & 4 Children		55	Female		do	do	do
	J. Corhl		23	Male		do	do	do
	J. Lentz		22	do		do	do	do
Brig Meridian	A. Rudly		36	Male	Shoemaker	Havre	Germany	United States
	K. Rudly		26	Female		do	do	do
	P. Almar		64	Male	Farmer	do	do	do
	K. Almar		60	Female		do	do	do
	P. Almar		16	Male		do	do	do
	J. Lentz		40	do	Weaver	do	do	do
	M. Lentz & 3 Children		37	Female		do	do	do
	J. Lentz		47	Male		do	do	do
	M. Lentz & 7 Children		45	Female		do	do	do
	M. Lentz		49	Male		do	do	do
	Mary Lentz & 5 Children		45	Female		do	do	do
	Mary Lang		26	do		do	do	do
	Fishburne		40	Male		do	do	do
	E. Fishburne & 4 Children		38	Female		do	do	do
	Jack Really		35	Male	Shoemaker	do	do	do
	Tracy Really & 4 Chil'n		36	Female		do	do	do
	Martha Wall		36	do		do	do	do
	Adaline Wall & 1 Child		34	do		do	do	do
	Lewis Farmes		47	Male		do	do	do

PASSENGERS ARRIVING AT THE PORT OF CHARLESTON 1820-1829

Name of vessel	Passengers' names	Date of arrival	Age	Sex	Occupation	Where from	Country-belong	Country-inhabit
Brig Meridian	Detia Farmes & 8 Child'n	June 1828	45	Female	Brick Maker	Havre	Germany	United States
	Jack Eckhart		36	Male		do	do	do
	Christian Eckhart		33	Female		do	do	do
	Joseph Hofman		23	Male	Joiner	do	do	do
	Jack Myer		35	do	Shoemaker	do	do	do
	M. Myer & 5 Children		34	Female		do	do	do
	D. Favion		45	Male	Taylor	do	do	do
	E. Favion & 8 Children		40	Female		do	do	do
	Chas Favion		26	Male	do	do	do	do
	G. Chaffer		35	do	Weaver	do	do	do
	Sof. Chaffer & 4 Chil'n		30	Female		do	do	do
	John Jonah		18	Male		do	do	do
	Vincent Barry		40	Male	Brassfounder	do	do	do
	Edw'd Barray		18	do	do	do	do	do
	Louisa Barray		16	Female	none	do	do	do
Brig Step'n Gerard	S. Airmar		42	Male	Shop Keeper	Havana	Havana	do
	J. B. Pilessure		30	do	Gold Smith	do	do	do
	J. Richardson		40	do	Merchant	do	United States	do
Sch'r Wm Winder	Joseph Obsie		35	do	Mariner	Cuba	Spain	do
Sch'r Toison	Margaret Ogden		19	Female	Merchant	Matanzas	United States	do
	Capt'n R. Wells		49	Male	Painter	do	do	do
	Thos T. Kid		21	do	Mechanic	do	do	do
Brig Gov Griswald	Mathew Allen		28	do	do	do	do	do
	J. R. Dusser		23	do	Mechanic	do	do	do
Sch'r	William Yodey		40	Male	do	Trinidad	United States	United States
Philadelphia	Saml Killbrook		28	do	do	do	do	do
	Saml Back		25	Male		do	do	do
Brig Stranger	Mrs. Gilbert & 5 Children		30	Female		Matanzas	France	do
	H. Gilbert		42	Male	Merchant	do	do	do
	John Hart		28	do	do	do		
	N. Doda		33	do	do	do	do	do
	A. Balca		27	do	do	do	Spain	do

PASSENGERS ARRIVING AT THE PORT OF CHARLESTON 1820-1829

Name of vessel	Passengers' names	Date of arrival	Age Sex	Occupation	Where from	Country- belong	Country- inhabit
Sch'r Philadelphia	William Yodey	June 1828	40 Male	Mechanic	Trinidad	United States	United States
	Saml Killbrook		28 do	do	do	do	do
	Saml Back		25 Male	do	do	do	do
Brig Stranger	Mrs. Gilbert & 5 Children		30 Female	Merchant	Matanzas	France	do
	H. Gilbert		42 Male		do	do	do
	John Hart		28 do				
	N. Doda		33 do	do	do	do	do
	A. Balca		27 do	do	do	Spain	do
Brig Catherine	John Seigling	July 1828	36 Male	Merchant	Havanna	U S	U S
	William Milne		40 do	do	do	do	"
	S. A. Woodburn		34 do	do	do	"	"
	Mathew Furlong		29 do	do	do	"	"
	William Frean		45 do	do	do	"	"
Sch. Marion	John Stewart		34 do	Surveyor	Glascow	Britain	do
Brig Retrench	William Burgess	August	45 do	Merchant	Havanna	Spain	Spain
Brig Mary	Gabra		45 do	Painter	do	do	do
	Appleton		18 do	do	do	do	do
Brig	T. Gabbey		40 do	do	do	France	U S
Genl Gadsden	Mrs. Gabbey 2 children		21 female	none	do	do	do
	Bartholomew Carpo		21 Male	Lawyer	do	do	do
	Rhubin Piket		40 do	Planter	do	do	U S
Schooner	John Ross		45 do	Merchant	do	U S	do
Billow	Mary Clifford		32 female	none	do	do	do
Brig Billow	C. Leheur Esasde		35 Male	Merchant	do	France	do
des. Nile	J. A. Roberts		28 do	none	do	U S	U S
Schooner Marion	Samuel Blois		35 do	Planter	do	"	"
	do Blois Jr.		9 do	none	do	"	"
Brig Emeline	James Montiford		30 do	Merchant	do	do	do
" Stranger	Antonio Dodey	April 1829	39 do	do	do	do	do
Brig Rose Bank	James Marlow		70 Male	Farmer	Matanzes	Britain	U S
	Bridget Marlow		65 Female	none	Belfast	Britain	do
	James Firth		22 Male	"	"	"	"
Brig	Sir William Edden		25 Male	none	Havanna	"	Britain
Genl Gadsden	C. W. Stoke		36 "	Merchant		Swiss	do
	Oliver OHarra		40 "	"		U S	U S
	M. L. Salandanger		32 "	"		"	"
Schooner	James Wiecard		22 "	Servant	Nieuvetas	Britain	Britain
Richm. Packet	James Porter		27 "	Trader		Spain	U S
	Antonio Miraga		46 "			"	"
Brig Retrench	Adam Weddell		14 "	Clerk	Glascow	Britain	Britain
	James Campbell		20 "	Labourer		do	"

83

PASSENGERS ARRIVING AT THE PORT OF CHARLESTON 1820-1829

Name of vessel	Passengers' names	Date of arrival	Age	Sex	Occupation	Where from	Country-belong	Country-inhabit	
Schooner	Eliza Burk	April 1829	35	Female	none	Matanzes	U S	U S	
Felicity	Andrew Burk		19	Male	clerk		"	"	
	T. P. Burk		22	"	Planter		"	"	
	Robt Mecklin		25		Lawyer		"	"	
Sch Lovely Kessia	Robt Miller		24	Male	Merchant	Havanna	"	"	
Brig Stranger	Edward Morris		25	"	do	Matanzes	"	"	
Ship Julian	James S. Mitchell		30	"	Cooper	Havanna	"	"	
Felucca Union	Antonio Aimar		40	"	Trader	St. Jago	Portugal	"	
	Perez		38				"	"	
Schooner Marion	John W. Henry		28	Male	none	St. Jago	Britain	U S	
	Thomas Murray		30	"	Mechanic		"	"	
Ship Andromachi	Charles Hadden		40	Male	Baker	London	"	"	
	Ann do & 4 children		35	Female	no		"	"	
	George Carpenter		41	Male	Stone Mason		"	"	
	Wm do		11	"	do		"	"	
Ship Leonidas	John Stoney Jr.	May	20	"	clerk	Liverpool	U S	"	
Brig Deligence	G. G. Crawford		22	"	Surgeon	Greenock	"	"	
	Mrs. M. Crawford		19	Female & child	none		"	"	
	Archibald Campbell		27	Male	none		"	"	
	Mrs. Campbell		25	Female	"		"	"	
Brig Mary	John Capo		28	Male	Merchant	Havanna	"	"	
	Ephanza Capo		24	Female	none		"	"	
	Roger Jones		42	Male	Carpenter		"	"	
	P. Jones		13	"	"		"	"	
Brig Jas & Isabella	Alex'r Harrang		40	Male	Planter	Porto Rico	"	"	
Brig Avis	James Dutch		Boy		none having)	Liverpool	British	British	Three died
	Peter McCardle		"		deserted from)				
	Arthur L'Estrange				their parents)				
Brig Atlantic	Duncan McCrea		56	Male	Planter	St. Batholome	U S	U S	
	A. G. Heldreth		30	"	Marriner		"	"	
Brig Genl	Francis C. Black		39	"	Merchant	Matanzes	"	"	
Gadsden	E. Dickinson		33	"	Physician		"	"	
	Hy. S. Richards		26	"	Atty at Law		"	"	
	Lewis Ebrintz		38	"	Merchant		"	"	
	O Sollett		31	"	do		"	"	
Ship Perfect	Danely Giles		29	"	Gentleman	Liverpool	Britain	Britain	
Sch'r Marion	Peter Fausan	June	40	"	Marriner	Havanna	U S	U S	
do Little William	James Munson		22	"	Mechanic	Matanzes	"	"	
Schooner	James G. Blois		35	"	Merchant	Havana	"	"	
United States	Mrs. Blance		32	"	none		"	"	

PASSENGERS ARRIVING AT THE PORT OF CHARLESTON 1820-1829

Name of vessel	Passengers' names	Date of arrival	Age	Sex	Occupation	Where from	Country- belong	Country- inhabit
Brig Lexington	Julia White	June 1829	18	Female	none		U S	U S
	Johanna White		16	"	"		"	"
	Catherine White		9	"	"		"	"
	Timothy White		25	"	Accomptant		"	"
	James White		22	"	do		"	"
Brig William	Alexander McDougald	July	34	Male	Farmer	Belfast	Britain	U S
Sch Lovely Kezia	L. Certagne		30	"	Merchant	Italy	Italy	"
	R. Sharpe[?]		21	"	none	Britain	Britain	"
Brig Genl Gadsden	John Seigling		38	Male	Musick Master	Havanna	U S	U S
	J. J. Valulle[?]		62	"	none			
Sch Liona (Spash)	J. A. Perret		29	Female	Planter		Spain	
Schooner	Sophia Richards		26	Female	none	Havanna	Spain	U S
Little William	Daughter		12	"	"	"	U S	"
Brig Mary	Vincent Barre	August	42	Male	Brass Founder	"	France	"
	J. Malzan		43	"	Marriner	"	U S	"
	R. A. Maicos		14	"	none	"	Spain	"
Schl. Forrester	Henry Cox		25	"	Merchant	Madeira	Britain	"
Brig Magnolia	Rosalea Ancoza		29	"	Trader	Havanna	U S	"
	Joseph Antonio		8	"	none		"	"
Brig Stranger	Alfred R. Drayton	September	19	"	Merchant	Matanzes	"	"
----	John Conly		27	"	do	"	"	"
----	----- Castilli		26	"	Marriner	"	"	"
Sch Sally Ann	James G. Bell		23	"	Mechanic	"	Spain	"
	James Roe		28	"	Speculator	Havanna	U S	"
	Mathew Reeves		29	"	Musician	Liverpool	"	"
	John Dunn		14	"	do		"	"
British Ship	Eliza Lewe		20	"	Labourer	Britain	Britain	"
Lady Roarna	Robert Lewe		26	Female	"	"	"	"
	Edward Lewe		3	Male	"	"	"	"
			2	"	"	"	"	"
Sch Waccanaw	William Hood		55	"	Merchant	St. Thomas	"	"
Ship Saml	T. Y. Henderson		23	"	Chymist	Havre	"	"
Robertson	J. F. Rest		33	"	Priest		Saxony	"
	Alex'r Gordon		42	"	Merchant	Liverpool	Britain	"
	Joel Stephens		40	"	"		U S	"
	James Black		38	"	"		"	"
Ship Majestic	Wm. Hemmingway		40	"	Cotton Manifact.		Britain	"
	Mrs. Ditto		35	Female	Ditto		"	"
	their children		dift ages				"	"
	John Steike		35	Male	Shoemaker		"	"
	wife		25	Female	"		"	"
	Four children				"		"	"

PASSENGERS ARRIVING AT THE PORT OF CHARLESTON 1820-1829

Quarter ending	Names	Age	Sex	Occupation	Country-belong	Country-inhabit	Vessel
March 31, 1820	Joseph Coppinger	18	Male	Merchant	Spain	Charleston	Schooner Margaret
	Joseph Guadarama	18	"	Ditto	Ditto	Ditto	
	Manuel Guere	30	"	Ditto	Ditto	Ditto	
	Michael Maslerson	30	"	Ditto	U. States	New York	Sloop Connecticut, master not ment'd
	Thomas Herbert	25	"	Carpenter	U. States	Salsbury	
	Mary Ann Eagan	25	Female	Lady	Britain	Baltimore	Brig Columbia, master not ment'd
	Margaret Eagan	under	"		Ditto	Ditto	
	John Eagan	nine	Male		Ditto	Ditto	
	Wm. Eagan	"		Ditto	Ditto		
	Therisa Eagan		Female		Ditto	Ditto	
	Eliza Eagan	years	Ditto		Ditto	Ditto	
	Mary Moss		Ditto	Servant	Ditto	Ditto	
	Thomas Moorhead	23	Male	Farmer	Britain	South Carolina	
	Eliza English	36	Female		Ditto	Ditto	
	John English	32	Male		Ditto	Ditto	
	John English	12	Ditto		Ditto	Ditto	
	Lawrence English	3	Ditto		Ditto	Ditto	
	Andrew English	3	Ditto		Ditto	Ditto	
	Ellen McCarren	7	Female		Ditto	Ditto	
	Margaret Woods	55	Ditto		Ditto	Ditto	
	James Emery	27	Male	Merchant	United States	United States	Sloop Ann, master not mentioned
	Patrick Dillon	28	Ditto	Ditto	Ditto	Charleston	
	Thomas McGowan	30	Ditto	Marriner	Ditto	Ditto	Sloop Adventure, master not mentioned
	Gilbert	28	Ditto	Ditto	Ditto	Ditto	
	Thomas Barnard	35	Ditto	Ditto	Ditto	Ditto	Brig Edw'd D. Douglass, master not mentioned
	William Parkham	43	Ditto	Carpenter	France	France	Sloop Jay, master not mentioned
	Issadore Gregnel	23	Ditto	Merchant	Ditto	Ditto	
	Charlotte F. Grognel	18	Female	Lady	Ditto	Ditto	
	Emel Marc Mandel	25	Male	Merchant	Ditto	Ditto	
	Joane Anto Enice	20	Ditto	Ditto	Ditto	Ditto	
	Edward E. Bungson	13	Ditto	Ditto	U. States	Charleston	Schooner Mary Ann
	William Miller	25	Ditto	Ditto	Ditto	Ditto	
	George Crombelholm	30	Ditto	Ditto	Ditto	New York	Brig Columbia, master not mentioned
	Samuel Mitchell	51	Ditto	Ditto	Ditto	Charleston	
	John F. Fortune	23	Ditto	None	Ditto	Ditto	Schooner Comet, master not mentioned
	Ann Charties	20	Female	None	Ditto	Ditto	
	Anthony Moore	30	Male	Marriner	Spain	Havanna	
	Garrer	25	Ditto	Ditto	Ditto	Ditto	
	Thomas Barnet	25	Ditto	Engineer	Britain	Liverpool	
	John Dies	21	Ditto	Marriner	Spain	Havanna	
	Granades	35	Ditto	Ditto	Ditto	Ditto	
	Anthony Triai	30	Ditto	Merchant	Ditto	St. Augustine	Schooner Jane, master not mentioned
	John Pelicia	21	Ditto	Ditto	Ditto	Ditto	

PASSENGERS ARRIVING AT THE PORT OF CHARLESTON 1820-1829

Quarter ending	Names	Age	Sex	Occupation	Country-belong	Country-inhabit	Vessel
March 31, 1820	John Warton	30	Ditto	Marriner	United States	United States	Schooner Ann, master not ment'd
	Andrew Gay	45	Ditto	Merchant	Ditto	Ditto	
	W'm Melly	22	Ditto	Ditto	Spain	St. Augustine	
	Manuel Giano Bly	21	Ditto	Ditto	Ditto	Ditto	
	John Kean	47	Ditto	Labourer	Britain	South Carolina	Brig Mary, master not mentioned
	Patrick Dempsey	20	Ditto	Ditto	Ditto	Ditto	
	Ann Burke	50	Female	Spinster	Ditto	Ditto	
	Mary Keary	22	Ditto	Mantuamaker	Ditto	Ditto	
	Thomas Bourke	17	Male	Labourer	Ditto	Ditto	
	Mary Thompson	5	Female	None	Ditto	Ditto	
	Eliza Fraizer	23	Ditto	Spinster	Ditto	Ditto	
	William Peacock	50	Male	Dancing Master	Ditto	Ditto	
	George Weir	22	Ditto	Farmer	Britain	South Carolina	Brig Angelina, master not ment'd
	Martha Weir	21	Female		Ditto	Ditto	
	John Weir	1	Male		Ditto	Ditto	
	Thomas Smith	31	Ditto	Farmer	Ditto	Ditto	
	Mary Smith	26	Female		Ditto	Ditto	
	Rebecca Smith	4	Ditto		Ditto	Ditto	
	Bess Smith	2	Ditto		Ditto	Ditto	
	Issabella Smith	4	Ditto		Ditto	Ditto	
	Hugh Moore	16	Male		Ditto	Ditto	
	William Fox	21	Ditto		Ditto	Ditto	
	Margaret Fox	19	Female		Ditto	Ditto	
	Mary Fox	50	Ditto		Ditto	Ditto	
	Joseph Sanchez	20	Male	Merchant	Spain	Charleston	Schooner Eudora, master not mentioned
	Samuel Yates	36	ditto	ditto	United States	ditto	Brig Catharine, master not ment'd
	Jane Yates	32	Female	Lady	ditto	ditto	
	E. Farley	26	ditto	ditto	ditto	ditto	
	Thomas Trink	22	Male		ditto	ditto	
	Bazil Gonzales	35	ditto	Merchant	France	France	
	Fontaine	36	ditto	ditto	ditto	ditto	
	L. H. C. Schutt	32	ditto	ditto	United States	Charleston	
	Isaac Luares	21	ditto	Servant	ditto	ditto	
	Lucifer	48	ditto	Merchant	France	France	Ship Java, master not mentioned
	William Arnott	36	ditto	Mason	Britain	United States	
	Prudence Hibbert	22	Female	Lady	United States	Boston	Schooner Sally, master not ment'd
	John P. Lavinciendiez	45	Male	Merchant	St. Domingo	Charleston	Schooner Mary, master not ment'd
	Jacques Biecies	30	ditto	Cabinet Maker	ditto	ditto	
	Chapman Levy	35	ditto	Lawyer	United States	ditto	Sloop Lawrence, master not ment'd
	Alexander McGilvery	40	ditto	Auctioneer	ditto	ditto	
	Stephen Lancaster	32	ditto	Merchant	ditto	ditto	
	Angulo Sante	40	ditto	ditto	ditto	ditto	
	Thomas Hindley	38	ditto	ditto	Britain	Britain	Ship Elizabeth, master not ment'd

PASSENGERS ARRIVING AT THE PORT OF CHARLESTON 1820-1829

Quarter ending	Names	Age	Sex	Occupation	Country-belong	Country-inhabit	Vessel
March 31, 1820	John Hall	28	ditto		Britain	Britain	
	William Mitchell	31	ditto		ditto	ditto	
	William Barber	28	ditto		ditto	ditto	
	Niel McNiel	18	ditto		ditto	Charleston	
	James McNamy	40	ditto	Merchant	United States	ditto	Ship Mary, master not ment'd
	James Hatch	33	ditto	Marriner	ditto	ditto	Schooner Mary Ann, master not ment'd
	John Helfred	21	ditto	ditto	ditto	ditto	
	Lorenzo Henry	34	ditto	Merchant	ditto	ditto	
	Alexander England	15	ditto		ditto	ditto	
	Samuel Porter	22	ditto	Planter	ditto	ditto	
	James Mathews	42	Male	Trader	ditto	ditto	Brig Perserverance, master not ment'd
	Manuel Fernandez	38	ditto	ditto	ditto	ditto	
	Joseph Squeber	25	ditto	Marriner	ditto	New York	
	Anthony Gray	48	ditto	ditto	ditto	ditto	
	Luther Whiting	30	ditto	Merchant	United States	New York	Schooner Echo, master not ment'd
	Jacobus	25	ditto	ditto	ditto	Charleston	
	Francis Bourke	25	ditto	ditto	ditto	ditto	
	Thompson	23	Female		ditto	ditto	
	James Flemming	45	Male	Merchant	ditto	ditto	Ship Charleston Packet, master not mentioned
	James P. Ripley	25	ditto	ditto	ditto	ditto	
	Joseph M. Mayhle	32	ditto	ditto	ditto	Boston	
	Pasquel Macalette	45	ditto	ditto	ditto	New York	
	Sextus Gaillard	19	ditto	Marriner	ditto	Charleston	Ship Montgomery, master not ment'd
	Samuel Gaillard	18	ditto	ditto	ditto	ditto	
	James Sligman	30	ditto	Soap Boiler	Germany	ditto	
	Anthony Yallick	50	ditto	Marriner	United States	New Orleans	Brig Eliza, master not mentioned
	Jose Frara	39	ditto	Merchant	ditto	ditto	
	William Brown	21	ditto	Shoe Maker	Britain	Charleston	
	George Burne	19	ditto	ditto	ditto	ditto	
	Anthony Morra	25	ditto	Merchant	Spain	Cadiz	
	Francis Perez	26	ditto	ditto	ditto	St. Cruix	
	John Senet	25	ditto	ditto	Britain	Charleston	
	John Patterson	24	ditto	ditto	ditto	ditto	
	John Morrisson	35	ditto	Marriner	United States	ditto	Schooner Mercury, master not ment'd
	Peter Coffin	45	ditto	Merchant	ditto	ditto	
	Catharine Duncan	27	Female	Spinster	ditto	ditto	Brig Harriot, master not mentioned
	John Haley	55	Male	Farmer	Britain	ditto	Brig Prince Leopold, master not ment'd
	James Mager	24	ditto	Merchant	ditto	ditto	
	John Owen Johnson	24	ditto	ditto	ditto	ditto	
	John McKelvey	47	ditto	Farmer	ditto	ditto	
	Robert Harper	45	ditto	ditto	ditto	ditto	
	John Malcolm	36	ditto	ditto	ditto	ditto	
	Peter Cad	18	ditto	ditto	ditto	ditto	

88

PASSENGERS ARRIVING AT THE PORT OF CHARLESTON 1820-1829

Quarter ending	Names	Age	Sex	Occupation	Country-Belong	Country-Inhabit	Vessel
March 31, 1820	John Young	63	ditto	ditto	Britain	ditto	
	Sarah Young	64	Female	none	ditto	ditto	
	Jane Young	24	Female	ditto	ditto	ditto	
	Ann Young	22	ditto	ditto	ditto	ditto	
	Margaret Young	20	ditto	ditto	ditto	ditto	
	John Wilson	25	Male	ditto	ditto	ditto	
	Jane Hare	20	Female	ditto	ditto	ditto	
	Margaret Hare	20	ditto	ditto	ditto	ditto	
	Alexander Hare	13	Male	ditto	ditto	ditto	
	Samuel Aiken	21	ditto	ditto	ditto	ditto	
	Nancy Aiken	65	Female	ditto	ditto	ditto	
	Margaret Aiken	30	ditto	ditto	ditto	ditto	
	Eliza Aiken	25	ditto	ditto	ditto	ditto	
	Nancy Aiken	23	ditto	ditto	ditto	ditto	
	John Aiken	5	Male	ditto	ditto	ditto	
	Matilda Crawford	9	Female	ditto	ditto	ditto	
	Alexander Rogers	17	Male	ditto	ditto	ditto	
	John Richardson	23	ditto	ditto	ditto	ditto	
	Robert Lynn	35	ditto	ditto	ditto	ditto	
	Daniel McCanty	24	ditto	ditto	ditto	ditto	
	John Henry	32	ditto	ditto	ditto	ditto	
	William Shegog	20	ditto	ditto	ditto	ditto	
	Jane Wilson	21	Female	ditto	ditto	ditto	
	Joseph Fernandes	40	Male	Marriner	United States	Philadelphia	Schooner Comet, master not mentioned
	Hugh Rogers	41	ditto	Merchant	ditto	Charleston	
	John Lopez	35	ditto	ditto	ditto	ditto	
	John Dias	44	ditto	ditto	Spain	ditto	
	John Shoulbread	25	Male	Surgeon	United States	ditto	Ship Octavia, master not ment'd
	Peter Neilson	23	ditto	Merchant	Britain	ditto	
	John Tudor	20	ditto	ditto	ditto	ditto	
	Frisbee	35	ditto	Marriner	U States	New Haven	
	Honble Patrick Brown	60	ditto	Judge	Britain	Nassau	Brig Arline, master not ment'd
	Sir Charles Saxton	50	ditto	Gentleman	ditto	London	
	Francois	40	ditto	Servant	Frances	ditto	
	Vincent Gonsales	25	ditto	Marriner	Portugal	Havanna	Schooner Margaret, master not mentioned
	Wm Ward	27	Male	Merchant	Britain	Charleston	
	Joseph Hodgson	34	ditto	Mechanic	ditto	ditto	Ship S. Ca. Packet, master not ment'd
	Wm Hodgson	11	ditto	ditto	ditto	ditto	
	Richard C. Codman	21	ditto	Merchant	U States	Boston	Brig Joseph, maser not mentioned
	James Dean	30	ditto	ditto	ditto	Charleston	Schooner Susan, master not ment'd

PASSENGERS ARRIVING AT THE PORT OF CHARLESTON 1820-1829

Quarter ending	Names	Age	Sex	Occupation	Country-belong	Country-inhabit	Vessel
June 30, 1820	Phillip Robinson	38	Male	Merchant	U States	U States	Brig Catharine, Wilsman M'r &c
	John De Sylva	33	do	do	do	do	
	F. Le Page	21	do	do	do	do	Sloop Lawrina, Buckley master
	Mary Lindsay	39	Female	Spinster	do	do	
	Harriet Frith	17	do	do	do	do	
	Peck	38	Male	Marriner	do	do	
	Charles Sully	36	do	Merchant	Spain	St. Augustine	
	Mrs. Williams	29	Female	Merchant	Britain	U States	Ship South Boston, Cambell &c
	Georgianna Buntin	12	do		do	do	
	Jesse do	8	do		do	do	
	William do	7	Male		do	do	
	Arsin Sortie	30	Male	Trader	France	St. Domingo	Sch'r Intrepid, Peizant master
	Francis Hogg	57	do	Farmer	Britain	U States	Ship Prince Madoc, F. Choate do
	William Ireson	30	do	Merchant	do	do	
	John Stewart	28	do	do	do	do	
	James McCully	18	do	Farmer	Britain	U States	Brig Susan, Pollock master
	Stephen do	17	do	do	do	do	
	Henry Irwin	22	do	do	do	do	
	John Murchie	28	do	do	do	do	
	Lepar Lefleur	21	Female	Spinster	U States	Nantz	Brig Confiance, Haraud do
	Galbaud	22	do	Servant	France	do	
	P. Machallette	40	Male	Merchant	U States	U States	Sch'r Fame, Sherry master
	John Sennett	25	do	Trader	Britain	U States	
	John Burk	23	do	do	do	do	
	Joseph Barden	28	do	do	Spain	Havanna	
	Gregory Hexenera	35	do	do	do	do	
	Antonio Moro	25	do	do	do	do	
	Aaron Lyon	30	do	Physician	U States	U States	died on his passage Brig Edward, Collier master
	Michael McCobb	35	do	Labourer	Britain	do	Ship Friend, Watson do
	James Maynard	37	do	Baker	do	do	
	William do	16	do	Barber	do	do	
	George Levan	39	do	Turner	do	do	
	Joseph Gilchrist	--	do		Spain	St. Augustine	Sch'r Margaret, master not mentioned
	John Durbec	13	do		U States	U States	Sch'r Mary, master not &c
	Mrs. Brown	30	Female	Lady	Britain	do	Ship Adriana, Drew master
	Harriott do	5	do		do	do	
	Augustus do	3	Male		do	do	
	Caroline do	2	Female		do	do	
	Francis Peyre Jr.	25	Male	Planter	U States	do	
	Robert Child	29	do	Mechanic	do	do	
	Joseph Dehagres	30	do	Merchant	Spain	do	
	Harriott	25	Female	Servant	Britain	do	
	Capt. L. Courtois	52	Male	Mariner	France	do	

PASSENGERS ARRIVING AT THE PORT OF CHARLESTON 1820-1829

Quarter ending	Names	Age	Sex	Occupation	Country-belong	Country-inhabit	Vessel
June 30, 1820	Madam Courtois	28	Female		France	U States	
	Lewis do	6	Male		do	do	
	Samuel Cook	37	do	Merchant	U States	do	
	Hugh McNary	26	do	do	do	do	
	Thomas Briggs	37	do	Planter	do	do	Ship Virginia, Martin master
	Monsieur Martin	25	Female	Doctor	France	do	
	Madam do	20	Female		do	do	
	Alexander Gregg	24	Male	Baker	Britain	U States	Brig Phebe, Anderson master
	Gilbert Taylor	24	do	Farmer	do	do	
	Henry Janny	60	do	Labourer	do	do	Ship Pocohontas, Howland m'r
	Robert do	55	do	do	do	do	
	Mary do	46	Female		do	do	
	Harriet do	23	do		do	do	
	Louisa do	20	do		do	do	
	Mary A. do	17	do		do	do	
	Ellen do	15	do		do	do	
	Elizabeth do	13	do		do	do	
	Margaret do	12	do		do	do	
	Michael Harvey	32	Male	Mechanic	do	do	Sch'r Comet, T. Bates master
	Polly Quick	30	Female	Spinster	U States	do	
	Rebecca Buire	45	do	do	do	do	
	James Chambore	38	Male	Dyer	do	do	
	And'w Friddle	30	do	Merchant	Germany	do	Sloop Gen'l Washington, S Bulkley do
	Nicholas Gardiner	30	do	Marriner	U States	do	
	John M. Sanchez	22	do	Merchant	Spain	do	
	John Pellisier	26	do	do	do	do	
	George W. Ogden	40	do	do	do	do	
	James Shaddock	18	Male	Marriner	U States	U States	Ship Roger Stuart, not &c
	James McGregor	30	do	Merchant	Britain	do	Sch'r Sisters, W. Green master
	Hepolite Grove	28	do	do	France	do	Brig Sea Gull, Hubble do
	John Stewart	28	do	do	Britain	do	
	Rachael DePass	18	Female		U States	do	Sch'r Jane, master not &c
	Adolphus Eschen	30	Male	Merchant	do	do	
	Samuel Goodrey	24	do	do	do	do	
	John Lopez	35	do	do	do	do	
	Henry Heldebram	32	do	do	Hambourgh	do	
	Issabella Do	45	Female		do	do	
	John Machoen	28	Male	do	Britain	do	Ship Ceres, master not &c
	Marshall Luker	23	do	Cabinet maker	U States	do	Schooner Mary Ann, J. Bonnell
	George Scott	22	do	Shoe maker	do	do	
	Joseph Mathews	45	do	Trader	do	do	
	Seth Austin	48	Male	Merchant	U States	U States	Sch'r Carrier, master not &c
	Jonathan Rathbone	28	do	do	do	do	

PASSENGERS ARRIVING AT THE PORT OF CHARLESTON 1820-1829

Quarter ending / Names	Age	Sex	Occupation	Country-belong	Country-inhabit	Vessel
June 30, 1820						
Edw'd King	15	do	Yeoman	Britain	do	
William Clark	15	Male	do	do	do	
Mrs. Dalton	45	Female	Lady	do	do	Ship Isabella, master not &c
David Wood & 2 child'n						
Hugh Livingston	25	Male	Tailor	do	do	
James Smith	45	Male	Marriner	do	do	Ship Jane, Cumming master
Hugh Oliver	23	do	Clerk	do	do	
Agnes do	25	do	do	do	do	
	24	Female		do	do	
William Craig	20	Male	Labourer	do	do	
William Jerry	28	ditto	none	U States	Kentucky	Brig Catherine, Wilson mas.
L. Blanten	35	ditto	ditto	ditto	ditto	
Antonio Garrier	35	ditto	Trader	Spain	Cuba	
Jacob Drummond	32	ditto	Mariner	U States	Bath	
William Dustch	28	ditto	Merch't	Holland	N York	Steam Ship Rob't Fulton, Inott mas
Manuel Fernandez	60	ditto		Spain		
Peter Pelow	35	ditto				
Pedres Isagalata	40	ditto				
Venison Salsald	--	Female				
Mrs. OBrian	55	ditto		U States		
Ingliso & Servant	--	Male	Servant	Spain		
Andrew Munroe	58	do	Labourer	Britain	N Carolina	Ship Mary & Susan, master not ment'd
Christiana Munroe	18	Female	none	ditto	ditto	
James OConnor	25	Male	Labourer	ditto	Charleston	Sloop Ja's Vincent, master &c.
Nathaniel Green Clary	35	ditto	Merchant	U States		
Andrew McDowell	32	ditto				
G. Ward	30	ditto		Spain	St. Augustine	
D. Sanchez	24	ditto		U States	Columbia	
John Taylor	25	Male		Spain	St. Augustine	
Devauraux		do	Merchant	do	Columbia	Sch'r Susan, Buscher master
Perrier		do	Mariner	do	St. Augustine	
Carrier		do	do	U States		
Fortune	24	do	Merchant	do	U States	Sch'r Mary Ann, Hilliard master
Francis Burke	24	do	Trader	Britain	do	
Asa Harmon	59	do	Mariner	do	U States	
Asa do Jr	19	do	Clerk	do	do	
William Kenneau	30	do	Merchant	U States	do	
James Hamelton	28	do	do	U States	do	Sch'r Antelope, Lewis master
Michael OConner	38	do	do	Britain	do	
John Curling	25	do	Mariner	U States	do	
John G. Wade	24	do	do	do	do	

PASSENGERS ARRIVING AT THE PORT OF CHARLESTON 1820-1829

Quarter ending	Names	Age	Sex	Occupation	Country-belong	Country-inhabit	Vessel
Sept'r 30 1820	Oliver OHarra	31	Male	Merchant	U States	Charleston	Sloop Lady Washington, Watterman do
	Charles Sully	36	do	do	do	St. Augustine	
	William Travers	30	do	do	do	Charleston	
	John Williams	24	do	Marriner	do		
	Mrs. McCauley	20	Female		Spain	St. Augustine	
	John Carraras	29	Male	Shoe Maker	do	do	
	Bartholomew Janeworth	20	do	do	do	do	
	Capt. Walton	27	do	Marriner	G Britain	do	Sch'r Mary, Coleman master &c.
	Madam Chimernard	28	Female		France	Charleston	
	John Oates	60	Male	Shop Keeper	G Britain	do	
	John Burke	28	do	do	do	do	
	Anthony Colingen	27	do	do	France	do	
	William Canuet	32	do	do	do	do	Sloop James, Vincent do
	Major Bird	42	Male	Officer USA	U States	U States	
	Lieutenant Leigle	20	do	do	do	do	
	Holmes	19	do	do	do		
	Humphreys	19	do	do	do		
	John Barclay	35	do	Merchant	do	do	Sch'r Comet, N. Forsyth &c.
	John Wheeler	33	do	do	do	Charleston	
	William Jerrassy	30	do	do	do	U States	
	Bottellier	38	do	Marriner	France	do	Ship Portia, Silliman master
	Fergerson	26	do	do	G. Britain	do	
	McGuire	30	do	Merchant	France	do	
	Arsdoff	32	do	do	do	do	
	Le Clair	27	do	Baker	do	do	
	Rachait	35	Female	Seamstress	U States	do	
	Niel Campbell	25	Male	Merchant	G Britain	U States	Sch'r Jane, Darling do
	James Pearson	44	Male	Mariner	U States	do	Sch'r Jane, McMillan do
	John Brown	25	do	do	do	do	
	William Marshall	35	do	do	do	do	
	James M. Mathewson	35	do	Gentleman	Hamburgh	St. Augustine	Ship Arab, Bingham do
	Pierce Rowe	26	do	Farmer	G Britain	Washington N C	Brig Christopher, Hayward do
	Franklin Goram	35	do	Merchant	U States	Washington NC	Sloop Genl Washington, Buckley do
	Joel Dickinson	40	do	Merchant	U States	N. York	Lady Washington, Waterman &c.
	John Andrews	30	do	Marriner		St. Augustine	
	Geo. Delespine	32	do	Merchant	Spain	do	
	Anthony Tray	28	do	do	do	do	
	Joseph Bunnett	25	do	Marriner	do	do	
	Francis Saltus	60	do	Merchant	U States	Charleston	Sch'r Planter, Osborn Do
	Mrs. Do	50	Female		do	do	
	Francis Yates	19	Male		do	do	
	Eliza Burch	40	Female		do	do	
	Ruth Righton	30	do		do	do	

93

PASSENGERS ARRIVING AT THE PORT OF CHARLESTON 1820-1829

Quarter ending: Sept'r 30 1820

Names	Age	Sex	Occupation	Country-belong	Country-inhabit	Vessel
B. Cooper	45	Male	Marriner	G Britain	do	Sloop James Vincent &c.
James Bentham	33	do	Merchant	U States	do	Sch'r Mary Ann, Hillard &c.
Joseph Elario	28	do	Marriner	Brazil	do	
C. Bowman	28	do	do	Charleston	Charleston	
John Henderson	24	do	Merchant	U States	N. Orleans	Brig Eliza, Chazell &c.
Bazella Gonzales	30	do	Merchant	Spain	U States	Brig Catharine, Welsman &c.
John Lopez	36	do	do	Portugal	Charleston	
William Phillbrick	27	do	do	U States	Savanna	
William Ward	27	do	do	G Britain	U States	
Mary do	26	Female	Lady	do	do	Ship S. Carolina, Easterby &c.
Eliza Ann do				do	do	
Jack Aiken	30	Male	Servant	U States	Charleston	
Theodore Sheafe	23	Male	Merchant	do	Portsmouth, N.H.	Brig Carolinian, McIntosh &c.
Gorham Bassett	32	do	Marriner	do	do	
Hugh Staples	23	do	do	do	U States	
Rufus S. Kidman	25	do	Gentleman	do	do	
Doctor	33	do	Physician	do	do	
James Bowers	34	do	Merchant	do	do	
Mrs. M. Belcher	32	Female	Lady	do	do	Ship Sybil, Belcher &c.
Mary Reed	28	do	do	do	do	
Anna Belcher	3	do		do	do	
Mary do	2	do		do	do	
Margaret Haise	19	do	Spinster	G Britain	do	Ship Octavia, Wilson &c.
Samuel Cook	35	Male	Shop Keeper	U States	Charleston	Sch'r Alexandria, Smith &c.
Joseph Argotie	25	do	do	Spain	Spain	
Daniel Gaillard	21	do	Gentleman	U States	Charleston	
William Parker	25	do	do	do	do	
James Magee	19	do	Farmer	G Britain	U States	Brig Susan, Pollock &c.
Mary McGuire	18	Female	Spinster	do	do	
Lucy Buntin	14	do	Marriner	do	do	
John F. Walker	23	Male	Merchant	do	Charleston	Ship Fama, Barry &c.
Henry Knust	47	do	do	do	do	
William H. Capers	19	do	Marriner	U States	do	
Mrs. Smith	26	Female	Spinster	G Britain	do	
& two children						
Mitchell	24	Male		do	do	
Joseph W. Clark	50	do	Mariner	U States	Charleston	Brig Commerce, Messervey &c.
Bernard Poll	18	do	Clerk	do	do	
Emills	20	do	do	France	do	
F. Monbrun	25	do	do	do	do	
M. Brodut	27	do		do	do	
Mr. Vanhaldren	38	Male	Tailor	Holland	do	Ship Charles & Henry, Carsdoff &c.
Mrs. Do	28	Female		do	do	

PASSENGERS ARRIVING AT THE PORT OF CHARLESTON 1820-1829

Quarter ending	Names	Age	Sex	Occupation	Country-belong	Country-inhabit	Vessel
Sept'r 30 1820	Michael Do	5	Male				
Dec'r 31 1821	And'w McMillan	67	Male	Farmer	G. Britain	U States	Brig George, Master not &c.
	Mrs. do & 8 Children	67	Female		do	do	
	Marg't McCoy & 5 Do	33	do		do	do	
	John Oneil	25	Male		do	do	
	Mary Do & 3 Children	34	Female		do	do	
	Peter Sharp	24	Male		do	do	
	Jane Do & 2 Children	26	Female		do	do	
	Wm McWhirr	64	Male		do	do	
	James Shannon	22	do		do	do	
	John Printer	60	do	Merchant	do	do	
	Stephen Miller	20	do	Confectioner	do	do	Sloop Cherub, not &c
	John Cattell	24	do	Merchant	do	do	Sch'r Emily, not &c
	Townson Moore	30	do	Clerk	do	do	Sch'r Liberty, Do
	Archibald Watson	20	do	Merchant	do	do	Ship Thos Gelston, Do
	Lewis Flemming	26	do		do	do	Sch'r Col. Ramsay, Do
	Mrs. do	20	Female		do	do	
	Thomas Donathan	28	Male	Merchant	do	do	Brig Harmony, Do
	Joseph Hogson	35	do	Taylor	do	do	
	Margaret do &	30	Female		do	do	
	4 children						
	James Ross	31	Male	Mariner	do	do	Sch'r Jane, Do
	Anthony Aymar	33	do	Trader	do	do	
	Alfred Woodhouse	24	do	Merchant	do	do	Ship So Boston, Do
	John Mahle	36	do	Do	Holland	do	
	Mrs. Dalton & child	21	Female		do	do	Ship Isabella, Do
	Campbell Douglass	40	Male	Grocer	Britain	do	
	Henry Middleton	19	do		do	do	
	R. O. Anderson	26	do	Trader	do	do	
	Robert Whitfield	25	do	Do	do	do	
	Thomas Jones	23	do	Do	do	do	
	Thomas Simmons	20	Male	Trader	G. Britain	U States	
	John Torrington	25	do	Do	do	do	
	Wm Cox	20	do	Do	do	do	
	John Rose	50	do	Carpenter	do	do	
	Eliza Do	40	Female		do	do	
	Mrs. Topham &	40	Female		do	do	
	5 Children						
	Edward Honewell	33	Male		do	do	Ship Hunter, Do
	Eliza Do	28	Female		do	do	
	& 2 Children						
	David Meyer	35	Male	Musician	do	do	

95

PASSENGERS ARRIVING AT THE PORT OF CHARLESTON 1820-1829

Quarter ending	Names	Age	Sex	Occupation	Country-belong	Country-inhabit	Vessel
Dec'r 31 1821	George Pritchard	24	do	Merchant		do	Sch'r Louisa, Do
	Joseph Veason	26	do	Do		do	
	T. H. Findley	40	do			do	Ship Mary & Susan, Do
	T. B. Clough	33	do			do	
	P. Fitzsimons	21	do			do	
	L. Moffat	32	do			do	
	Alfred Huger	33	do	Planter		do	Brig Catharine, Do
	M. Richard	40	do			do	
	Mrs. Do & child	45	Female			do	
	M. Sosie	45	Male	Tinner		do	
	Mrs. Do & 6 Children	45	Female			do	
	M. E. Levy	45	Male	Trader		do	
	M. Rutaut	27	Do	Merchant		do	
	James Miller	26	Do	Do		do	
	M. Brush & child	20	Do	Tailor		do	
	John Lowden	34	Do	Merchant		do	Ship Corsair, Do
	Don Diago Carrare	47	Do		Spain	do	
	Mrs. do	30	Female		Britain	do	
	And'w McDowall	31	Male	Merchant		do	
	Mrs. do	24	Female			do	
	And'w Henderson	25	Male	Merchant		do	
	Joseph Harrison	21	do	Mechanic		do	
	Stephen Watson	24	do	Do		do	
	Geo Grairson	22	do	Do		do	
	Mathewson	24	do	Do		do	
	S. Domingo	35	do	Trader	Portugal	do	Sloop Ann, Do
	Louisa Vensey & child	33	Female		Spain	do	
	B. Gonsalves	38	Male	Trader	France	do	Sch'r Mary Ann, Do
	J. P. Barre	28	Do	Do	U States	do	
	E. Chisolm	16	Do	Mariner		do	
	Samuel Corman	22	Do	Do		do	
	Edw'd Buckler	24	do	Merchant		do	Sch'r Eudora, Do
	J. Stanter	35	do	Clerk		do	
	Manuel Fernandez	39	do	Trader	Portugal	do	Sch'r Betsy & Peggy, Do
	George Welden	23	do	Labourer	Britain	do	Ship Homer, Do
	Niel McDuffee	24	Male	Labourer	G Britain	U States	
	John Patterson	22	do			do	
	Niel McPhail	26	Male	do		do	Brig Phebe, Do
	James do	40	do	do		do	
	Janett McNair & 4 child	40	Female			do	
	Maria Douglass	23	do			do	
	James Wilson	25	Male	Labourer		do	

PASSENGERS ARRIVING AT THE PORT OF CHARLESTON 1820-1829

Quarter ending	Names	Age	Sex	Occupation	Country-belong	Country-inhabit	Vessel
Dec'r 31 1821	Elizabeth Marshal & 3 child.	28	Female		G Britain	do	
	William Shields	35	Male	Labourer	do	do	Ship Adriana, Do
	R. Cheves	34	do	do	do	do	
	H. N. Vest	35	do	do	do	do	
	Jonathan Cooper	20	do	Planter	do	do	Sch'r Decatur, Do
	John Noga	36	do	Mariner	do	do	
	John Salter	35	do	Do	U States	do	
	James L. Brown	35	do	Merchant	G Britain	do	Sloop Genl Washington, Do
	Mrs. do	38	Female		do	do	
	William Welsh & child	35	Male	Tailor	do	do	
	Joseph Delamore	22	do	Planter	do	do	Sch'r Comet, Do
	Thomas Mara	19	do	Do	do	do	
	C. M. Dumoulin	22	do	Merchant	do	do	
	J. Ross	27	do	Mariner	do	do	
	Dr. Richardson	50	do	Physician	U States	do	Ship S. Carolina
	Mrs. Do & Child	35	Female		do	do	
	Miss Coffin	19	do		do	do	
	Miss Field	30	do		do	do	
	Dr. Hannah	24	Male	Physician	do	do	
	John Paul	37	do	Merchant	do	do	
	John McKenzie	41	do		do	do	
	Charles Goodshee	21	do	Shoemaker	G Britain	do	Sch'r Eliza, Do
	Edward Phillips	21	do	Farmer	do	do	Ship James Bailey, Do
	Samuel Adams	36	do	Do	do	do	
	Robert Wilson	30	do	Do	do	do	
	John Adams	24	do	Do	do	do	
	Mrs. Do	25	Female		do	do	
	Isaac Walker	14	Male	Farmer	do	do	
	Samuel Ewart	23	do	Do	do	do	
	Wm Kennedy	22	do	Do	do	do	
	Samuel McCohet	21	do	Do	do	do	
	William Dunlop	19	do	Do	do	do	
	Thomas Bogs	32	do	Do	do	do	
	Martha Do &3 Children	32	Female		do	do	
	James McClure	60	Male	Apothecary	do	do	
	Mrs. Do & 4 Children	60	Female		do	do	
	Jane Harper & 6 Do	45	Female		do	do	
	Betty McFee	24	do		do	do	
	Robert Irwin	47	Male	Labourer	France	U States	
	James Irwin	22	Male	Labourer	do	do	
	Daniel McClowell	20	do	Do	do	do	
	Wm Charles	23	do	Do	do	do	

PASSENGERS ARRIVING AT THE PORT OF CHARLESTON 1820-1829

Quarter ending	Names	Age	Sex	Occupation	Country-belong	Country-inhabit	Vessel
Dec'r 31 1821	John Houtain	25	do	Labourer	France	U States	Ship Jane, Do
	Thomas Kennedy	27	do	Do	do	do	
	Rich'd do	21	do	Do	do	do	
	Henry McGrahagan	22	do	Do	do	do	
	James Haslett	20	do	Do	do	do	
	Marg't Davidson & 3 Children	44	Female		G. Britain	do	
	James Carlisle	56	Male	Labourer	do	do	
	Mary Do & 4 Children	53	Female		do	do	
	Wm Martin	25	Male	Labourer	do	do	
	Susanna Do	23	Female		do	do	
	And'w Dool	42	Male	Labourer	do	do	
	Phillip McClery	25	Do	Do	do	do	
	Alex'r Henderson	21	Do	Do	do	do	
	Philip Raney	20	Do	Do	do	do	
	Mary Burns & 3 children	42	Female		do	do	
	Rob't McMaster	26	Male	Labourer	do	do	
	Wm Owens	25	Do	Do	do	do	
	Wm Dunn & 3 Children	30	Do	Do	do	do	
	Wm Fullerton	21	Do	do	do	do	
	Henry Caulfield	20	Do	do	do	do	
	Robert Dobbin	20	Do	do	do	do	
	John Blair	60	Do	do	do	do	
	Jane Do & 3 Children	55	Female		do	do	
	P. Mannock	49	Male	Labourer	do	do	
	Mrs. Do & 5 Children	45	Female		do	do	
	James McNeilly	20	Male	Labourer	do	do	
	Wm Riddon	26	Do	Do	do	do	
	Wm White	18	Do	Do	do	do	
	Wm Scott	24	Male	Do	do	do	
	Ellen Do	26	Female		do	do	
	Wm McGowan	20	Male	Labourer	do	do	
	John McKissick	25	Do	Do	do	do	
	Robert Larney	67	Do	Do	do	do	
	Mrs. Do & 3 Children	53	Female		do	do	
	David McCallish	18	Male	Labourer	do	do	
	William Hugh	26	Male	Do	do	do	
	James Do	27	Do	Do	do	do	
	Wm. Do & 5 Children	29	Do	Do	do	do	

PASSENGERS ARRIVING AT THE PORT OF CHARLESTON 1820-1829

Quarter ending	Names	Age	Sex	Occupation	Country-belong	Country-inhabit	Vessel
April 1st 1822	Joseph Urban	30	Male	Merchant	France	U States	Sloop Ann, Master not &
	Peter Monqued	32	Do	Do	Britain	do	
	Henry Goldsmith	16	Do	Do	U States	do	
	John Dash	20	Do	Do	do	do	
	Geo. Phillips	18	Do	Do	do	do	
	John Damon	40	Do	Do	do	do	Sch'r Mary Ann, &c
	John Shegog	28	Do	Merchant	do	do	Sch'r Comet &c
	B. Gonsally	30	Do	Do	Spain	do	
	John Howard	25	Do	Cabinet maker	U States	do	Sch'r Sarah Ann &c
	John F. Ohl	30	Do	Merchant	Hamburgh	do	Brig Philad'a &c
	William Phillpot	30	Do	Do	G Britain	do	
	William C. Kausler	40	Do	Do	Germany	do	
	Mary Ann Magnan	35	Female		West Indies	do	
	A. Segar	30	Male	Trader	U States	do	
	L. C. Gross	40	Do	Do	Germany	do	
	Charles Meyo	30	Do	Mariner	U States	do	Brig Ann &c
	E. C. Brire	28	Do	Merchant	Holland	do	Brig Gov'r Brooks &c
	John Oaks	25	Do	Do	U States	do	Sch'r Sampson &c
	Wm Hall	24	Do	Mariner	do	do	
	Baldwin M. Halsey	24	Do	Merchant	do	do	Sch'r Larch &c
	Thomas Barnett	28	Do	Engineer	G. Britain	do	Sch'r Elisa & Polly &c
	Henry Brookins	50	Do	Mariner	do	do	
	John Anthony	25	Do	Do	do	do	
	Roger Harriett & 2 Child	58	Do	Merchant	do	do	Sch'r Sam'l Smith &c
	Daniel Allen	30	Do	Physician	do	do	
	S. C. Potter	26	Do	Merchant	do	do	
	J. Mathews	50	Do	Do	do	do	Brig Catharine &c
	A. Forsyth	52	Do	Mariner	do	do	
	Adam McClaren	45	Do	Merchant	G. Britain	do	Ship Jane &c
	Agnes McClaren & 8 Children	45	Female		G. Britain	U States	
	George Shaw	28	Male	Butcher	do	do	
	James Phillips	35	Do	Baker	do	do	
	Thomas Hemmingsway	21	Do	Lawyer	G. Britain	do	Ship Bayard, &c
	Pat. McBreet	27	Male		do	U States	
	Mary do	22	Female	Farmer	do	do	
	Thomas Latu	24	Male	Do	do	do	
	James Carroll	28	Do	Do	do	do	
	Edmund Dyer	44	Do		do	do	
	Ann Do & 2 children	36	Female		do	do	
	John Duffy	45	Do		do	do	
	Ellen Do & 4 children	38	Female		do	do	

99

PASSENGERS ARRIVING AT THE PORT OF CHARLESTON 1820-1829

Quarter ending	Names	Age	Sex	Occupation	Country-belong	Country-inhabit	Vessel
April 1st 1822	Wm Lamb	24	Male	Farmer	G. Britain	U States	
	B. Sweeny	20	Do	Do	do	do	
	Mich'l Smith	22	Do	Do	do	do	
	Pat. Naughton	27	Do	Do	do	do	
	James Phalen	22	Do	Do	do	do	
	Pat. Lahy	30	Do	Do	do	do	
	Michael Carroll & Child	13	Do	Do	do	do	
	Charles Freebody	23	Do	Do	do	do	Brig Mary &c
	Stephen Singleton	36	Do	Mariner	do	do	Ship Johnson &c
	David Canter	42	Do	Do	do	do	Sch'r Content &c
	Nathan Bacon	43	Do	Trader	do	do	Sch'r Philader &c
	Hugh Graham	30	Do		G. Britain	do	Brig Leopold &c
	Mary do	25	Female		do	do	
	Edward do	28	Male	Grocer	do	do	
	Alex'r Holstrum	19	Do	Clerk	do	do	
	James Logan	30	Do	Baker	do	do	
	Marg't Larman & 2 Child	28	Female		do	do	
	P. Macalette	55	Male	Mariner	Portugal	do	Brig Neptune's Barge &c
	Lewis do	28	Do	Do	do	do	
	D. Bolston	25	Do	Physician	U States	do	Ship Lucius &c
	Francis de Castro	44	Do	Planter	Spain	do	
	G. W. de Roche	40	Do	Merchant	France	do	
	M. Gouche	19	Do	Do	do	do	
	John Oats	60	Do	Publican	U States	do	
	John Urban	28	Do	Tailor	France	do	Sch'r Bee &c
	Fred'k Monquet	35	Do	Do	do	do	
	Abel Harris	60	Do	Merchant	U States	do	Sch'r Rosby &c
	Sam'l Snoddy	20	Do	Labourer	G. Britain	do	Sch'r Grace &c
	Jane McIrish	35	Female	Spinster	do	do	
	Martha Do	29	Do	Do	France	do	
	M. Montanden	32	Male		do	do	Sch'r Comet &c
	M. Brandt	40	Do		do	do	
	John Dunscomb	40	Male	Merchant	do	do	Sch'r Industry &c
	C. Baker	50	Do	Mariner	G. Britain	U States	
	Joseph Hammond	24	Do	Merch't	do	do	Ship Porteu &c
	Thomas Williams	26	Do	Broker	do	do	Sch'r Mary Ann &c
	L. Monseur	50	Do	Trader	France	do	
	Lyebodiere	28	Do	Merch't	do	do	Died 13 March
	Robert Wallace	63	Do	Farmer	G. Britain	do	Ship Jesse & Flora &c
	Mrs. Do & 5 Children	45	Female		do	do	
	John Robinson	30	Male	Farmer	do	do	

100

PASSENGERS ARRIVING AT THE PORT OF CHARLESTON 1820-1829

Quarter ending	Names	Age	Sex	Occupation	Country-belong	Country-inhabit	Vessel
April 1st 1822	Mary, Do & 2 children	26	Female		G. Britain	do	Ship Trajan &c
	Alex'r McPhaul	18	Male	Do	do	do	
	David Brown	25	Do	Do	do	do	
	Wm Snoddy	68	Do	Do	do	do	
	Mrs. Do & 2 children	62	Female		do	do	
	John McKeown	23	Male	Farmer	do	do	
	John Shaw	35	Do	Do	do	do	
	Mrs. Do & Child	30	Female		do	do	
	Adam Wallace	24	Male		do	do	
	John McCormick	36	Do		do	do	
	Mrs. Do & 5 children	35	Female		do	do	
	Thomas McCoy	50	Male		do	do	
	Mrs. Do & 3 child.	40	female		do	do	
	Thomas Hart	27	Male	Merchant	U States	do	Sch'r Col. Ramsay &c
	Simeon Barthe	66	Do	Do	do	do	
	James Lawson	20	Do	Do	do	do	
	Wm R. Faber	27	Do	Do	do	do	
	A. Geraldo	30	Do	Mariner	do	do	
	John Langenette	27	Do	Merchant	Spain	do	Sch'r Jane &c
	Wm Eckel	28	Do	Do	U States	do	Do Sarah Ann &C
	John Dominique	40	Do	do	Italy	do	Brig Ann &c
	Robert McFannen	24	Do	Farmer	G Britain	do	
	James Kinsey	25	Do	do	do	do	
	Ann Do	22	Female		do	do	
	James McCann	30	Male	Farmer	do	do	
	Issabella do & Child	21	Female		do	do	
	Samuel McKey	20	Male		do	do	
	Robert Harrit	30	Do		do	do	Ship Orion
	Mrs. Balker & Child	42	Female		do	do	
	Henry Dreffren	35	Male		do	do	
	Maria do & child	20	Female		do	do	
	Samuel M. Smith	36	Male	Trader	U States	do	Sloop Emily &c
	Peter do	24	Do	Do	do	do	
	Charles Hawkins	28	Do	Do	do	do	
	Barnard do	26	Do	Do	do	do	
	George Beale	25	Do	Do	do	do	
	Otho Laurence	38	Male		do	do	Ship Perfect &c
	Charles Maxwell	25	Do	Teacher	G Britain	do	
	Bernard Chenee	28	Do		France	do	
	John James Appleton	30	Do	Sec'y of Legation	U States	do	Brig Deux Freres &c
	Nicholas Aquitar	26	Do	Merchant	do	do	Brig Standard &c
	St. Jago Tabara	29	Do	Do	Spain	do	
	Herman H. Green	23	Do	Do	U States	do	

Quarter ending	Names	Age	Sex	Occupation	Country-belong	Country-inhabit	Vessel
April 1st 1822	Thomas Munroe	27	Do		U States	do	
	Peter Barrett	37	Do	Mariner	do	do	
	Samuel Stimson	30	Do	Do	do	do	
	John Nolan	27	Do		do	do	
	Josia Calliona	35	Do		do	do	
	Michael Praya	29	Do	Mariner	Spain	do	
	R. Pease	25	Do	Do	U States	do	
	Wm Fox	30	Do	Do	do	do	
	Charles Gedding	19	Do	Physician	do	do	
	Huger	30	Do	Merchant	do	do	Brig Catharine &c
	M. Simonton	34	Do	Do	do	do	
	Keith	24	Do	Do	do	do	
	Depass	25	Do	Do	do	do	
	Alexander	28	Do	Do	do	do	
June 30, 1822	W. R. Smith	28	Male	Merchant	Havana	U States	Sch'r Eliza & Polly, Master not &c
	John Halden	35	Do	Do	Trinidad	do	Sch'r Col. Geo. Armstead Do
	M. Stevenson	38	Do	Carpenter	Germany	do	
	Jacob Gilbert	25	Do	Do	U States	do	
	Sarah do	20	Female		do	do	
	John W. Trott	40	Male	Merchant	England	do	Sch'r Betsy & Pegy, not &c
	Henry Goldsmith	17	Do	Do	do	do	
	John Norga	45	Do	Mariner	Portugal	do	
	Antonio Pannell	15	Do	Do	Spain	do	
	H. Eymar	30	Do	Shop keeper	do	do	Sch'r Comet, not &c
	H. Debal	21	Do	Do	do	do	
	Augustus Linguart	30	Do	Merchant	Austria	do	Sch'r Neptune, not &c
	Francis Prioye	32	Do	Do	do	do	
	E. Emenes	60	Do		Denmark	do	
	John Wurner	23	Do	Merchant	U States	do	Sch'r Emeline, not &c
	Mrs do	21	Female		do	U States	
	Piene	30	Male	Merchant	U States	do	
	D. Montgomery	40	Male	Planter	do	do	
	G. W. Geddes	22	Do	Lawyer	do	do	
	John Gill	25	Do	Planter	do	do	
	Manuel Piera	38	Do	Mariner	Spain	do	
	Fred'k Polles	27	Do	Do	do	do	
	P. Reynal	46	Male	Merchant	U States	do	Brig Commerce, not &c
	John Chartran	35	Do	Planter	France	do	Sch'r Mary, not &c
	Louisa do & child	20	Female		do	do	
	Monquoit	38	Male		do	do	
	Wm Sullivan	26	Do		England	do	
	Jose A. Iswaga	26	Do	Merchant	Spain	do	Sch'r Louise, not &c

PASSENGERS ARRIVING AT THE PORT OF CHARLESTON 1820-1829

Quarter ending	Names	Age	Sex	Occupation	Country-belong	Country-inhabit	Vessel
June 30, 1822	F. Delahanka	25	Do	Do		do	Sch'r Jane, not &c
	Benj. Buchannan	45	Do	Do	Scotland	do	Ship Boston, not &c
	P. J. Lorent	60	Do	Merchant	Germany	do	
	H. T. Faber	23	Do	Do	U States	do	Brig Catharine, not &c
	Henry Rolando	28	Do	Do	do	do	
	Joseph Mathews	25	Do	Do	do	do	
	Charles Mugridge	20	Do	Blacksmith	Britain	do	Ship Isabella, not &c
	John Anderson	21	Do	Sugar baker	do	do	
	Claude Rache	20	Do	Do	do	do	
	C. Vigue	18	Do	Do	do	do	
	Henry Shoretts	24	Do	Do	do	do	
	John Loconro	22	Do	Do	do	do	
	Wm Callender	38	Do	Merchant	U States	do	Ship Sally, not &c
	Townsend Moore	36	Do	Do	do	do	Sloop Liberty, not &c
	John Coleman	24	Do	Watchmaker	do	do	Sch'r Fama, not &c
	Patrick McClevanty	34	Do	Shoemaker	G Britain	do	
	David Mitchell	32	Do	Farmer	do	do	Ship Triton
	James J. Lawson	20	Do	Merchant	U States	do	Sch'r Sally, not &c
	Morgan Jones	52	Do	Do	do	do	
	B. Gonsales	29	Do	Do	Spain	do	
	J. Cardoza	35	Do	Trader	Do	do	Sch'r Eliza & Polly &c
	James Todd	40	Do	Farmer	G Britain	do	
	Wm Stewart	45	Do	Mariner	U States	do	Ship Bayard, &c
	Francis Falio	35	Do	Merchant	Spain	do	Sch'r Comet, &c
	Patrick Gilmore	28	Do	Do	G Britain	do	
	J. A. Barelli	21	Do	Do	Italy	do	
	Lewis Pilaluguer	35	Do	Do	do	do	
	N. Rutal & 2 children	40	Female	Trader	France	do	
	John Barelli	40	Male	Merchant	do	do	
	C. H. Riley	40	Do	Mariner	U States	do	Sch'r Bee, &c
	D. Canton	40	Do	Traveller	do	do	Sch'r Mechanic &c
	P. Munoz	30	Do	Shoemaker	do	U States	
	John Dell	35	Male	Do	do	do	
	Mrs. Do	18	Female	Do	do	do	
	Timothy White	19	Male	Planter	do	do	
	C. Pevaso	35	Do	Merchant	Spain	do	Sch'r Joseph not &c
	John Chaves	22	Do	Do	do	do	
	Francisco Fernandez	28	Do	Do	do	do	
	Francis Mearandez	25	Do	Do	do	do	

PASSENGERS ARRIVING AT THE PORT OF CHARLESTON 1820-1829

Quarter ending	Names	Age	Sex	Occupation	Country-belong	Country-inhabit	Vessel
Sept 30, 1822	G. Del Roches	37	Male	Farmer	France	France	Brig Mary, Master not &c
	Urban	30	Do	Trader	Matanzes	do	Sch'r Sally & Polly &c
	Madam Toumassen	31	Female		do	do	
	J. H. Magwood	27	Male	Merchant	do	do	Sloop Victory &c
	Jno Routledge	27	Do	Mariner	U States	U States	Brig Catharine &c
	Mrs. Hamilton & child	30	Female		Havana	G. Britain	Sch'r Felix &c
	John Rodrigues	30	Male	Trader	Porto Rico	do	
	Samuel Withington	30	Do	Merchant	G. Britain	U States	Sch'r Fama &c
	David Tirundale	31	Do	Do	U States	do	
	Charles Delorme	18	Do			do	
	J. J. Vollee	13	Do	Trader		do	Ship S. Carolina &c
	Isaac Wolf	38	Female			do	
	Mrs. Do & 5 children	28	Female			do	Sch. Louisa &c
	E. Morris	25	Male	Merchant	Spain	do	
	Antonio Ramerez	35	Do	Planter	Spain	do	Sch'r Eliza & Polly &c
	Thomas Legium	30	Do	Trader	France	U States	
	Louis Vegin	29	Do	Carpenter	do	do	Brig Neptune's Barge &c
	Anthony Bragas	30	Do	Merchant	Spain	Spain	
	Joaquim Savater	33	Do	Do	do	do	
	Tho's Swain	35	Do	Mariner	do	do	Sloop Jane &c.
	Archibald McFarlane	54	Do	Farmer	G. Britain	do	
	Mary Do & Child	29	Female		do	do	
	George Do	29	Male	Cooper	do	do	Sloop Endeavor &c
	John Watson	27	Do	Mariner	do	do	Sch'r Sarah Ann &c
	John Noga	40	Do	Do	Spain	do	Ship Ceres &c
	John Lomis	22	Do	Millwright	G. Britain	do	
	John Davis	41	Do	Shop keeper	do	do	Ship Perfect &c
	John C. Beale	46	Do	Do	U States	do	
	Henry Noyes	32	Do	Mariner	do	do	Sch'r Betsey & Peggy &c
	John Geddes	50	Do	Lawyer	do	do	
	G. H. Geddes	17	Do		do	do	
	H. Do	19	Female		do	do	
	M. Montgomery	40	Male	Planter	do	do	
	Henry Goldsmith	19	Do	Trader	do	do	Sch'r Mechanic &c
	John B. Rogers	28	Do	Merchant	do	do	
	Hugh Shannon	36	Do	Mechanic	G. Britain	do	
	John Arthur	32	Do	Do	do	do	Ship Fama &c
	Rob't Holbertin	30	Do	Hozier	do	do	
	Ch. McDonald	19	Do	Farmer	do	do	
	Gallagher	32	Do	Trader	do	do	
	Mrs. Do & 2 children	28	Female		do	do	
	John C. Ross	27	Male	Merchant	G. Britain	U States	
	Mrs. Do & child	20	Female		do	do	

Quarter ending	Names	Age	Sex	Occupation	Country-belong	Country-inhabit	Vessel
Sept 30, 1822	L. Y. Abrahams	45	Male	Trader	G. Britain	U States	Ship Charles & Henry &c
	H. J. Janke	22	Do		Amsterdam	U States	
	Jennet DeWolf	30	Female		do		
	James Ross	36	Male	Mariner	G. Britain	do	Sch'r Felix &c
	James Green	25	Do	Merchant	do	do	Sch'r Fate &c
	J. Flint	40	Do	Do	do	do	
	Thomas McCreedy	24	Do	Do	do	do	
Dec'r 31, 1822	M. Sarrazen & child	70	Female		Havana	U States	Sch'r Eudora, master &c
	P. Packet	40	Male	Tailor	do	do	
	Mrs. Do	40	Female		do	do	
	M. Fernandez	45	Male	Mariner	do	do	
	John M. Hopkins	55	Male	Merchant	U States	U States	Ship Bayard, master not &c
	Wm Timmond	50	Do	Do	do	do	
	Wm McKenzie	55	Do	Do	G. Britain	do	
	Robert Horrey & child	24	Do	Farmer	do	do	
	Daniel Nicholson	20	Do		do	do	
	John Nevill	45	Do	Merchant	do	do	
	Joseph Sampson	28	Do	Do	do	do	Sch'r Col. G. Armistead Do
	N. Cohen	15	Do	Do	do	do	Brig Leopold Do
	J. Lee	18	Do	Do	do	do	
	John Lowden	35	Do	Do	do	do	
	Ann Do	35	Female		do	do	Ship Corsair Do
	Alex'r Black	33	Male		do	do	
	Eliza Do	30	Female		do	do	
	Seth Watson	25	Male		do	do	
	J. S. Vaughn	18	Do		do	do	
	J. Howe	20	Do		do	do	
	Elisha Larnerd	25	Do	Mechanic	do	do	Sch'r Eliza & Polly Do
	J. D. Hamilton	24	Do	Merchant	do	do	
	James Brown	21	Do	Clerk	do	do	Ship Roger Stewart Do
	James Smith	22	Do	Lawyer	do	do	
	Wm Anderson	22	Do	Clerk	do	do	
	Wm Kennedy	19	Do	Clerk	do	do	
	Jno B. Thompson	23	Do	Do	do	do	
	Alex'r Campbell	30	Do	Farmer	do	do	
	Dougald McIntire	28	Male	Do	do	do	Ship Plantaganet Do
	Letty Do & 2 children	28	Female		do	do	
	Geo W. Frost	25	Male	Merchant	do	do	
	Hugh Wilson	45	Do	Farmer	do	do	
	Jennet Do & 3 Childr	45	Female		do	do	
	Y. Isnaga	18	Male	Planter	Trinidad	do	Sch'r Louisa Do
	M. Menici	30	Do	Painter	Havana	do	Sch'r Comet Do

105

PASSENGERS ARRIVING AT THE PORT OF CHARLESTON 1820-1829

Quarter ending	Names	Age	Sex	Occupation	Country-belong	Country-inhabit	Vessel
Dec'r 31, 1822	M. Theodore	30	Male		U States	U States	Sch'r Mary Do
	Catharine Pritchard	25	Female		do	do	
	John Smith	30	Male	Mariner	do	do	
	James Emelly	28	Do	Planter	France	do	
	Urban Grain	28	Do	Mariner	do	do	
	J. P. Lavencendue	28	Do	Merchant	do	do	
	P. Cassen	32	Do	Do	G. Britain	do	Sch'r Felix Do
	Cork	45	Do	Do	do	do	
	Kesler	30	Do		do	do	
	S. B. Benoist	54	Do	Trader	France	do	Ship Portea Do
	Mrs. Do & child	22	Female		do	do	
	M. Petit	28	Male	Merchant	do	do	
	Mrs. Do	23	Female		do	do	
	James Tenmouth	38	Male	Merchant	G. Britain	U States	Ship Newberryport Do
	Mary Do & 2 children	38	Female		do	do	
	John George	25	Male	Mariner	do	do	Sch'r Swift Do
	Marg't McAllister	25	Female		do	do	Ship James Bailey Do
	& 2 Do						
	Hans Do	25	Male	Farmer	do	do	
	Elizabeth Elliott	18	Female	Spinster	do	do	
	James Reid	27	Male	Farmer	do	do	
	Robert Kidd	22	Do	Do	do	do	
	John Caldwell	24	Do	Do	do	do	
	Thomas Palmer	22	Do	Do	do	do	
	Hugh Kelly	30	Do	Do	do	do	
	George Ferguson	19	Do	Do	do	do	
	Andrew McGill	36	Do	Do	do	do	
	Agnes Do & 2 children	25	Female		do	do	
	Francis Joseph	26	Male	Trader	U States	do	Brig If &c
	Philip Martinet	25	Do	Do	do	do	
	John Woodrop	69	Do	Merchant	G. Britain	do	Ship So Carolina &c
	C. Fitzsimmons	22	Do	Do	do	do	
	Wm. Gibson	38	Do	Do	do	do	
	James Moodie	32	Do	Do	do	do	
	Robert Chisolm	25	Do	Do	do	do	
	A. Hutchins	43	Do	Do	do	do	
	C. Todd	35	Male	Mariner	U States	U States	Sch'r Comet &c
	Wm. Cobbs	30	Do	Do	do	do	
	Eliza Theus	27	Female	Servant	G. Britain	do	Ship Mary Beach &c
	Isabella Perry	70	Do	Midwife	do	do	
	James Maggee	25	Male	Merchant	do	do	
	John Kerr	21	Do	Do	do	do	Brig Laura
	Robert Alexander	28	Do	Do	do	do	

PASSENGERS ARRIVING AT THE PORT OF CHARLESTON 1820-1829

Quarter ending	Names	Age	Sex	Occupation	Country-belong	Country-inhabit	Vessel
Dec'r 31, 1822	John Reside	22	Do	Do	G. Britain	U States	
	Robert Gunning	25	Do	Do	do	do	
	John McKelvan	25	Do	Farmer	do	do	
	Thomas Williamson	45	Do	Do	do	do	
	James McLarklin	18	Do	Do	do	do	
	John Russell	18	Do	Do	do	do	
	Wm. Burtin	30	Do	Do	do	do	
	Wm. McWhinney	28	Do	Do	do	do	
	Mrs. Do	20	Female		do	do	
	Marg't Duffey & 3 child	30	Do		do	do	Ship Cleveland &c
	Thomas Collard	32	Male	Farmer	do	do	
	Thomas Jones	63	Do	Do	do	do	
	Robert Burrell	66	Do	Do	do	do	
	Edw'd do	46	Do	Do	do	do	
	M. Morgan	45	Do	Do	do	do	
	J. Berlant	60	Do	Merchant	France	do	Brig Catharine &c
	Thomas Germaine	40	Male		G. Britain	U States	Ship Caledonian &c
	John Campbell	20	Do	Do	do	do	
	Thomas Scott	16	Do	Do	do	do	
	George Hunter	16	Do	Do	do	do	
	George Scott	20	Do	Do	do	do	
	Robert Small	25	Do	Do	do	do	
	Ann Do	20	Female		do	do	
	James Stewart	24	Male	Clerk	do	do	
	John McBride	20	Do	Do	do	do	
	McAdam Smith	20	Do	Do	do	do	
	Henry Bell	20	Do	Do	do	do	
	John Wright	18	Do	Do	do	do	
	John Robinson	19	Do	Farmer	do	do	
	James Miller	30	Do	Do	do	do	
	Wilson Dalrymple	25	Do	Do	do	do	
	Rob't Hutchinson	24	Do	Do	do	do	
	Daniel Finis	24	Do	Do	do	do	
	Alexander McGrady	19	Do	Do	do	do	
	John Diolin[?]	35	Do	Do	do	do	
	James Smith	32	Male	Do	do	do	
	Thomas Caulfield	30	Do	Do	do	do	
	Mary A. Do & child	23	Female		do	do	
	Geo. Johnson	20	Male	Farmer	do	do	
	Eliza Do & child	23	Female		do	do	
	David Watson	17	Male	Farmer	do	do	

PASSENGERS ARRIVING AT THE PORT OF CHARLESTON 1820-1829

Quarter ending	Names	Age	Sex	Occupation	Country-belong	Country-inhabit	Vessel
Dec'r 31, 1822	Thomas Castles	40	Male	Farmer	G. Britain	U States	
	Mary Do & child	28	Female		do	do	
	Wm. Willis	21	Male	Do	do	do	
	John Greenlee	23	Do	Do	do	do	
	Geo. Stewart	23	Do	Do	do	do	
	Thomas Neilson	45	Do		do	do	
	Jane Do & child	36	Do[sic]	Do	do	do	
	Adam Crawford	41	Male		do	do	
	Mary Do & child	35	Female		do	do	
	Sam'l Duncan	45	Male	Do	do	do	
	Samuel Pearson	50	Do	do	do	do	
	Mary Do & 6 child.	45	Female		do	do	
	Rob't Beggs	19	Male	Do	do	do	Brig Centurion, Master not &c
	Jno Smith	22	Do	Do	do	do	Sch'r Horatio Do
	And'w Orr	28	Do	Do	do	do	
	Hugh Logan	23	Do	Do	do	do	Ship Bingham Do
	David Henderson	25	Do	Do	do	do	
	James Robinson	22	Do	Do	do	do	Brig Rachael & Sally Do
	John Do	20	Do	Do	do	do	
March 31, 1823	James Gracia	30	Male	Mariner	St. Bartholomew	U States	Ship Corsair Do
	Edw'd Goware	35	Do	Merchant	Aquadilla	Spain	Schr Maid of the Mill Do
	John Rodriguez	32	Do	Mariner	do	do	Ship Perfect, Master not &c
	E. Bordier	35	Do	Merchant	Geneva	U States	
	Jean Baptist	22	Do	Painter & Glazier		do	
	Joseph Markilola	23	Do	Do	do	do	
	Gardner	35	Do	Mariner	U States	do	
	Urban	28	Do	Trader	France	do	
	Wm Holetear	22	Do		do	do	
	John Brown	30	Do	Do	G. Britain	do	Sch'r Abigail Do
	B. Young	30	Do	Military	Columbia	Columbia	Sch'r Col. Armstead Do
	James B. Clough	38	Male	Merchant	G. Britain	G. B.	
	Mrs. Do & 4 Children	28	Female		do	do	
	Mary Marshall	39	Do		do	do	
	Ann Bennett	19	Do		do	do	
	Thos H. Hindley	43	Male	Merchant	do	do	
	Alex'r Adam	21	Do	Do	do	do	
	Isaac Silliman & child	32	Do	Officer	U. States	U. States	
	Henry Goldsmith	18	Do	Trader	do	do	
	Henry Brown	35	Do	Merchant	Germany	do	
	Isabella Do	38	Female			do	
	Joseph Lopez	35	Male	Do	Portugal	do	
	Joseph Matthews	40	Do	Do	Spain	do	

PASSENGERS ARRIVING AT THE PORT OF CHARLESTON 1820-1829

Quarter ending	Names	Age	Sex	Occupation	Country-belong	Country-inhabit	Vessel
March 31, 1823	Nathan'l Lopyez[?]	32	Do	Planter	Spain	U. States	
	Thos Marld	45	Do	Merchant		do	
	J. Gonsales	35	Do	Lawyer	do	do	
	H. Forester	20	Female	Milliner	do	do	
	Ann Wilson	25	Do	Do	U States	do	Sch'r Eliza & Polly Do
	Diego Marso	27	Male	Military	Chili	Chili	
	John Herspool	30	Do	Merchant	U States	U States	Sch'r Bellona Do
	A. H. F. L. Changuian	22	Do	Do	Netherlands	do	Sch'r Sarah Ann Do
	John Crosbie	55	Do	Farmer	G. Britain	do	Ship Mary &c
	John Pierce	28	Do	Do	do	do	Ship Hannah Do
	Sam'l McCullough	55	Do	Do	do	do	
	John G. Beale	26	Do	Mariner	do	do	
	John Thompson	22	Do	Farmer	do	do	
	Wm. Rowland	21	Do	Surveyor	do	do	Bark Jane Do
	James Maloney	35	Do	Farmer	do	do	
	John Williams	19	Do	Clerk	do	do	
	Charles Maghim	43	Do	Merchant	France	do	Sch'r Mechanic Do
	M. Lorent	30	Do	Do	do	do	
	F. Caura	30	Do	Do	Spain		
	John Calabra	30	Male	Merchant	Spain	U States	Sch'r Nancy & Felix Do
	John Caladara	20	Do	Do	do	do	Brig Rosina Do
	Geo Lowe	33	Do	Columbian officer	Columbia	Columbia	
	John Finlay	21	Male	Merchant	G. Britain	U States	Brig Charles Do
	Jane McMoran & child	45	Female		do	do	
	Wm. B. Hall	32	Male	Do	do	do	
	J. S. Russell	25	Do	Do	do	do	Sch'r Midas Do
	Sally Vincent & child	40	Female		Guadaloup	do	Brig Ann Do
	L. Sproll	20	Male	Farmer	G. Britain	do	
	Moses Do & 3 children	21	Do	Do	do	do	Brig Sall & Hipe Do
	R. McColum	40	Do	Do	do	do	
	Benj. Chapman	43	Do	Do	do	do	Sch'r Felix Do
	A. Henry	24	Do	Do	do	do	
	David Canter	40	Do	Merchant	do	do	
	J. Ross	33	Do	Do	do	do	
	William Humble	22	Male	Merchant	G. Britain	U States	Brig Francis Do
	Martin Long	45	Do	Do	do	do	Sch'r Phoenix Do
	John McGowan	45	Do	Do	do	do	Brig Pelgrim Do
	Doctor Monet	44	Do	Physician	U States	U States	Sch'r Marion
	Mrs. Do	16	Female		do	do	
	R. Fontenroy	24	Male	Planter	do	do	
	J. Denaco	24	Do	Merchant	Italy	do	
	J. Sperow	20	Do	Trader	Spain	do	
	Francis Joseph	30	Do	Do	Portugal	do	Sch'r Eliza & Polly Do

PASSENGERS ARRIVING AT THE PORT OF CHARLESTON 1820-1829

Quarter ending	Names	Age	Sex	Occupation	Country-belong	Country- inhabit	Vessel
March 31, 1823	Charles Lowry	50	Do	Tailor	U States	U States	Sch'r Swift Do
	Henry Austin	41	Do	Merchant	do	do	Ship St. Peter Do
	A. Putman	41	Do	Do	do	do	
	John Ward	32	Do	Do	G. Britain	do	Ship Mary Catharine Do
June 30, 1823	John Ward	32	Male	Merchant	England	U States	Ship Mary, Master Not &c
	John Donaughan	45	Do	Do	do	do	Brig Clarissa Ann &c
	John Routiers	25	Do		Holland	do	Ship Thalia &c
	D. McGinn	36	Do	Physician	do	do	Brig Cha's Coffin &c
	Mrs. Do & 2 children	24	Female				
	Christopher Castino	32	Male	Merchant	Spain	Spain	
	Antonio Aimar	28	Do	Trader	Portugal	U States	
	Peter Dordelay	23	Do	Mariner	do	do	
	D. Smith	30	Do		Germany	do	Schooner Favourite &c
	Mr. Smith & child	20	Female		Great Britain	U States	
	M. Samporac	30	Male	Merchant	Great Britain	do	Brig Caroline Ann
	Mariana Pala	22	Female		France	Spain	Schooner Leopard &c
	J. Harrizle	22	Male		Spain		
	Ann Anderson	32	Female		do	G. Britain	Brig Minerva &c
	John Ross	20	Male	Labourer	G. Britain	U States	Brig Columbia &c
	Antonio Cabal	48	Do		France	do	Brig Alexander le Grande &c
	F. Samiento	32	Do		do	do	
	J. Couffon	30	Do	Merchant	do	do	
	R. Danviers	24	Do	Do	do	do	
	Henderson Ferguson	60	Do	Planter	U States	do	Schooner Swift &c
	Mrs. Do	50	Female		do	do	
	Theodore Gaillard	50	Male	Factor	U States	do	
	L. Watkins	28	Do	Do	do	do	
	Sextus Gaillard	26	Do	Do	do	do	
	John Warner	50	Do	Commerc'l agent	do	do	Schooner Jane &c
	Charles Starr	23	Do	U. S. Navy	do	do	
	D. Bett	28	Do	Do	do	do	
	Francis Marshall	52	Do	Planter	do	do	Schooner Harriet &c
	Thomas D. Loughany	35	Do	Merchant	do	do	Schooner Wicker &c
	Isaac Suthram	44	Do	Manufacturer	do	do	Sloop Providence &c
	John Murphy	22	Do	Merchant	do	do	
	L. R. Strong	27	Do	Do	do	do	
	Mr. Jove & child	39	Female		France	do	Brig Catherine &c
	M. Galuchat	35	Male		do	do	
	A. Schult	27	Do	Planter	do	do	
	La Maitre	25	Do	Merchant	do	do	
	Urban	30	Do	Do	do	do	
	Gaillard	35	Do	Do	do	do	

PASSENGERS ARRIVING AT THE PORT OF CHARLESTON 1820-1829

Quarter ending	Names	Age	Sex	Occupation	Country-belong	Country-inhabit	Vessel
June 30, 1823	Peter Macatelle	45	Do	Mariner	U States	U States	Schooner Harriet &c
	Walter Wilkie	33	Do	Trader	do	do	
	John Shuburk	27	Do	Mariner	do	do	
	Henry Little	48	Do	Farmer	do	do	
	Jean Little & 8 children	30	Female		do	do	Brig Phoebe &c
	Joseph Espina	50	Male	Merchant	G. Britain	U States	Brig Rachael & Sally &c
	Stephen Anderson	25	Do	Do	Spain	do	
	Anthony Purdy	35	Do	Do	U States	do	
	Stephen Burrows	32	Do	Do	do	do	
	John Morriston	27	Do	Do	do	do	
	M. Aiken	50	Do	Do	do	do	Sloop Norfolk &c
	T. Tomaison	38	Do	Do	do	do	Brig Charles Coffin &c
	Charles OSullivan	32	Male	Painter	G. Britain	U States	
	Mrs. Do & 3 children	23	Female		do	do	
	Anthony Aymar	30	Male	Trader	Italy	do	
	Madame Delorme	55	Do [sic]		France	do	
	Peter Dordeily	24	Do		do	do	
	J. B. Zegniags	23	Do		do	do	
	John Stoddard	26	Do		do	do	
	C. Martinelli	35	Do	Mariner	do	do	
	William Kerr	40	Do	Merchant	G. Britain	do	
	Jesse Livingston & child	32	Do		do	do	Ship Roger Stewart &c
	Mrs. Lowe & 2 children	35	Female		do	do	Ship Isabella &c
	M. Somerville	32	Male	Butcher	do	do	
	M. Halman	25	Do	Sugar baker	Germany	do	
	M. Ficksman	26	Do	Do	do	do	
	James Magill	22	Do	Farmer	G. Britain	do	Ship Phaeson &c
	E. Do	21	Female	Do	do	do	
	Francis LaRouselier	33	Male	Merchant	France	do	Brig Fanny
	Joseph Barriele	32	Do	Do	do	do	
	James Gordall	29	Do	Do	do	do	
	M. Mendoza	35	Do	Do	Spain	do	
	Mrs. Do & 3 children	28	Female		do	do	
	Mrs. Rosetta	28	Do		do	do	
	S. E. Lightburn	37	Male	Do	Britain	do	Schooner Dolphin &c
	James Greese	30	Do	Do	do	do	
	H. Junge	22	Do	Do	U States	do	Schooner Return &c
	M. Brown	48	Do	Do	do	do	Brig Catharine &c
	M. Cloth	35	Do	Do	Germany	do	
	J. Tholosan	30	Do	Do	France	do	

PASSENGERS ARRIVING AT THE PORT OF CHARLESTON 1820-1829

Quarter ending	Names	Age	Sex	Occupation	Country-belong	Country-inhabit	Vessel
June 30, 1823	A. Forsyth	55	Do	Mariner	France	U States	Sch'r Eliza &c
	R. F. Martin	28	Do	Trader	do	do	Sch'r Aurora &c
	Wm S. Barton	34	Do	Do	do	do	
Sept 30, 1823	Dominic Divison	28	Male	Merchant	Spain	U States	Sch'r Mary, master not &c
	Madam Mulando	28	Female		do	do	
	M. Dordelly	26	Male	Tobacconest	U States	do	
	Alex'r Banneter	24	Do	Merchant	do	do	
	Hugh Bowley	22	Do	Do	do	do	Ship Hunter, Do
	A. Hernandez	25	Do	Do	Spain	U States	Sch'r Adeline, Do
	Jno Fenwehe	28	Do	Do	do	do	
	Isaac Martin	30	Do	Cooper	U States	do	
	Joseph Jewett	24	Do	Do	do	do	
	John Beursille[?]	28	Do	Mariner	do	do	Sch'r Swift, Do
	John M. Hardy	32	Do	Do	do	do	Sch'r Marion, Do
	David Canter	45	Do	Do	do	do	
	John Oates	60	Do	Do	do	do	
	Don A. Zeno Saldaner	34	Do	Do	Spain	do	
	Francis C. Black	30	Do	Merchant	U States	do	Sch'r Fish Hawk, Do
	L. Fresbie	27	Do	Do	do	do	
	D. Thompson	50	Do	Lawyer	G. Britain	do	
	Wm. J. Rowe	30	Do	Merchant	do	do	
	John Douglass	25	Do	Clerk	do	do	
	Wm. Ascoot	30	Do	Mariner	U States	do	Sch'r Eliza & Polly, &c
	Thomas Budd	30	Do		do	do	
	Thomas Hatch	34	Male	Trader	do	do	
	Jno P. Barrie	28	Do	Do	do	do	
	Antonio Domingo	19	Do	Do	do	do	Sch'r Dolphin, &c
	Wm Oats	25	Do		do	do	
	Joseph Penera	30	Do		do	do	
	Sam'l Philbrick	29	Do		do	do	Sch'r Elvia & Maria, &c
	Silvester Murphy	26	Do		do	do	
	Wm. R. Peyton	26	Do		do	do	
	John Stone	35	Do	Physician	do	do	Sch'r MacDonough, &c
	Charles Prevost	40	Do	Carpenter	do	do	
	John Hambelton	26	Do	Farmer	do	do	
	B. McGinn	24	Do	Mariner	do	do	Sloop Norfolk, &c
	John Clark	50	Do	Do	do	do	
	Geo. Armstead	30	Do	Do	do	do	
	Thos Jackson	26	Do	Merchant	do	do	Sch'r Marion, &c
	Chil. Magnier	25	Do	Do	do	do	
	Francis Deval	21	Do	Do	do	do	
	Jno Fabrack	50	Do	Mariner	do	do	

112

PASSENGERS ARRIVING AT THE PORT OF CHARLESTON 1820-1829

Quarter ending	Names	Age	Sex	Occupation	Country-belong	Country-inhabit	Vessel
Sept 30, 1823	Joseph Sylvia	28	Male	Mariner	U States	U States	Sch'r Eudora, &c
	Joseph Johnson	38	Do	Do	do	do	Sch'r Oleander, &c
	Chas Lowry	40	Do		do	do	
	Wm. P. Young	20	Do		do	do	
	H. A. do	24	Do		do	do	
	Arthur Oconnor	20	Do		do	do	
	Mrs. Do	18	Female		do	do	
	Jno La Fontaine	28	Male		do	do	
	Joseph A. Allen	44	Do		do	do	
	Benj. Briton	31	Do		do	do	
	Thos Sinclair	42	Do		do	do	Ship Fama, &c
	A. Lyon	28	Do		do	do	Brig Commerce, &c
	Peter Lawrence	60	Do		do	do	Sch'r Eliza & Polly, &c
	Geo Sutton	37	Do	Mariner	do	do	
	Emanuel Orban	28	Do	Do	do	do	Ship Perfect, &c
	E. Stephens	35	Do	Minister	do	do	Ship Ceres, &c
	Jon Lutes	44	Do	Physician	do	do	
	A. Weshuley	18	Do	Merchant	do	do	
	Ab. Buckin	58	Do	Labourer	do	do	
	Hodge Pinkney	50	Do	Planter	do	do	
June 30, 1824	D. Mayat	35	Male	Physician	Havana	U States	Brig Catherine
	C. Magnan	28	Do	Planter	do	do	
	Charles Winthrop	25	Do	Merchant	do	do	Sch'r Esther &c
	Madam Luchaise	50	Female		France	do	
	James McElorm	32	Male	Merchant	do	do	
	Antonio Bauderot	35	Do	Tailor	do	do	Sch'r Eudora &c
	Edward Baker	30	Do	Mechanic	U States	do	Sch'r Franklin &c
	Lemartie	22	Do	Merchant	France	do	Brig Only Daughter &c
	Thomas Cooper	29	Do	Do	G. Britain	do	Brig Gen'l Brown &c
	Robert King	82	Do		do	do	Brig Panther &c
	A. Lambert	27	Do	Do	U States	do	
	Phillip Young	40	Do	Do	do	do	
	Henry Do	18	Do	Do	do	do	Sch'r Rabit &c
	Paul Thomason	41	Do	Mariner	do	do	
	J. B. F. Fubachet	45	Do		do	do	
	James Ward	21	Do		do	do	
	A. Locur	52	Do		do	do	Ship Favorite &c
	Samuel Karrs	30	Do	Do	do	do	Sch'r Betsy &c
	Mrs. Levi & child	25	Female		do	do	
	Theodore Flotard	25	Male	Merchant	do	do	
	Louis Burtell	24	Do	Do	do	do	
	John Murrechen	24	Do	Physician	do	do	

PASSENGERS ARRIVING AT THE PORT OF CHARLESTON 1820-1829

Quarter ending	Names	Age	Sex	Occupation	Country-belong	Country- inhabit	Vessel
June 30, 1824	John Ross	45	Do	Merchant	U States	U States	Sch'r Lovely Kesiah &c
	John Lopez	40	Do	Do	do	do	
	B. Durban	35	Do	Do	do	do	
	Valentine Sala	38	Do	Do	do	do	
	Anthony Brayas	45	Male	Merchant	Spain	Spain	
	George French	40	Do	Do	Switzerland	U States	Ship Conova &c
	P. Hailfort	25	Do	Farmer	do	do	
	John Schifer	23	Do	Do	do	do	
	Frederick Miller	19	Do	Do	do	do	
	A. Eymar	30	Do	Merchant	France	do	Brig Charles &c
	M. Hatten	26	Do	Do	do	do	
	R. Perrot	19	Do	Mechanic	do	do	
	J. Aspero	39	Do	Merchant	U States	do	
	Alex'r McBeath	45	Do	Planter	G. Britain	do	Sch'r Esther &c
	Mrs. Do & 2 children	22	Female	Merchant	do	do	
	James Green	26	Male	Do	do	do	Sch'r Chase &c
	John Scott	26	Do	Do	do	do	
	M. Orr	28	Do	Do	do	do	
	George DeRoche	45	Do	Do	do	do	Brig Orient &c
	Joseph Fernandez	45	Do	Stone cutter	Spain	do	Ship Corsair
	Jeremiah Connelly	25	Do	Farmer	G. Britain	do	
	Thomas Do	30	Do	Do	do	do	
	And'w Crothy	17	Do	Do	do	do	
	Joseph Cullina	41	Do	Do	do	do	
	C. Milligut	35	Do	Merchant	France	do	Sloop Mercantor &c
	Elizabeth Richards	32	Do[sic]	Do	G. Britain	do	Brig James Munroe &c
	J. Urban	35	Do	Do	U States	do	
	P. J. F. Soltomayer	40	Do	Minister	St. Domingo	do	
	Jose Bouchet	32	Do	Cutter	U States	do	
	Rich'd Zimmerman	35	Do	Merchant	do	do	
	L. Michalette	40	Do	Do	do	do	
	M. Houserman	42	Do	Mariner	Holland	do	Sch'r Chase &c
	S. C. Tennant	24	Do	Merchant	G. Britain	do	
	M. ODonald	32	Do	Teacher	do	do	
	M. M. Kelly	28	Do	Do	Holland	do	
	J. M. Tuesky	31	Do	Merchant	Holland	do	
	A. R. Fernandez	40	Do	Clerk	Spain	do	Ship Issabella &c
	J. S. Cohen	24	Do	Merchant	G. Britain	do	
	A. Do	18	Female		do	do	
	Martin Pendegrass	20	Male	Clerk	U States	do	Brig Panther &c
	Charles Conyers	25	Do	Merchant	do	do	Brig Carolina Ann &c
	Alex'r Harang	50	Do	Planter	do	do	
	Edward G. Lightburn	19	Do	Do	do	do	

114

PASSENGERS ARRIVING AT THE PORT OF CHARLESTON 1820-1829

Quarter ending	Names	Age	Sex	Occupation	Country-belong	Country-inhabit	Vessel
June 30, 1824	James Magniar	33	Male	Merchant	U States	U States	Sch'r Louisiana &c
	J. C. Jenkins	28	Do	Do	G. Britain	do	Ship Marion &c
	Michael OReilly	22	do		do	do	Brig Atlas &c
	Joseph Wompomus	40	Male	M. Officer	Spain	U States	Ship Tarantula &c
	Mrs. Do & child	35	Female		do	do	
	Augustine Ordonoro	39	Male		Spain	U States	
	F. Bravo	35	Do		do	do	
	G. Gaizo	65	Do	Merchant	do	Spain	
	R. Olivea	40	Do	Priest	do	do	
	Pedro Orago	39	Do	Merchant	do	do	
	J. Miatas	35	Do	Merchant	do	do	
	R. Salegas	40	Do	Surgeon	do	do	
	G. Lopez	33	Do	Soldier	do	do	
	C. Do & child	27	Female		do	do	
	C. Oliva	40	Male	Do	do	do	
	P. Orago	39	Do	Do	do	do	
	Antonio Pena	37	Do	Do	do	do	
	Manuel Gill	36	Do	Do	do	do	
	J. Vayoas	39	Do	Do	do	do	
	Diego Tolino	40	Do	Do	do	do	
	M. Martinez	37	Do	Do	do	do	
	A. Herrera	40	Do	Do	do	do	
	F. Cartu	47	Do	Do	do	do	
	Herman Follin	35	Do	Merchant	U States	do	
	Wm. G. Lowry	22	Do	Physician	do	do	Sch'r Mary &c
	U. Romylac	22	Do	Merchant	do	do	
Sept'r 30 1824	Juane Xene	19	Male		Spain	Spain	Brig Catherine, master not &c
	Dronicio Mantella	20	Do		do	do	
	Joaquim Penalvers	22	Do		do	do	
	Miguel de Corderos	10	Do		Havanna	do	
	J. P. Bane	29	Do	Merchant	France	U States	
	M. Obegnaud	48	Female		do	do	
	James Pepnot	31	Male	Mechanic	U States	do	Brig Charles &c
	Wm G. Barney	31	Do	Mariner	France	do	
	M. Barre	33	Do	Merchant	France	do	
	M. Durban	26	Male	Merchant	Spain	U States	Brig Trader &c
	Nicholas Sergas	15	Do	Do	do	do	
	Anthony Felzer	45	Do	Teacher	Scotland	do	
	Henry Cockroft	52	Do	Mechanic	U. States	do	Ship Charles & Henry &c
	M. Do	14	Do		do	do	
	James Downes	15	Do	Do	G. Britain	do	
	Robert Warren	16	Do	Do	do	do	

PASSENGERS ARRIVING AT THE PORT OF CHARLESTON 1820-1829

Quarter ending	Names	Age	Sex	Occupation	Country-belong	Country-inhabit	Vessel
Sept'r 30 1824	Miguel de Fernandez	30	Do	Merchant	Cuba	Cuba	Sch'r Speedwell &c
	B. S. Grimke	27	Do	Naval officer	do	do	Sch'r Marion &c
	Baptist Goeres	57	Do	Merchant	U States	U States	
	D. Ciolan	38	Do	Do	Spain	Spain	Sch'r Leopardo &c
	M. Ogelby	38	Do		U States	U States	Brig Catharine &c
	John W. Bradley	22	Do	Do	G. Britain	U States	Ship Criere &c
	G. A. Love	40	Do	Soldier	do	do	
	John Albert	35	Do		do	do	Sch'r Mary &c
	Mrs. Do & daughter	35	Female		do	do	
	Is. Lorrella	40	Male	Mariner	Spain	Spain	
	Nicholas Rey	18	Do	Lawyer	do	do	Sch'r Sally & Polly &c
	P. Sanchez	27	Do	Merchant	do	do	
	J. Alvaraz	23	Do	Do	do	do	
	Antoine Aymar	30	Do	Do	do	do	
	James Green	27	Do	Do	do	do	
	James Himely	29	Do	Planter	U States	U States	Sch'r Mary &c
	John Lopez	35	Do	Trader	do	do	Sch'r Eliza &c
	M. Burgar	22	Do	Merchant	do	do	Sch'r Eliza & Jane &c
	Thomas Davis	37	Do	Mariner	do	do	
	M. Johns	40	Do	Do	do	do	Ship Triton &c
	Margaret Mitchell	30	Female		do	do	
	Jose Olibe	29	Male	Merchant	Spain	Spain	
	M. Laman	27	Do	Do	do	do	Sch'r Eliza &c
	Juan Alvez	22	Do	Do	do	do	
	John Saldwar	17	Do	Do	do	do	
	J. de Pamdeda	39	Male	Merchant	Spain	Spain	
	Francis Rye	35	Do	Do	U States	do	
	John Parcle	21	Do	Do	do	do	
	George Bell	36	Do	Do	do	do	Sch'r James Madison &c
	Nicholas Grand	30	Do	Do	do	do	
	James Robertson	30	Do	Do	do	do	
	Charles E. Miller	20	Do	Do	do	do	Brig Trader &c
	Geo. Relph	38	Do	Do	do	do	
	Thomas Walton	38	Do	Do	G. Britain	do	Ship Perfect &c
	Madam Bollineau	46	Female		France	do	
	Julianna Chereugh	16	Do		do	do	
	Francois Do	18	Male		do	do	
Dec'r 31, 1824	Robert Burger	30	Male	Mariner	U States	U States	Sch'r Eagle, master not &c
	J. P. Bean	30	Do	Mechanic	do	do	
	Jacob Hyams	24	Do	Trader	Poland	do	Ship Ceres, Do
	Catherine Appleton	17	Female		G. Britain	do	Brig Antelope Do

PASSENGERS ARRIVING AT THE PORT OF CHARLESTON 1820-1829

Quarter ending	Names	Age	Sex	Occupation	Country-belong	Country-inhabit	Vessel
Dec'r 31, 1824	John Gemmell	22	Male	Farmer	G. Britain	U States	Ship Corsair Do
	Jane Do	21	Female			do	
	Martin Meritt	36	Male	Merchant	do	do	
	W. C. Mollineau	30	Do	Do	do	do	
	Edward Menlove	25	Do	Do	do	do	
	Stephen Watson	26	Do	Do	do	do	
	Thomas Bridgewood	30	Do	Do	do	do	
	James Brown	20	Do	Do	do	do	
	Fred'k Miller	24	Do	Teacher	do	do	
	Charles Brenan	33	Do	Merchant	do	do	
	J. Oneale	27	Do	Comedian	do	do	
	Thomas Faulkner	48	Do	Do	do	do	
	James Howard	28	Do	Carpenter	do	do	
	Charles Hood	25	Do	Do	do	do	
	John Syle	28	Do	Clerk	do	do	
	Edward Henry	21	Do	Farmer	do	do	
	Patrick Dixon	30	Do	Do	do	do	
	James Do	30	Do	Tailor	do	do	
	And'w Do	26	Do	Do	do	do	
	John Do	26	Do	Farmer	do	do	
	Daniel Conelly	20	Do	Do	do	do	
	Alex'r Campbell	24	Do	Artist	G. Britain	U States	
	John Flaherty	27	Male	Clerk	do	do	
	John Kelly	26	Do		do	do	
	Mary Do & child	26	Female				
	Eliza Hughes	34	Do				
	& 3 children ages 10, 7, 6						
	Mary Ann Tardy	22,		Mariner	Spain		Brig Catherine Do
	John Missroon	19	Male	Mariner	U States	do	
	F. de Sylva	35	Do	Trader	do	do	
	P. Roerigues	26	Male		U States	U States	Sch'r Eliza Do
	J. Martinelle	42	Do		do	do	
	Susan Nichols	31	Female		do	do	
	C. Lawrence	35	Male	Mariner	do	do	
	D. Carreased	38	Do	Do	Spain	do	Sch'r Eudora Do
	D. Gonzales	40	Do	Do	Spain	do	
	J. C. Stewart	24	Do	Merchant	do	do	
	John Clark	56	Do	Surveyor	G. Britain	do	
	Robert Featherington	24	Do	Merchant	do	do	Brig Traveller &c
	Wm. B. Yates	18	Do		do	do	
	John Longmer	21	Do		do	do	

117

PASSENGERS ARRIVING AT THE PORT OF CHARLESTON 1820-1829

Quarter ending	Names	Age	Sex	Occupation	Country-belong	Country-inhabit	Vessel
Dec'r 31, 1824	John Lowden	40	Do	Do	G. Britain	U States	Ship Ganges &c
	Mrs. Do	38	Female		do	do	
	George Do	18	Male		do	do	
	Mrs. Martin	60	Female		U States	do	
	Miss Campbell	19	Do		do	do	
	Mr. Isaac	40	Male	Do	G. Britain	do	Ship Minerva &c
	M. Higginbottom	50	Do	Do	do	do	
	M. Smith	23	Do	Do	do	do	
	Mrs. Carvin	45	Do [sic]		France	do	
	A. LaBarbeire	24	Do	Do	do	do	
	J. Le Martre	16	Do	Do	do	do	
	J. Antoine Moore	25	Do	Do	do	do	
	Peter Poria	55	Do	Do	do	do	Scho'r Thos Washington, &c
	H. Newman	40	Do	Brit. Consul	G. Britain	do	
	Mrs. Do &	35	Female		do	do	
	3 children ages 11, 9, 3½ fem.						
	Mr. McClure	33	Male	Mariner	U States	do	
	Mrs. Do & Infant	27	Female		do	do	
	Mrs. Harrison	31	Do		G. Britain	do	Ship Robt. Edwards &c
	Miss Giles	29	Do		do	do	
	M. Fistre	40	Male		do	do	
	Mrs. Reily & 2 child.	33	Female		do	do	
	Mrs. Clark & child	35	Do		U States	do	
	J. J. Middleton	22	Male		G. Britain	do	
	Mr. Cullen	34	Do		do	U States	
	John Cook	24	Do		do	do	
	John Brown	16	Do		do	do	
	Don Rogue Quintan	27	Do	Planter	Spain	Spain	Ship Eagle &c
	Jesse Edwards	28	Do	Do	do	do	
	Jon G. Areayo	21	Do	Military officer	do	do	
	Manuel Arcaya	21	Do	Do	do	do	
	Dr. Rauot	40	Do	Physician	France	U States	Brig Doug Trouen &c
	Wm Longsdon	45	Do	Merchant	G. Britain	G. Britain	
	G. H. Bacot	47	Do	Lawyer	U. States	U. States	
	T. H. Hindsley	45	Do	Merchant	G. Britain	do	Ship Majestic &c
	Wm. Hume	25	Do	Physician	U. States	do	
	Alex. Mazyck	24	Do	Lawyer	do	do	
	Thomas Boyd	28	Do	Farmer	G. Britain	do	
	Mary Boyd &	26	Female		G. Britain	U. States	Brig Caledonia &c
	2 children ages 3 & 1 fem.						
	Alexander Henry	21	Male	Farmer	do	do	
	M. Do &	20	Female		do	do	
	Infant 3 months						

118

PASSENGERS ARRIVING AT THE PORT OF CHARLESTON 1820-1829

Quarter ending	Names	Age	Sex	Occupation	Country-belong	Country-inhabit	Vessel
Dec'r 31, 1824	Ellen Harper	20	Do		G. Britain	U. States	
	William Thompson	24	Male		do	do	
	George Craig	26	Do		do	do	
	Ann Do	24	Female		do	do	
	& 2 child. 3yrs & 2 months						
	John Marks	26	Male		do	do	
	Margaret Do	20	Female		do	do	
	John Morran	24	Male		do	do	
	Marg't Moran	22	Female		do	do	
	Esther Gribben	22	Do		do	do	
	Catherine Murray	34	Do		do	do	
	James Do	16	Male		do	do	
	Pat Rob't & Elen Do	12 2 9f			do	do	
	William McCand	28	Male		do	do	
	William Taylor	24	Do		do	do	
	John Elder	32	Do		do	do	
	Wm McRee	30	Do		do	do	
	Ellen Do	24	Female		do	do	
	& 2 children 1, 2 months						
	James Barnett	27	Male	Merchant	do	do	Ship Georgiana &c
	Jane Eccles	18	Female		do	do	
	John Rowand	35	Male	Farmer	do	do	
	Sarah Do	32	Female		do	do	
	& 3 children Eliza Jane 9, Jane 9, James 7 & Margaret 4						
	Edward Lathers	14	Male		G. Britain	U. States	
	Richard Do	9	Do		do	do	
	B. Mitchell	19	Female		do	do	
	Timothy Dodd	38	Male		do	do	
	& 6 child. John 14, Sam'l 4, Eliza 12, Maria 9, Jane 6, Isabella 2						
	Wm. G. Scott	30	Male	Farmer	do	do	Ship Margaret Bogle &c
	Robert McIntosh	45	Do	Do	do	do	
	James Porter	23	Do	Do	do	do	
	John Miller	40	Do	Do	do	do	
	Mary Brown	34	Female		do	do	
	Elizabeth Hazard	16	Do		do	do	
	Elizabeth Patterson	35	Do		do	do	
	Mary Tshudy	34	Do		do	do	
	Mrs. Finn	45	Do		do	do	
	John Rodgers	52	Male		do	do	Ship Mary Catherine &c
	James Gafney	18	Do		do	do	
	Mr. Hutton	28	Do	Merchant	do	do	
	Mrs. Do	56	Female		do	do	
	J. Baptist Cousa	60	Male	Do	Spain	do	

PASSENGERS ARRIVING AT THE PORT OF CHARLESTON 1820-1829

Quarter ending	Names	Age	Sex	Occupation	Country-belong	Country-inhabit	Vessel
Dec'r 31, 1824	Thomas Ferash	40	Do	Baker	Spain	U. States	Sch'r Marion &c
	Samuel Reed	30	Do	Merchant	G. Britain	do	
	& child 11 yrs						
	John J. Cassedy	23	Do	Do	do	do	
	Mrs. Cassidy	19	Female		G. Britain	U. States	
	William Logan	28	Male	Merchant	do	do	
	Preston Charters	21	Do	Farmer	do	do	
	John Walker	34	Do	Do	do	do	
	James Aiken	36	Do	Do	do	do	
	Joseph Biggart	67	Do	Do	do	do	
	Alex'r Do	38	Do	Do	do	do	
	6 sons James 21, Joseph 19, John 17, Archy 14, Alexr 9, Wm 3						
	B. Haggy	20	Female		do	do	
	Daniel Stewart	45	Male	Do	do	do	
	Robert Do	20	Do	Do	do	do	
	James Do	18	Do	Do	do	do	
	Martha Do	15	Female		do	do	
	Jane Do	13	Do		do	do	
	Mary Do	10	Do		do	do	
	Eliza Do	6	Do		do	do	
	Mary Collins & Infant	25	Female		do	do	
	Mary Adams &	34	Do		do	do	
	children Ann 13, John 6 & Esther 3						
	William Wylee	35	Male	Farmer	do	do	
	David Hupper	30	Male	Farmer	G. Britain	U. States	
	Samuel Rath	20	Do	Do	do	do	
	Bernard Henry	30	Do	Do	do	do	
	Samuel Reenan	30	Do	Do	do	do	
	Elizabeth Do &	30	Female		do	do	
	4 children Mary 9, Michael 8, Jno 7 & Geo. 4						
	N. Boulton	20	Male		do	do	
	Thomas Orr	18	Do	Do	do	do	
	Betty McCoy	18	Female		do	do	
	James McLane	22	Male	Do	do	do	
	Elizabeth Do	19	Female		do	do	
	James Johnson	21	Male		do	do	
	William Walker	21	Do		do	do	
	Wm Smith	23	Do		do	do	
	Robert Boyd	21	Do		do	do	
	Samuel May	40	Do		do	do	
	Dennis ODonald	28	Do		do	do	
	Thomas McCarven	28	Do		do	do	
	John McCormick	16	Do		do	do	

PASSENGERS ARRIVING AT THE PORT OF CHARLESTON 1820-1829

Quarter ending	Names	Age	Sex	Occupation	Country-belong	Country-inhabit	Vessel
Dec'r 31, 1824	Joseph Davis	18	Do		do	do	
	Jane Harkell	53	Female		do	do	
March 31, 1825	Henry M. Watson	35	Male	Lawyer	U States	U States	Brig Cha's Coffin, Master not &c
	Wm Symes	30	Do	Mechanic	do	do	
	Anthony Aymar	39	Do	Trader	do	do	
	Matheu Dustass	55	Do	Do	do	do	
	R. G. Wallace	30	Do	Do	do	do	Scho'r Eagle master not &c
	William Foster	28	Do	Inspector	do	do	
	Alex'r Harang	32	Do	Pilot	do	do	
	Joab Blackman	30	Do	Carpenter	do	do	Scho'r Susan not &c
	Mrs. Do & 2 children	25	Female		do	do	
	O. H. Middleton	25	Male	Factor	U States	U States	Ship Sarah & Caroline &c
	C. J. Manigault	29	Do		do	do	
	J. C. Vanderhorst	43	Do		do	do	
	M. Gray	26	Do		do	do	
	G. Dates	35	Do		do	do	
	Ann Peak	25	Female		do	do	
	Wm Bunney	20	Male	Clerk	do	do	Ship Thornton &c
	P. O. Reilley	30	Do	Do	G. Britain	do	
	Major Williside	30	Do	Farmer	do	do	Brig Ariel not &c
	Mary Do	35	Female		do	do	
	A. Richardson	30	Male	Slater	France	do	Ship Lucius not &c
	John Feteau	30	Do	Tailor	do	do	Sch'r Eliza not &c
	Robert Hunter	26	Do	Merchant	G. Britain	do	Sch'r Endeavour not &c
	Augustus Certenger	35	Do	Mariner	Spain	do	Brig Emeline &c
	Charles Isham	35	Do	Clergyman	U States	do	Brig Pomona &c
	Mr. Victor	35		Mechanic	France	do	
	Mrs.Moss & 3 children	30	Female		U States	do	Sch'r Col. Armstead &c
	Mr. Gilmore	28	Male		do	do	Brig Azores &c
	James Minot	22	Do		do	do	
	Richard Goldsmith	35	Do	Cab. Maker	do	do	Sch'r Wicker
	B. Tickner	40	Do	N. Officer	do	do	
	G. Weems	22	Do	Do	do	do	
	A. Wood	29	Do	Trader	do	do	
	A. Roberts	35	Do	Do	do	do	
	P. Ficardo	35	Do	Do	do	do	
	Wm Kerr	37	Do	Merchant	G. Britain	do	Brig Leod &c
	James E. Durrell	15	Do	Mariner	U. States	do	
	Godfrey Schutt	25	Do	Planter	do	do	Sch'r Marion *c
	James Reynolds	40	Do	Merchant	do	do	
	J. L. Peizant	45	Do	Do	do	do	
	Wm Harper	47	Do	Planter	do	do	Brig Miller &c

121

PASSENGERS ARRIVING AT THE PORT OF CHARLESTON 1820-1829

Quarter ending	Names	Age	Sex	Occupation	Country-belong	Country-inhabit	Vessel
March 31, 1825	Mr. McCarty	30	Do	Priest	G. Britain	do	Ship Hannah &c
	Mr. Lewis	46	Male	Merchant	do	do	
	J. B. LeMaitre	24	Do	Do	do	do	Brig Silvester Healey &c
	Peter Norman	28	Do	Mariner	U. States	do	
	Joseph Elzurde	28	Do	Merchant	Spain	do	Sch'r Eagle &c
	Lalemand Lamont	45	Do	Gardner	France	do	Brig Amiable Victoire &c
	S. Chatran	35	Do	Trader	do	do	Sloop Venus &c
	Mr. Aimar	35	Do	Do	do	do	
	E. Graham	31	Do	Carpenter	do	do	
	J. Atland	22	Do	Trader	Spain	do	
	D. S. Anderson	22	Do	Merchant	U States	do	Schooner Albion &c
	N. Swift	41	Do	Do	do	do	
	Joseph Ingersoll	45	Do	Do	do	do	Ship Robin Hood &c
	A. Buria	28	Do	Do	Spain	do	
	A. Jove	17	Do	Do	U States	do	
	J. Lopez	40	Do	Do	do	do	
	Alwin Ball	17	Male	Student	U States	U States	Ship Perfect &c
	Elias Ball	15	Do	Do	do	do	
	Matthew Coates	23	Do	Farmer	G. Britain	do	Ship Mary Cathar. &c
	Patrick Hearty	37	Do	Do	do	do	
	Mary Hearty Do & 7 Children 2 Males 5 females	37	Female			do	
	Wm Lang	28	Male	Do	do	do	
	Bridget Adams & child.	33	Female		do	do	
	Wm. C. Do	40	Male	Do	do	do	
	R. Maxwell	32	Do	Do	do	do	
	Edward Dwight	45	Do	Merchant	U. States	do	Brig Elizabeth &c
	Mrs. Do	32	Female		do	do	
	N. Kennedy	25	Male		do	do	
	Mozes Mapora	45	Do	Teacher	G. Britain	do	Sch'r Waterloo &c
	Mrs. Do & 6 children	40	Female		do	do	
	Mr. Mensh	29	Male	Merchant	Germany	do	Sch'r Col. Armstead &c
	Edward Tennant	26	Do	Do	do	do	
	Isaac Young	36	Do	Mechanic	do	do	
	Michael Fronteneau	58	Do	Merchant	do	do	Brig Carolina Ann &c
	Mr. Chanson	66	Do	Do	France	do	
	Mr. Crouchois	19	Do	Do	U. States	do	
	Mr. Fernandez	40	Do	Teacher	Portugal	do	
	Mr. Almeida	40	Do	Mariner	U States	do	
	Mr. Roberts	40	Do	Do	do	do	
	Mr. Pink	30	Do	Do	do	do	Sch'r Marion &c
	Mr. Fennick	55	Do	Clergyman	do	do	
	J. H. Lewis	35	Do	Trader	do	do	

PASSENGERS ARRIVING AT THE PORT OF CHARLESTON 1820-1829

Quarter ending	Names	Age	Sex	Occupation	Country-belong	Country-inhabit	Vessel
March 31, 1825	Thomas Hill	40	Do	Do		do	Ship Dunlop &c
	Sidney Brooks	26	Male	Do		do	
	J. P. Barr	28	Do	Do		do	
	James Moer	26	Do	Farmer	G. Britain	do	
	Margaret Do	26	Female	Do		do	
	Matthew Crawford	24	Male	Do		do	
	Wm Do	19	Do	Do		do	
	Wm Thompson	25	Do	Do		do	
	Joseph Nooks	22	Do	Do		do	Schooner Ranger &c
	Charles Delorme	23	Do	Upholsterer		do	
	G. Dalini	34	Do			do	
	G. Untesed	42	Do	Distiller	Spain	do	
	C. Uspolele	40	Do	Mariner	France	do	
June 30, 1825	J. Degasser	45	Male	Merchant	France	U. States	Brig Catharine &c
	Wm. Raser	34	Do	Do	U. States	do	
	Mrs. Do & child	25	Female		do	do	
	R. W. Dayton	28	Male	Mariner	do	do	
	Mr. Lazarus	33	Male	Merchant	U. States	U. States	Sch'r Felix &c
	Thomas Robson	30	Do	Do	do	do	
	John B. Gilbert	40	Do	Do	do	do	Brig Hope & Polly &c
	Antonio Flores	35	Do	Carpenter	Spain	Spain	Sch'r Leopardos &c
	H. Crosthwite	30	Do	Do	U. States	U. States	Sch'r Susan &c
	Robert Pearson	28	Do	Do	do	do	
	Terrence Fernan	16	Do	Labourer	G. Britain	do	Bark Caledonian
	Daniel Holland	35	Do	Shoemaker	do	do	
	R. D. Lawrence	25	Do	Merchant	U. States	do	Sch'r Cora &c
	M. Morgan	30	Do		U. States	do	Sch'r Eagle &c
	Fred'k Grenell	28	Do	Do	do	do	Brig Hannah &c
	Louis Abarante	35	Do	Do	do	do	Brig Catharine &c
	James Barker	43	Do	Mechanic	do	do	
	John E. Roe	54	Do	Do	do	do	
	Thomas Mercan	37	Do	Merchant	do	do	Sch'r Col. Geo. Armstead &c
	Alex'r Slidell	22	Do	U. S. Navy	do	do	Brig Pomona &c.
	Wm. Frean	38	Do	Merchant	do	do	Brig Trader &c
	John Clendennen	29	Do	Do	do	do	Brig Charles Coffin &c
	John Gonsales	36	Do	Do	do	do	Sch'r Susan &c
	T. Thorne	37	Do	Do	do	do	
	Y. Lawson	30	Do	Do	do	do	
	Antonio Manden	36	Male	Do	do	do	Schu'r Ursula &c
	M. A. Dewolf	20	Male	Do	do	do	
	John F. Russell	20	Do	Do	do	do	
	Antonio Ayman	40	Do	Trader	do	do	

PASSENGERS ARRIVING AT THE PORT OF CHARLESTON 1820-1829

Quarter ending	Names	Age	Sex	Occupation	Country-belong	Country-inhabit	Vessel
June 30, 1825	John Cooksa	50	Do	Merchant	do	do	Sch'r Union &c
	Joseph Merrick	50	Do	Do	do	do	
	Peter Boudo	30	Male	Mariner	U. States	U. States	
	A. Berhman	30	Do	Merchant	Holland	do	Brig Emeline &c
	E. Fernandez	40	Do	Do	Spain	do	
	T. Michallette	28	Do	Do	do	do	
	Henry Brookins	48	Do	Do	do	do	
	T. Shearer	26	Do	Planter	U. States	do	
	Joseph Bosa	30	Do	Merchant	do	do	
	Joseph Beyer	35	Do	Do	do	do	
	John Couehaes	19	Do	Do	do	do	
	Peter Boudo	30	Do	Mariner	Spain	Spain	Sch'r Union &c
	Joseph Maxby	28	Do	Do	do	do	
	And'w Burnett	40	Do	Farmer	G. Britain	U. States	Ship Dudean &c
	Ann Do & 5 children ages 15, 12, 10, 6, 3 yrs males	45	Female		do	do	
	Mary McCullen & child 3 yrs. male	30	Do		do	do	
	Ann Stully	45	Do				
	Nancy Do & 3 children aged 9, 7, 5, males	23	Do				
	Rob't Thompson	30	Do				
	James Kermgan	30	Do				
	Martha Kennedy	25	Female				
	Mary Do	32	Do				
	Daniel Cook	32	Male				
	Samuel McNeck	40	Male		Ireland	U. States	
	David McBerney	19	Do		do	do	
	Ann Do	34	Female		do	do	
	James Richardson	35	Male	Merchant	do	do	
	Philip Young Jr.	48	Do	Do	do	do	
	Henry Do	20	Do	Do	do	do	
	F. Winthrop	28	Do	Do	do	do	
	A. Parrara	23	Do	Mariner	do	do	
	Michael Berlo	24	Do	Merchant	Spain	do	
	David Pollock	31	Do	Do	do	do	
	A. B. Crens	27	Do	Physician	G. Britain	do	
	Joseph Cooksin	25	Do	Shoemaker	U. States	do	
	H. McAllister	30	Do	Lawyer	do	do	
	James Corkey	45	Do	Merchant	do	do	
	Francis Wallis & son 14 years	44	Do	Do	do	do	
	John Baring	28	Do	Do	do	do	

124

PASSENGERS ARRIVING AT THE PORT OF CHARLESTON 1820-1829

Quarter ending	Names	Age	Sex	Occupation	Country-belong	Country-inhabit	Vessel
June 30, 1825	Thomas Oliver	25	Do		do	Spain	
	John Roderigues	35	Do	Do	do	Spain	
Sept 30 1825	M. R. L. Echenique	45	Male	Merchant	Vera Cruz	Spain	Ship Galatea, Master not &c
	N. W. Ollis	52	Do	Planter	U States	U States	Sch'r Cadnecus
	V. Diez	26	Do	Officer	Spain	Spain	Brig Carolina Ann &c
	Madame Mettland	20	Female		do	do	
	Madame Lelimends	20	Do		do	do	Brig Catharine &c
	Joseph Howland	36	Male	Merchant	U States	U States	
	Emanuel Sell	22	Do	Do	Spain	Spain	
	Louis Grognet	27	Do	Mechanic	U States	U States	Sch'r Polly &c
	Joseph Chresto	22	Do	Merchant	Spain	Spain	Brig Mary &c
	Thomas F. Bailey	22	Do	Mariner	U States	U States	Sch'r Susanna &c
	James Ross	22	Do	Merchant	do	do	Sch'r Sally & Polly &c
	Don Manuel	32	Do	Do	Spain	Spain	Brig Rachel & Sally &c
	Wm. Johnson	36	Do	Mariner	U States	U States	Sch'r Eclipse &c
	V. D. Massau	32	Do	Merchant	do	do	
	D. Wodden	26	Do	Do	do	do	
	John Markinson	35	Do	Farmer	do	do	
	Elizabeth Markinson & 3 children	27	Female		do	do	
	John	35	Male	Do	do	do	
	Mary Markin	27	Female		do	do	
	John Carler	27	Female		do	do	
	Robert Carty	40	Male	Farmer	G. Britain	U States	Ship Lucius &c
	Laurence Marky	26	Do	Do	do	do	
	John Mansey	50	Do	Do	do	do	
	A. Aimar	40	Do	Do	do	do	
	R. Randall	25	Do	Mariner	U States	do	Sch'r Caduceus &c
	M. Goldsmith	50	Do		do	do	Brig Emeline &c
	W. McMillan	33	Do		do	do	
	Mrs. Do	25	Female		do	do	
	Miss Belcher	18	Do		do	do	Ship Isabella &c
	Mrs. Wheldon	22	Do		do	do	
	Samuel McNeil	45	Male	Merchant	do	do	
	John Moore	35	Do	Do	do	do	
	Alex'r Watson	25	Do	Farmer	do	do	Ship Sarah & Caroline &c

PASSENGERS ARRIVING AT THE PORT OF CHARLESTON 1820-1829

Quarter ending	Names	Age	Sex	Occupation	Country-belong	Country-inhabit	Vessel
Dec'r 31, 1825	L. C. Harley	18	Male	Mariner	U. States	U States	Brig Carolina Ann &c
	F. C. Black	32	Do	Merchant	do	do	Brig Catharine &c
	Mrs. Carne & child	21	Female			do	
	Mrs. Welsby	20	Do			do	
	Miss R. Abrahams	17	Do		G. Britain	do	Ship Niagara &c
	J. Welsby	25	Male	Do	do	do	
	John Robson	30	Do	Do	do	do	
	E. Abrahams	37	Do	Do	do	do	
	Wm. Hall	48	Do	Do	do	do	
	John McIver	25	Do	Do	do	do	
	Francis Muge	25	Do	Do	do	do	
	Alex'r Shime	45	Do	Do	do	do	
	George Relph	36	Do	Do	do	do	
	Jacob Harris	56	Do	Do	do	do	
	John G. Fraser	28	Do	Do	do	do	
	Gabriel Murray	26	Do	Do	do	do	
	Stephen Watson	25	Do		do	do	
	James Nicholson	65	Do		do	do	
	Nathan Fosdick	22	Do		do	do	Sch'r Four Sisters &c
	John Valentine	32	Do		do	do	
	John Richard	40	Do		do	do	
	Jacob Depass	28	Male	Saddler	France	U. States	Brig Catharine &c
	John E. Bonneau	40	Do	Factor	do	do	
	Thomas Ashby	42	Do	Planter	do	do	
	M. Redmond	26	Do	Merchant	G. Britain	do	
	M. Evans	56	Do	Do	U. States	do	
	M. Wilkinson	26	Do	Do	do	do	
	M. Leppet	26	Do	Do	do	do	
	M. Dreghorn	26	Do	Physician	do	do	
	D. Porcher	26	Do	Merchant	do	do	
	S. Getty [Gelly?]	36	Do		do	do	Ship Mary Catharine
	Mrs. Do & 5 children	36	Female		do	do	
	Wm. Clannegan	36	Male	Do	do	do	
	John Smith	26	Do	Do	do	do	
	S. King	12	Do		do	do	
	R. Do	15	Do		do	do	
	L. Ganahle	35	Do	Do	France	do	Brig Solide &c
	M. Park	35	Do	Mariner	U. States	do	Sch'r Susan &c
	Wm. Hall	30	Do	Do	do	do	
	Joshua Conlee	25	Do	Trader	do	do	Sch'r Marion &c
	Isaac Suares	22	Do	Do	do	do	
	B. Clark	38	Do	Merchant	do	do	
	James Black	47	Do	Mechanic	do	do	

126

PASSENGERS ARRIVING AT THE PORT OF CHARLESTON 1820-1829

Quarter ending	Names	Age	Sex	Occupation	Country-belong	Country-inhabit	Vessel
Dec'r 31, 1825	Samuel McNight	24	Male	Merchant	U. States	U. States	Ship So Carolina &c
	Wm. Carson	30	Do	Do	do	do	
	Isaac P. Wheeler	32	Do	Do	Cuba	do	Brig Emeline &c
	P. Parranconni	23	Do	Do	do	do	
	A. Candonuel	32	Do	Mariner	France	do	
	S. Roberts	45	Do	Do	do	do	
	Wm. Hume	25	Do	Physician	U. States	do	
	Mrs. Do	20	Female		do	do	
	John Lucas	50	Male	Miller	G. Britain	do	
	Thomas Higham	50	Do	Merchant	do	do	Ship Tallyho &c
	S. Lamburch	11	Do		do	do	
	Thomas Brooks	40	Do	Do	do	do	
	Thomas Scott	40	Do	Do	do	do	
	John West	40	Do	Do	do	do	
	H. Roman	23	Do	Mariner	Spain	Spain	
	P. Herrera	28	Do	Do	do	do	
	T. R. Seran	33	Do	Do	Germany	U. States	
	L. Meyer	35	Do	Do	do	do	
	Wm. A. Donaldson	55	Do	Merchant	G. Britain	do	
	Geo. McKinnie	27	Do	Do	do	do	
	John Mathewson	44	Do	Do	do	do	
	Mrs. Do	44	Female		do	do	
	Peter Cook	56	Male	Labourer	do	do	
	Mrs. Do & 2 children	54	Female		do	do	
	James McIntosh	35	Male	Merchant	do	do	
	Mrs. Do	30	Female		do	do	
	Sarah Brown	45	Female		G. Britain	U. States	Brig Export &c
	Charles McIver	14	Male		do	do	
	D. Mathewson	16	Do		do	do	
	John Do	19	Do	Farmer	do	do	
	John Do Jr.	17	Do		do	do	
	R. McCulloch	16	Female		do	do	
	Thomas Fraser	17	Male	Do	do	do	
	Hugh Beattie	28	Do	Tailor	do	do	
	R. Bright	55	Do	Apothecary	do	do	
	M. Stedley	52	Do	Do	do	do	
	M. Iveson	25	Female	Milliner	do	do	
	P. Duncan	60	Male		do	do	
	G. W. Lee	45	Do		do	do	Bark Bramin &c
	H. Yonge	40	Do		do	do	
	J. Arne	40	Do	Merchant	U. States	do	
	B. Clifford	38	Do	Do	do	do	Brig Gen'l Brown &c
	V. Pegere	30	Do	Do	do	do	

PASSENGERS ARRIVING AT THE PORT OF CHARLESTON 1820-1829

Quarter ending	Names	Age	Sex	Occupation	Country-belong	Country-inhabit	Vessel
Dec'r 31, 1825	Eugene Were	25	Male	Merchant	U. States	U. States	
	Mrs. Green & child	35	Female		do	do	
	Mrs. Lowden	38	Do		do	do	Brig Romulus &c
	Mrs. Chesolm	40	Do		do	do	Ship Marmion &c
	Mrs. Keith	46	Do		U. States	do	
	Mrs. Anone	46	Do		do	do	
	S. Chisolm	19	Do		do	do	
	J. Do	18	Do		do	do	
	S. Millikin	19	Do		do	do	
	E. Do	16	Do		do	do	
	M. Gracie	38	Do		do	do	
	Mr. Broadfoot	46	Male		do	do	
	Mr. Bacot	50	Do		do	do	
	Mr. McNeil	46	Do		do	do	
	Mr. Moodie	26	Do		do	do	
	Mr. Forrest	38	Do		G. Britain	do	
	Mr. Herbert	26	Do		do	do	
	Mr. Gough	19	Do		U. States	do	
	Mr. Purves	16	Do		do	do	
	George Lowden	18	Do	Linendraper	G. Britain	do	
	Henry Hare	25	Do	Merchant	do	do	
	J. H. May	30	Do		U. States	do	Brig Charles & Henry &c
	John Welsh	30	Do		do	do	
	John Rowland	30	Do	Mariner	do	do	Brig Miller &c
	Geo. Williche	25	Do	Physician	do	do	Ship Majestic &c
	John Mitchell	25	Do	Merchant	do	do	Sh'r Merit &c
	Joseph Sheng	25	Do		do	do	
March 31, 1826	J. A. Graser	50	Male	Merchant	Bremen	U. States	Brig Germania &c
	C. A. Bieben	25	Male	Merchant	Bremen	U. States	
	J. H. Hindley	50	Do	Do	England	England	Ship Hannah &c
	J. H. Do Jr	16	Do		do	do	
	Thos Eswine	28	Do	Physician	Havana	U. States	Ship Amelia &c
	Ira Saville	26	Do	Merchant	St. Thomas	do	Sch'r Washington &c
	A. Fromaget	34	Do	Hatter	Amsterdam	do	Brig Jasper &c
	C. Kelly	47	Do	Mariner	Havana	do	Brig Catharine &c
	D. C. Blanco	18	Do		do	do	
	E. Paiver	30	Do	Do	Matanzas	do	Sch'r Perry &c
	S. Eymar	40	Do	Do	do	do	Brig Scion &c
	John Batist	35	Do	Merchant	do	Spain	
	John Lopes	40	Do	Trader	do	do	
	M. Essner	24	Do	Merchant	Havana	do	Sch'r Eclipse &c
	___ Lorilla	43	Do	Mariner	do	do	

128

PASSENGERS ARRIVING AT THE PORT OF CHARLESTON 1820-1829

Quarter ending	Names	Age	Sex	Occupation	Country-belong	Country- inhabit	Vessel
March 31, 1826	Emanuel Hurnandes	38	Male	Merchant	Havana	U. States	Brig Mary &c
	Francisco Romero	50	Do	Mariner	do	Spain	
	L. Chastean	30	Do	Do	do	U. States	Sloop Enterprise
	George Thrasher	40	Do	Do	Nassau	do	
	George Fitz	30	Do		do	do	
	Jacob Walker	40	Do	Teacher	Scotland	Prussia	Brig Deveron &c
	Cha's Benick	20	Do	Merchant	Bermuda	G. Britain	Brig Atlantic &c
	R. Boot	50	Do		do	do	
	Benjamin Adair	23	Do	Physician	Scotland	Scotland	Ship Roger Stuart &c
	R. H. Gryer	25	Do	Merchant	Matanzas	U. States	Brig Charles &c
	Geo. W. Johnson	62	Do	Do	England	do	Ship Sarah & Caroline
	A. M. Williams	48	Do	Do	do	do	
	E. Morris	25	Do	Do	Havana	do	
	Jane do	35	Do	Do	do	do	Ship Langdon Chevis
	Christie	35	Do	Do	do	do	
	Poria	46	Do	Do	do	do	
	David Couan	20	Do	Farmer	Ireland	do	
	Jane do	26	Female	do	do	do	Brig Somoset &c
	Patrick McVeagh	30	Male	Do	do	do	
	James McMullan	32	Do	Do	do	do	
	Wm Elliot	60	Male	Do	do	do	
	Agnes do	60	Female		do	do	
	do do	30	Do		do	do	
	Rich'd do	28	Male		do	do	
	Matilda do & child	26	Female		do	do	
	Robert Davis	18	Male		do	do	
	Margaret Buchanan	40	Female		do	do	
	& 2 children fem.	16, 11 years			do	do	
	William Allen	30	Male	Do	G. Britain	do	
	Randal Stuart	20	Do	Do	do	do	
	William Do	22	Do	Do	do	do	
	Wm Davis	21	Do	Do	do	do	
	Jane McClure	32	Female	Do	do	do	
	Ellen Maguire	28	Do	Do	do	do	
	James Mullan	25	Male	Do	do	do	
	L. Hoey	21	Do	Do	do	do	
	James Conner	26	Do	Do	do	do	
	James McDermot	22	Male	Farmer	G. Britain	U. States	
	Mary Collins &	26	Female		do	do	
	3 Children fem.	5, 3, 8 years					
	Thomas Campbell	19	Male	Do	do	do	
	James Maguire	65	Do	Do	do	do	
	Catharine do	55	Female		do	do	

PASSENGERS ARRIVING AT THE PORT OF CHARLESTON 1820-1829

Quarter ending	Names	Age	Sex	Occupation	Country-belong	Country-inhabit	Vessel
March 31, 1826	John do	28	Male	Farmer	G. Britain	U. States	
	Margaret do	30	Female		do	do	
	Eliza Scott	19	Do		do	do	
	Ann McLane	22	Do		do	do	
	Mary Rutledge	25	Do		do	do	
	& Child fem. 4 years						
	Jane Allen	21	Do		do	do	
	Mary McVeight	24	Do		do	do	Ship Xenophon &c
	R. Askew	40	Male	Shoemaker	do	do	
	Sophia do	38	Female		do	do	
	Robt Turner	25	Male	Farmer	Ireland	do	Ship Dunlop &c
	John Johnson	22	Do	Do	do	do	
	James Carsinell	30	Do	Do	do	do	
	Theodore Verslays	32	Do	Supercargo	Holland	do	Ship Pauline &c
	Steven S. Tardy	26	Do	Painter	do	do	Brig Catharine &c
	Jane Roderigues	51	Female		Florida	do	
	Wm Williamson	26	Male		do	do	
	F. de Sueze	30	Do	Trader	do	do	
	A. Do	40	Do	Mariner	Havana	do	
	Robert Ross	35	Do	Merchant	Scotland	do	Brig Marcia
	William Wilkinson	40	Do	Do	do	do	
	Peter Zealand	25	Do	Trader	East Indies	do	
	Edward Delorme	25	Do	Musician	U. States	do	
June 30, 1826	Oliver Southwick	26	Male	Mariner	U. States	U. States	Ship Armadillo &c
	Fred'k Blamquist	50	Do	Do	do	do	
	A. Wathington	55	Do	Merchant	do	do	Sch'r Jane &c
	Margaret Babcock	20	Female		do	do	
	Mary Do	18	Do		do	do	
	Mrs. Sweet	60	Do		do	do	
	F. Antonio	38	Male	Do	do	do	Brig Miller &c
	Edward Morris	24	Do	Do	do	do	
	T. Martinelle	35	Do	Trader	do	do	Brig Emeline &c
	Mrs. Do	33	Female		do	do	
	Arthur McGwin	30	Male	Physician	U. States	U. States	
	Mr. Pinton	28	Do	Merchant	do	do	
	Leonard Ponham	40	Do	Pedlar	France	do	Brig Mary &c
	Theresa Do	35	Female		do	do	
	W. Phillips	30	Male	Merchant	England	do	Ship S. Robinson &c
	Godfrey Schutt	30	Do	Planter	U. States	do	Brig Catharine &c
	F. Clark	20	Do		do	do	
	H. Schutt	23	Female		do	do	
	W. J. Cinkin	27	Male	Mariner	do	do	Sch'r Sally & Polly &c

PASSENGERS ARRIVING AT THE PORT OF CHARLESTON 1820-1829

Quarter ending	Names	Age	Sex	Occupation	Country-belong	Country-inhabit	Vessel
June 30, 1826	John Chartrand	40	Male	Planter	U. States	U. States	Brig Charles &c
	Mrs. Do &	30	Female		do	do	
	3 children fem. 6, 4, 2, years						
	Francis Plaza	26	Male		do	do	
	Francis Bulta	19	Do		do	do	
	Manuel Cotta	45	Do	Merchant	Cuba	do	
	J. Corsuner	38	Do	Do	do	do	
	C. Vidal	22	Do	Do	do	do	Sch'r Lovely &c
	M. Dupont	30	Do	Do	France	do	
	J. Pergani	35	Do	Do	do	do	
	Alex'r Feraud	45	Do	Do	Spain	do	Sch'r Catharine & Jane
	J. G. Cooper	20	Do	Planter	U. States	do	
	A. Caehon	25	Do	Merchant	France	do	
	Giles Lathe	50	Do	Do	U. States	do	Brig Phoebe &c
	David Bucket	35	Do	Do	do	do	Brig Catharine &C
	Henry Yonge	21	Do	Do	do	do	
	P. H. Huie	25	Do	Mariner	do	do	
	John Albert	30	Do		do	do	Brig Scion &c
	Antonio Eymar	30	Do	Merchant	do	do	Ship Mary Catharine
	Thomas Shuthoree	50	Do	Do	do	do	
	Thomas Mair	50	Do	Do	do	do	
	Thomas Horan.	20	Do		G. Britain	do	
	John Booth	40	Do	Do	do	do	
	Edward Mentorie	25	Do	Do	do	do	Brig Lucy &c
	John Eckles	25	Do	Do	U. States	do	Ship South Boston &c
	Chauncey Cleyes	24	Do	Painter	G. Britain	do	
	John Miller	49	Do	Planter	do	do	
	Wm. Stephens	22	Do	Do	U. States	do	Sch'r Perry &c
	Wm. S. Sanches	21	Do	Mariner	G. Britain	do	Brig Mary &c
	Donald McDonald	35	Do	Traveller	do	do	
	Robert Latta	37	Do	Planter	do	do	
	Mary Do	35	Female		do	do	Brig Emeline &c
	G. M. Bethune	23	Male	Clergyman	U. States	do	
	Mrs. Do	20	Female		do	do	
	R. S. Boggs	21	Male		do	do	
	Emelia Gerard	17	Female		do	do	
	James Dailey	25	Male		do	do	Sch'r Fox &c
	G. M. Norres	30	Do	Mariner	do	do	Sch'r Phaeton &c
	James McCall	35	Do	Merchant	do	do	Sch'r Col. Geo. Armstead &c
	Mrs. Do & child	30	Female		do	do	
	E. Geddings	27	Male		do	do	Ship Ceres &c
	William Sanches	21	Male	Merchant	U. States	U. States	Sch'r Rising States &c
	Francis Cordes	45	Do	Do	do	do	

131

PASSENGERS ARRIVING AT THE PORT OF CHARLESTON 1820-1829

Quarter ending / Names	Age	Sex	Occupation	Country-belong	Country-inhabit	Vessel
June 30, 1826						
Wm. B. Hall	22	Male	Merchant	U. States	U. States	Brig Charles &c
F. Dupont	30	Do	Do	do	do	
D. Mentere	26	Do	Do	do	do	
C. Magnan	35	Do	Do	France	do	
L. Carter	26	Do	Do	Tenneffee[?]	do	
A. Eymar	30	Do	Do	U. States	do	Brig Scion &c
Sept. 30, 1826						
E. Verdery	21	Male	Painter	Jamaica	U. States	Sch'r Marion &c
George Relph	25	Do	Merchant	England	do	Ship Majestic &c
Mrs. Do	30	Female		do	do	
Wm Sebereau	28	Male		France	France	
Thomas Maw	40	Do	Do	England	England	
Alex'r Grant	40	Do	Do	do	do	
Edward Nelson	30	Do	Do	U. States	U. States	
John Seigling	32	Do	Do	do	do	Brig Stephen Gerard &c
Levi Hart	25	Do	Do	do	do	
Edward Darrell	26	Do	Do	do	do	Ship Isabella &c
George Tippets	40	Do	Mechanic	do	do	Sch'r Joseph &c
John Clevenger	30	Do	Do	do	do	
Wm. Hall	20	Do	Do	do	do	
L. Woodrow	26	Do	Do	do	do	
John Jackson	27	Do	Do	do	do	
John Samuel	21	Do	Do	do	do	
Richard Forrest	42	Do	Do	do	do	
Francis Leverick	25	Do	Do	do	do	
Henry Clark	30	Do	Do	do	do	
Lewis Newton	32	Do	Do	do	do	
John Morris	28	Do	Do	do	do	
George Gosley	23	Do	Do	do	do	
Richard Adams	22	Do	Do	do	do	
A. L. Stiner	45	Do	Clockmaker	Germany	do	Brig Wade &c
Joseph Evott	22	Do	Do	do	do	
F. Miscker	22	Do	Do	do	do	
John Tourner	40	Do	Do	do	do	
Wm Young	30	Do	Farmer	U. States	do	
John Berre	40	Do	Merchant	Spain	do	Sch'r Eliza Ann &c
James P. Wood	25	Do	Carpenter	U. States	do	Sch'r Lucinda &c
L. Farel	19	Do	Planter	do	do	
P. C. Verger	45	Do	Merchant	France	do	Brig James Munroe &c
G. E. King	18	Do	Do	U. States	do	Ship Perfect &c
Carlo Delle	54	Do	Do	Spain	do	Brig Catharine &c
R. Carell	32	Do	Do	do	do	
A. R. Drayton	18	Do	Do	U. States	do	

PASSENGERS ARRIVING AT THE PORT OF CHARLESTON 1820-1829

Quarter ending	Names	Age	Sex	Occupation	Country-belong	Country-inhabit	Vessel
Sept. 30, 1826	L. Sanchez	20	Male	Merchant	Florida	U. States	
	F. Peaza	18	Do	Do	Cuba	do	
	F. Pereno	30	Do	Mariner	France	do	
	D. Clar	55	Do	Merchant	France	do	
	F. P. Sanches	27	Do	Do	Spain	U. States	Brig Steph'n Gerard &c
	A. Eymar	32	Do	Do	do	do	
	Charles Deloram	60	Do	Do	do	do	Sch'r Bolina &c
	Mary do	21	Female		do	do	
Dec. 31, 1826	L. Mulholland	15	Male	Merchant	Ireland	U. States	Ship Bolivar master &c
	Charles Scott	15	Do	Planter	do	do	
	James Thompson	22	Do		do	do	
	Robert Moor	30	Do		do	do	
	Wm Todd	45	Do	Weaver	do	do	
	John Clarke	30	Do	Farmer	do	do	
	Robert White	25	Do	Do	do	do	Ship Jupiter master &c
	M. de Fougers	50	Do	F. Consul	France	do	
	John Parker	45	Do	Planter	do	do	
	L. Bignon	50	Do	Merchant	do	do	
	Francis Duboc	50	Do	Do	do	do	
	C. G. A. Lacoske	49	Do	Do	do	do	
	A. Ladeveze	16	Do	Do	do	do	
	N. Raynal	52	Do	Do	do	dc	
	T. Bourdon	45	Do	Do	do	do	
	T. Moger	27	Do	Do	do	do	
	Elisha Arnold	48	Do	Mariner	U. States	do	Brig Clarrissa Ann &c
	M. Lausand	37	Do	Merchant	France	do	Brig Catharine &c
	John Woodrup Jr	19	Do	Do	U. States	do	
	James Parker	50	Do	Do	do	do	
	Seth Woodberry	30	Do	Mariner	do	do	Brig Ocean &c
	John Coskary	19	Do	Farmer	Ireland	do	
	Wm. Wiley	40	Do	Do	do	do	
	Molly Do	40	Female		do	do	
	William Lamuer	30	Male	Do	do	do	
	Cornelius Guffigan	45	Do	Do	do	do	
	P. Carr	30	Do	Do	do	do	
	John Campbell	20	Do	Do	do	do	
	Jane Do	21	Female		do	do	
	Pat Coree	20	Male	Do	do	do	
	Hugh McClerlon	22	Do	Do	do	do	
	Pat Ryan	21	Do	Do	do	do	
	John Canavah	20	Do	Do	do	do	
	Frank Corree	25	Do	Do	do	do	

133

PASSENGERS ARRIVING AT THE PORT OF CHARLESTON 1820-1829

Quarter ending	Names	Age	Sex	Occupation	Country-belong	Country-inhabit	Vessel
Dec. 31, 1826	Elizabeth do	21	Female		Ireland	U. States	
	Mary do	3	Do		do	do	
	Francis Conolly	30	Male	Taylor	Ireland	U. States	
	Daniel Welch	45	Do	Farmer	do	do	
	James McIver	30	Male	Do	do	do	
	Conrad Parker	30	Do	Locksmith	Germany	do	
	Charles Scott	42	Do	Mariner	U. States	do	Sch'r Lucinda &c
	P. E. Sevard	30	Do	Farmer	do	do	
	Elias Boston	32	Do	Mariner	do	do	Sch'r Ranger &c
	Edmd Gelarson	28	Do	Do	do	do	Brig Catharine &c
	James Smith	33	Do	Farmer	Ireland	do	Brig William &c
	Elizabeth Do	35	Female		do	do	
	John Do	30	Male	Do	do	do	
	John Reed	40	Do	Do	do	do	
	William Kane	40	Do	Do	do	do	
	Margaret Do	41	Female		do	do	
	Hugh Do	12	Male		do	do	
	Rebecca Do	7	Female		do	do	
	Mary Do	2	Do		do	do	
	Daniel McCregan	36	Male	Do	do	do	
	Wm Asherhurst	30	Do	Do	do	do	
	Thomas Do	12	Do		do	do	
	John McClough	22	Do	Do	do	do	
	James Do	18	Do	Do	do	do	
	Wm Do	29	Do	Do	do	do	
	Arthur Hare	21	Do	Do	do	do	
	Ann Randles	25	Female		do	do	
	James Gill	22	Male	Do	do	do	
	Henry Harper	40	Do	Do	do	do	
	John Fraser	30	Do	Do	do	do	
	Mary Reddoch	35	Female		do	do	
	Margaret Do	12	Do		do	do	
	Harriet Waters	18	Do		do	do	
	John McCulloch	26	Male	Merchant	Scotland	do	Barque Herald
	M. Ogilvie	17	Do	Do	do	do	
	Alex'r Collie	43	Do	Laborer	do	do	
	Wm Stewart	40	Do	Merchant	U. States	do	
	M. Moult	38	Do	Do	do	do	Ship Samuel Robertson &c
	D. Dickson	33	Do	Physician	do	do	
	Wm. McWhinnee	28	Do	Merchant	do	do	
	Mr. Hamilton	25	Do	Do	do	do	
	Mrs. Do	30	Female		do	do	
	Miss Kidale	17	Do		do	do	

134

PASSENGERS ARRIVING AT THE PORT OF CHARLESTON 1820-1829

Quarter ending	Names	Age	Sex	Occupation	Country-belong	Country- inhabit	Vessel
Dec. 31, 1826	Mr. Crosby	30	Male		U. States	U. States	Barque Oxford &c
	James Hamilton	31	Do	Painter	Ireland	do	
	John Do	25	Do	Do		do	
	William Wilkie	20	Male		Ireland	U. States	
	N. J. Goodrich	35	Do		Scotland	do	
	Joseph Aiken	35	Do		do	do	
	Mary Do	22	Female		do	do	
	And'w Thetford	33	Male	Carpenter	Ireland	do	Brig Mary &c
	William Foster	28	Do	Mariner	U. States	do	
	A. Durban	35	Do	Merchant	do	do	
	Ann Graves	17	Female		do	do	
	Mary Ellis	31	Do		do	do	Brig Emeline &c
	Benjamin Do	15	Male		do	do	
	Mary Ranger	33	Female		do	do	
	Sarah Ledder	15	Do		do	do	
	Matilda Do	7	Do		do	do	
	Emma Calvo	25	Do		do	do	
	John Do	5	Male		do	do	
	Charles Do	3	Do		do	do	
	Catharine Douglas	32	Female		do	do	
	Jane Do	7	Do		do	do	
	Mary Do	3	Do		do	do	
	John McKenzie	45	Male	Do	do	do	
	L. B. Clough	40	Do	Do	do	do	
	William Young	52	Do	Do	do	do	
	John Bird	40	Do	Do	do	do	
	Wm. Mitchel	32	Do	Do	do	do	
	Wm. Broadfoot Jr.	14	Do		do	do	
	Miss Do	12	Female		do	do	
	Henry Newman	35	Male	Brit. Consul	England	do	Ship Robert Edwards
	Charles Baring	55	Do	Merchant	do	do	
	Jane Hughs	25	Female		do	do	
	George Jackson	30	Male		do	do	
	Robt. Pringle	30	Do		do	do	
	Benj. Lucas	21	Do		do	do	
	John Mill	45	Do	Do	do	do	
	Joseph Mill	35	Do	Do	do	do	
	Wm. W. Ball	30	Do	Do	do	do	
	C. Schroder	22	Do	Do	do	do	
	Wm. Do	25	Do		do	do	
	John H. Hammond	28	Do		do	do	
	J. H. Hinman	20	Do		do	do	
	L. Lulcher	24	Male		do	do	

PASSENGERS ARRIVING AT THE PORT OF CHARLESTON 1820-1829

Quarter ending	Names	Age	Sex	Occupation	Country-belong	Country-inhabit	Vessel
Dec. 31, 1826	B. Do	21	Female		England	U. States	Brig Andromeda &c
	A. P. R. Granden	28	Male		do	do	
	K. Macral	24	Do		France	do	
	L. Jones	40	Do		Scotland	do	
	R. M. Laren	43	Do		do	do	
	Pat McIver	20	Do		Ireland	U. States	
	Mrs. Do	15	Female		do	do	
	Samuel Lamburn	18	Male	Merchant	G. Britain	do	Ship Mary Catharine
	W. C. Molyneaux	28	Do	Do	do	do	
	E. Moyleaux	27	Do	Do	do	do	
	E. Menlove	28	Do	Do	do	do	
	James Robertson	29	Do	Do	U. States	do	
	Edward Hughes	45	Do	Do	G. Britain	do	
	James Nicholson	60	Do	Do	do	do	
	R. C. Cunningham	32	Do	Do	do	do	
	Thomas Gates	27	Do	Do	do	do	
	S. Woodward	40	Do	Do	do	do	
	Mary Cameron	16	Female		do	do	Ship Lydia &c
	James Hall	25	Male	Mariner	U. States	do	
	W. Crawford	26	Do	Do	do	do	
	John L. Hubbard	42	Do	Do	do	do	
	Wm. Johnson	32	Do	Do	do	do	Brig Retrench
	B. F. McDonald	25	Do	Clerk	Ireland	do	
	A. W. Wiley	26	Do	Do	do	do	Ship Commerce
	James Gordon	27	Do	Merchant	G. Britain	do	Brig Stephen Gerard &c
	Richd Gray	40	Do	Mariner	U. States	do	Sch'r Lucinda &c
	George E. Carter	25	Do	Merchant	do	do	
	Rich'd Norton	21	Do	Clerk	do	do	
	Ann M. Burk	18	Female		do	do	Ship Eliza Grant
	Jacob Eggart	50	Male	Merchant	do	do	Ship Lycurgus &c
	P. R. Yonge Jr	18	Do	Do	Florida	do	
	P. R. Do	50	Do	Do	do	do	
	F. Do	49	Do		do	do	
	Eliza Do	19	Female		do	do	
	J. A. Barretie	26	Male	Do	U. States	do	Sch'r Alfred &c
	H. Bates	29	Do	Mariner	do	do	
	Nathan Foster	21	Do	Do	do	do	
	Daniel Richardson	31	Do	Do	do	do	
	T. Ney	20	Do	Do	do	do	
	Joseph Class	21	Do	Do	do	do	
	H. Brackenbridge	50	Do	Judge	do	do	Sch'r Bolivar &c
	Henry Nelson	35	Do	Planter	do	do	
	Thaddeus Chambers	18	Do	Mariner	do	do	

PASSENGERS ARRIVING AT THE PORT OF CHARLESTON 1820-1829

Quarter ending	Names	Age	Sex	Occupation	Country-belong	Country-inhabit	Vessel
March 31, 1827	F. Dupont	28	Male	Merchant	U. States	U. States	Sch'r Sally & Polly &c
	J. P. Gardner	30	Do		England	do	Ship Home &c
	E. Mazy	40	Do		do	do	
	Francis Geram	40	Do		U. States	do	Sch'r Arrozana &c
	Samuel Pedrick	35	Do		do	do	
	J. Morris	25	Do	Do	do	do	Brig Sall & Hope &c
	J. Bonhonom	25	Do	Do	do	do	
	Mrs. Do	38	Female		do	do	
	Ezra Field	26	Male	Do	do	do	Brig Hesper &c
	T. Powell	28	Do	Planter	do	do	
	Daniel McLaughlin	19	Do	Merchant	Ireland	do	
	Richard Morgan	58	Do		do	do	Ship William Dawson
	Sarah Do	50	Female		do	do	
	Eliza Sawyer	54	Do		do	do	
	John Lafon	55	Male	Cooper	U. States	do	Brig Atlantic &c
	E. Gergand	55	Do		Bordeaux	Bordeaux	
	E. Do	45	Female		do	do	
	E. Fayalle	30	Male	Merchant	U. States	U. States	
	S. Buran	24	Do	Ship carpenter	do	do	
	J. Cherry	24	Male	Blockmaker	U. States	U. States	
	Lucas Frederick	32	Do	Locksmith	Bordeaux	Bordeaux	
	James Fowler	28	Do	Bricklayer	do	do	
	Wm. McKessick	40	Do	Farmer	Ireland	U. States	Brig Rose Bank &c
	Martin Do	30	Do	Do	do	do	
	David Cowan	25	Do	Do	do	do	
	Isabella Do	20	Female		do	do	
	Jane Do	16	Do		do	do	
	Sarah Do	15	Do		do	do	
	Mary Do	13	Do		do	do	
	John Do	21	Male	Do	do	do	
	Thomas Maxwell	35	Do	Do	do	do	
	Thomas Kerrion	30	Do	Do	do	do	
	Agnes Kerrion	31	Female		do	do	
	Robt Kervion	46	Male	Do	do	do	
	Robert Do	40	Male	Do	do	do	
	Ann Beattie	20	Female		do	do	
	James Richardson	23	Male	Do	do	do	
	Ralph Bamford	22	Do	Do	do	do	
	Eliza Coulter	25	Female		do	do	
	Susannah Coulter	19	Do		do	do	
	Saml Sports	18	Male	Do	do	do	
	David Caron	20	Do	Do	do	do	
	James Mooney	16	Do	Do	do	do	

PASSENGERS ARRIVING AT THE PORT OF CHARLESTON 1820-1829

Quarter ending	Names	Age	Sex	Occupation	Country-belong	Country- inhabit	Vessel
March 31, 1827	James McKibber	28	Do	Farmer	Ireland	U. States	
	Edward Gellan	30	Do	Do	do	do	
	G. B. Claxton	29	Do	Merchant	U. States	do	
	James Dorman	23	Male		Scotland	do	Barque Aurora &c
	Mrs. Beveridge	25	Female		U. States	do	Brig Chas Forbes &c
	Mrs. Mugridge	30	Do		England	do	Brig General Brown &c
	& 2 children						
	Thomas Hindley	45	Male	Merchant	do	do	
	Thomas Do Jr.	18	Do	Do	do	do	
	A. Watson	30	Do	Do	do	do	
	A. Low	45	Do	Do	do	do	
	Mr. Buckham	46	Do	Do	do	do	Sch'r Juno &c
	Mr. Cunnigan	40	Do	Do	U. States	do	
	Rich'd Welch	23	Do	Laborer	Ireland	do	Brig Varonica &c
	Andrew Mantand	40	Do	Merchant	do	do	
	Wm Close	22	Do	Do	do	do	Ship Perfect &c
	James Hassett	14	Do		U. States	do	
	Michael Do	10	Do		do	do	Ship Lucus &c
	Mr. Hartley	40	Do	Planter	do	do	
	Mrs. Cleland	30	Female		do	do	
	& 4 children						
	Mrs. Boyer	25	Do		do	do	
	John Kelly	18	Male		do	do	
	Harriet Harper	50	Female		U. States	do	Sch'r Planter &c
	T. Thompson	22	Male	Clerk	do	do	
	Mr. Lamothe	30	Do	Mariner	do	do	
	Wm. Campbell	35	Do	Merchant	do	do	
	C. G. Carbajet	25	Do	Do	Spain	do	Brig Mary &c
	Wm. Carter	30	Do	Do	U. States	do	Sch'r Lucinda &c
	A. Roberts	25	Do	Do	do	do	Sch'r Saluda &c
	J. A. Darby	36	Do	Do	do	do	
	V. Velbassa	40	Do	Do	do	do	
	James York	26	Do	Do	do	do	
	James Easton	35	Do	Mariner	do	do	Ship Telegraph &c
	John Pleasant	23	Do	Merchant	do	do	Sch'r Ranger &c
	E. Small	29	Do	Mariner	do	do	
	James Anderson	22	Do	Do	do	do	Brig Catharine &c
	F. C. Blanco	28	Do	Do	do	do	
	Thos S. Danforth	23	Do	Merchant	do	do	Brig Native &c
	Jos Revera	25	Do	Do	Havana	Havana	
	M. Johnson	21	Do	Do	U. States	U. States	
	S. Chappels	40	Do	Do	do	do	
	John S. Lynn	26	Do	Shipwright	do	do	Brig Stephen Gerard &c

138

PASSENGERS ARRIVING AT THE PORT OF CHARLESTON 1820-1829

Quarter ending	Names	Age	Sex	Occupation	Country-belong	Country-inhabit	Vessel
March 31, 1827	I. W. Lord	21	Male	Merchant	U. States	U. States	Brig Sophia &c
	James Marsh Jr	26	Do	Shipwright	do	do	Brig Marcia &c
	B. Bianco	24	Do	Merchant	Spain	Havana	
	Henry Catlin	31	Do	Do	France	U. States	Brig Mary &c
	F. Mont	44	Do	Do	Spain	Spain	
	E. Sanches	18	Do	Servant	do	do	
	Joseph Tomlinson	16	Do	Clerk	England	U. States	Brig Apthorp &c
	J. D. Wolfe Jr	25	Do	Merchant	U. States	do	Brig Scion &c
	M. Roberts	35	Male	Mariner	do	do	Sch'r Lovely Kezia &c
	Henry Yonge	25	Do	Merchant	do	do	Sch'r Ranger &c
	Alex'r Kindill	45	Do	Physician	do	do	Brig Jean &c
	C. D. Hight	18	Do	Merchant	Ireland	do	Ship Francis &c
	S. Davis	34	Do		Scotland	do	
	J. F. Williams	18	Do		England	do	
	Wm Raney	25	Do	Mariner	U. States	do	Sch'r Juno &c
	John Philip	20	Do	Laborer	G. Britain	do	
June 30, 1827	G. Relph	40	Male	Merchant	G. Britain	U. States	Ship Mary Catherine &c
	John Jones	67	Do	Do	do	do	
	Robert Brunnell	71	Do	Do	do	do	Brig Catherine
	C. A. Stott	30	Do		Germany	U. States	Brig Sophia, master not &c
	M. Petit	48	Do	Merchant	U. States	Mexico	
	Silva	35	Do		do	U. States	Brig Catherine &c
	Bonhommie	26	Do	Trader	do	do	
	O Reilley & 2 children	32	Female		do	do	
	Henry Von Glahn	23	Male	Sugar baker	do	do	Ship Jupiter &c
	John Muller	20	Do	Do	Hanover	do	
	J. Meyer	23	Do	Do	do	do	
	Henry Bure[?]	22	Do	Do	do	do	
	James Usher	38	Do	Merchant	U. States	do	
	A. Barrelle	25	Do	Do	do	do	
	D. Thompson	30	Do	Do	do	do	
	E. Murford	43	Do	Do	do	do	Sch'r Lovely Kezia &c
	D. Montero	27	Do	Do	do	do	
	J. Chartrand	40	Do	Planter	do	do	
	N. Burrell	35	Do	Merchant	do	do	Sch'r Sally & Polly &c
	S. S. Slice	25	Do	Do	do	do	
	T. Dupont	30	Do	Do	do	do	
	A. Barbot	40	Do	Do	do	do	Sch'r Lucinda &c
	Mrs. Gardere	55	Female		do	do	
	Miss Do	30	Do		do	do	
	M. Delerme	60	Male	Planter	do	do	Brig Mary &c
	M. Lafette	40	Do	Mariner	do	do	

PASSENGERS ARRIVING AT THE PORT OF CHARLESTON 1820-1829

Quarter ending	Names	Age	Sex	Occupation	Country-belong	Country-inhabit	Vessel
June 30, 1827	Mrs. Morrisson	28	Female		G. Britain	U. States	Brig General Brown &c
	A. P. Jive	22	Male		U. States	do	Brig Catherine &c
	M. McNab	50	Female		do	do	Brig Retrench &c
	Archibald Campbell	30	Male	Clerk	G. Britain	do	
	Wm White	25	Do	Do	do	do	Ship Roger Stewart &c
	M. Robertson	50	Do	Physician	do	do	
	Wm Relly	26	Do	Farmer	do	do	
	Arthur Connell	23	Do	Do	do	do	Brig Andromac &c
	John Fitzpatrick	20	Do	Do	do	do	
	T. McNaldre	49	Do	Merchant	do	do	
	Juan Valdez	37	Do	Planter	Spain	do	
	Manuel	35	Do	Do		do	
	A. de Salva	54	Female		do	do	Brig Catharine
	D. Valdez	24	Do		do	do	
	L. Do & 3 children	27	Do		do	do	
	Le Sage	65	Male	Merchant	France	do	Brig Sophia
	Berlin	22	Do	Mariner	U. States	do	
	E. Elewart	22	Do	Merchant	do	do	
	E. Hodskin	27	Do	Mechanic	do	do	Sch'r Planter &c
	A. Eymar	45	Do	Mechanic	do	do	
	Anton Feymel	30	Do	Mechanic	do	do	
	M. Jarvis	27	Male	Planter	G. Britain	U. States	Bark Agnes &c
	Don R. Perez	33	Do		Spain	do	Sch'r Lovely Kezia &c
	B. W. Barden	33	Do	Merchant	U. States	do	
	Geo. T. Carter	25	Do	Do	do	do	Sch'r Lucinda &c
	F. Yturran	30	Do	Do	Spain	do	
	J. W. Mitchell	30	Do	Do	G. Britain	do	
	C. M. Stoney	35	Do	Do	U. States	do	Brig Emeline
	M. Fernandez	30	Do	Do	Spain	do	
Sept. 30, 1827	H. H. Martins	22	Male	Merchant	Germany	U. States	Brig Mary, Master not mentioned
	M. Aymar	42	Do	Do	France	do	Sch'r Marion Do
	M. Blanchet	28	Do	Do	do	do	
	Francis Dupont	30	Do	Supercargo	U. States	do	Sch'r Sally & Polly &c
	James Richardson	40	Do		England	England	Brig Catherine &c
	N. Grand	35	Do	Merchant	Cuba	Cuba	Sloop Huntress &c
	Joseph Howland	40	Do	Do	U. States	U. States	Sch'r Lovely Kezia &c
	John H. Lorance	25	Do	Do	do	do	Sch'r Franklin &c
	M. Wagner	28	Do	Do	Hamburg	Havana	Brig Sophia &c
	Fred'k Bowman	40	Do	Do	U. States	U. States	Sch'r Jane
	Patrick Kelly	30	Do	Do	Ireland	do	
	Thos Lesesne	20	Do	Do	U. States	do	Sch'r Johanna &c
	John Collins	35	Do	Do	Ireland	do	

PASSENGERS ARRIVING AT THE PORT OF CHARLESTON 1820-1829

Quarter ending	Names	Age	Sex	Occupation	Country-belong	Country- inhabit	Vessel
Sept. 30, 1827	George Brown	27	Male	Merchant	U. States	U. States	Brig Mary &c
	M. Bonhomme	32	Do	Do	France	do	
	J. H. Debloist	17	Do	Mariner		do	Brig Orient
	Wm. Smiellie	30	Do	Mason	Scotland	do	Brig Wade
	J. P. Beaufelt	30	Do	Watchmaker	U. States	do	Sch'r Jane
Dec'r 31, 1827	James Benny	45	Male	Mason	Scotland	U. States	Brig Czar, master not &c
	John Do	30	Do	Farmer	do	do	
	James Adam	22	Do	Blacksmith	do	do	
	John Dennie	20	Do	Mason	do	do	
	Alex'r Mackie	23	Do	Do	do	do	
	Rob't Taylor	22	Do	Do	do	do	
	Isabella Do	18	Female		do	do	
	David McNell	55	Male	Farmer	do	do	
	A. Do	21	Do	Do	do	do	
	John Reston	35	Male	Farmer	Scotland	U. States	
	P. McLean	18	Do	Do	do	do	
	Herbemont	19	Do	Cab. maker	France	do	Sch'r Pilgrim
	Moses Smith	35	Do	Merchant	U. States	do	
	Charles Howe	27	Do	Do	do	do	
	John Wall	44	Do	Do	do	do	
	A. R. Drayton	20	Do	Do	do	do	Brig Catharine &c
	John Watson	36	Female	Tailor	Ireland	do	Ship Rob't Kerr &c
	Jane Do	30	Female		do	do	
	Tho's McCartney	20	Male		do	do	
	Wm. Rutherford	28	Do		do	do	
	A. Robert	30	Do	Merchant	do	do	Brig Stephen Gerard &c
	J. Vebaseca	28	Do	Do	do	do	
	Wm. Hunter	30	Do	Do	do	do	Brig William &c
	Joseph Burns	25	Do	Clerk	do	do	
	H. Lowry	14	Do	Do	do	do	
	And'w Reed	17	Do	Do	do	do	
	Mrs. Evans & child	25	Female	Spinster	do	do	
	Nancy McFadden	42	Do	Do	do	do	
	Mary McCrea	23	Do	Do	do	do	
	L. Do & child	30	Do		do	do	
	Sarah Magee	20	Do		do	do	
	Jane Do	21	Do		do	do	
	Wm. Hunter	35	Do		do	do	
	E. Do & child	38	Female		do	do	
	A. McKinsie	36	Male	Mechanic		do	Sch'r Pilgrim, Master not &c
	Thomas Mair	48	Do	Merchant	do	do	Mary Susan &c
	Wm Flinn	32	Do	Do	Ireland	do	

PASSENGERS ARRIVING AT THE PORT OF CHARLESTON 1820-1829

Quarter ending	Names	Age	Sex	Occupation	Country-belong	Country-inhabit	Vessel
Dec'r 31, 1827	J. D. Brower	25	Do	Mariner	U. States	U. States	Ship South Boston &c
	James Morgan	30	Do	Merchant	do	do	Brig Mary &c
	Alex'r Campbell	21	Do	Clerk	Scotland	do	Brig Retrench &c
	Wm McMillen	40	Do	Carpenter	U. States	do	Sch'r Marion &c
	A. Aimar	38	Do	Merchant	Cuba	Cuba	Brig Emeline &c
	Wm. Dick	40	Do	Do	Scotland	U. States	Brig Isabella &c
	B. Dempsey	30	Do	Do	England	do	
	Edw'd Morris	25	Do	Do	U. States	do	Sch'r Johanna &c
	Jacob Schoeler	39	Do	Stone cutter	Germany	do	Ship Lathalia &c
	Francis Xavier	23	Do		do	do	
	T. Schoeler & 6 children	40	Female		do	do	
	David Philp	22	Male	Carpenter	U. States	do	Bark Herald &c
	Mrs. Stephens	45	Female		do	do	Ship Majestic &c
	Miss Do	18	Do		do	do	
	Mrs. Lowden	42	Do		do	do	
	Miss Do	18	Do		do	do	
	Wm Do	48	Male	Merchant	do	do	
	R. Campbell	28	Do	Do	do	do	
	Wm. C. Molyneau	35	Do	Do	do	do	
	J. G. Moodie	27	Male	Merchant	U. States	do	
	J. Lowden	22	Do	Do	do	do	
	Tho's Walton	30	Do	Do	do	do	
	J. McDougald	25	Do	Do	do	do	
	G. J. Lowden	20	Do	Do	do	do	
	John Keller	37	Do	Do	do	do	
	Wm. Reddish	22	Do	Do	do	do	
	Elisha Solomons	38	Do	Do	do	do	
	M. Ourauchal[?]	26	Do	Farmer	Ireland	do	
	Rob't McMurray	40	Male	Do	do	do	
	Marg't Do & Child	30	Female		do	do	
	Rob't Arnold	22	Male	Do	do	do	
	Wm Yelly	50	Do	Do	do	do	
	Jane Do	50	Female		do	do	
	Joseph Cameron	20	Male	Do	do	do	
	Wm. Whitaker	35	Do	Do	do	do	
	Mrs. Do & 2 children	30	Female		do	do	
	C.Dickey & 5 children	30	Do		do	do	
	C. Atkinson	20	Male		G. Britain	do	Bark Mary &c
	Isaac Smith	35	Do	Merchant	U. States	do	Sch'r Hope &c
	Rich'd Hill	25	Do	Do	do	do	
	Edm'd Hamilton	30	Do	Do	do	do	
	Rich'd Bearns	28	Do	Do	do	do	

142

PASSENGERS ARRIVING AT THE PORT OF CHARLESTON 1820-1829

Quarter ending	Names	Age	Sex	Occupation	Country-belong	Country-inhabit	Vessel
Dec'r 31, 1827	Thomas Meacher	35	Male	Merchant	U. States	U. States	Brig Jane Velet &c
	Peter Finland	40	Do	Do	do	do	
	Mrs. McDonald & 5 children	37	Female			do	
	Mary Polson	50	Do		do	do	Ship Mary &c
	James Evans	50	Male	Do	Scotland	do	
	Rob't Muir	16	Do	Do	do	do	
	Mrs. Meacher & 2 children	36	Female		do	do	
	Wm. Blythe	40	Male	Baker	do	do	
	Mrs. Do	38	Female		do	do	
	John Daniel	45	Male	Tailor	do	do	Brig Rose Bank &c
	T. Cawon	20	Do	Watchmaker	Ireland	do	
	And'w Little	22	Do		do	do	
	And'w Logan	19	Do	Farmer	do	do	
	M. Mooney	25	Do	Mechanic	do	do	
	Peter Swan	60	Do	Merchant	France	do	Ship Eucharis &c
	Rose Do & 4 children	35	Female		do	do	
	L. Marchand	50	Male	Do	do	do	Ship Amelie &c
	Mrs. Do & child	35	Female		do	do	
	J. Geneste	17	Male	Silversmith	do	do	
	F. Baum	18	Do	Clerk	Bremen	do	Ship Jupiter &c
	Cha's Smilger	18	Do	Do	do	do	
	J. Nickleson	70	Do	Merchant	U. States	do	Ship Science &c
	James McDonald	30	Do	Do	do	do	
	Henry Wright	50	Do	Do	do	do	
	John Bird	30	Male	Merchant	U. States	U. States	
	Sarah Do	45	Female		do	do	
	M. J. George	35	Male	Do	do	do	Ship Sarah Ralston &c
	C. Myrick	35	Do	Mariner	do	do	
	Abraham Wolfe	45	Do	Merchant	do	do	
	Wm. McKay	46	Do	Do	do	do	
	Mrs. Do	25	Female		do	do	
	L. Barwith	27	Male	Clerk	Germany	do	Brig Henrietta &c
	J. Mathea	36	Do	Physician	U. States	do	Sch'r Lovely Kezzia &c
	John West	26	Do	Merchant	do	do	
March 31, 1828	J. G. Blois	35	Male	Planter	U. States	U. States	Brig Mary, Master not &c
	M. Gibson	42	Do	Merchant	do	do	
	Antonio Eymar	34	Do	Do	Portugal	do	Brig Scion &c
	Alex'r M. Edwards	50	Do	Judge	G. Britain	Nassau	Brig Philadelphia &c
	John McEncroe	45	Do	Priest	do	U. States	

143

PASSENGERS ARRIVING AT THE PORT OF CHARLESTON 1820-1829

Quarter ending	Names	Age	Sex	Occupation	Country-belong	Country-inhabit	Vessel
March 31, 1828	S. Auger Salazor	40	Male	Mariner	Spain	Spain	Sloop Connecticut &c
	J. Jones	30	Do	Merchant	U. States	U. States	
	Wm Rogers	20	Do	Merchant	do	do	Sch'r Marion &c
	Wm Martin	28	Do	Do	G. Britain	do	Ship Perfect &c
	J. Thayer	42	Do	Do	U. States	do	Brig Stephen Gerard &c
	Mrs. Maxwell	20	Female		do	do	
	Mary Scannell	36	Do		do	do	Brig Miles Standish &c
	Sophia Barker	38	Do		do	do	
	Jesse Ossward	22	Male		do	do	
	Matthew Hunt	40	Do	Engineer	do	do	
	Phillip Sullivan	51	Do	Drover	do	do	
	E. W. Horton	35	Male	Drover	U. States	U. States	
	Nathaniel Rogers	20	Do	Do	do	do	
	Dougald Mathewson	25	Do	Merchant	Scotland	Scotland	Brig Shakespear
	T. H. Hindley	50	Do	Do	do	do	Lady Rowena &c
	Th. H. Do Jr.	20	Do	Do	do	do	
	Wm Carlyon	20	Do	Do	U. States	U. States	Brig Stranger &c
	John Chartrar	40	Do	Planter	Cuba	do	
	Lewis Dubois	62	Do	Merchant	U. States	do	
	Ambrose Do	30	Do	Do	do	do	
	M. Gilson	30	Do	Do	do	do	
	J. M. McKie	30	Do	Physician	do	do	
	Charles Esnard	25	Do	Merchant	do	do	Bark Wm. Booth &c
	Dennis L. Kelly	24	Do	Laborer	G. Britain	do	
	Mary Do	17	Female		do	do	
	Wm Latham	25	Male	Do	do	do	Brig Stephen Gerard &c
	John Shefner	25	Do	Merchant	Germany	do	Brig Scion &c
	Antonio Eymar	33	Do	Do	Portugal	do	Brig Atlantic &c
	John Bass	39	Do	Do	U. States	do	
	M. Saventem	24	Do		do	do	Ship Unicorn &c
	Charles Newman	26	Do		do	do	Brig Sally Barker &c
	Edward Morris	28	Do	Do	do	do	
Sept. 30, 1828	John Seigling	36	Male	Merchant	U. States	U. States	Brig Catherine
	William Milne	40	Do	Do	do	do	
	S. A. Woodburne	34	Do	Do	do	do	
	Matthew Furlong	29	Do	Do	do	do	
	Wm Frean	45	Do	Do	do	do	Sch'r Marion &c
	John Stewart	34	Do	Surveyor	G. Britain	do	Brig Retrench &c
	Wm Burgess	45	Do	Merchant	Spain	Spain	Brig Mary &c
	Mr. Gabra	45	Do	Painter	do	do	
	Mr. Appleton	18	Do	Do	do	do	

144

PASSENGERS ARRIVING AT THE PORT OF CHARLESTON 1820-1829

Quarter ending	Names	Age	Sex	Occupation	Country-belong	Country-inhabit	Vessel
Sept. 30, 1828	T. Gabbey	40	Do	Painter	France	U. States	Brig Gen'l Gadsden &c
	Mrs. Do & 2 children	21	Female		do	do	
	B. Carpo	21	Male	Lawyer	do	do	
	R. Piket	40	Do	Planter	do	do	
	John Ross	45	Do	Merchant	do	do	Sch'r Billow &c
	Mary Clifford	32	Female		do	do	
	C. L. Esasde	35	Male	Do	do	do	
	J. A. Roberts	28	Do		U. States	do	
	Samuel Blois	35	Do	Planter		do	Sch'r Marion &c
	S. Do Jr.	9	Do			do	
	James Monteford	30	Do	Merchant	do	do	
	Antonio Dodey	39	Do	Do	do	do	
March 31, 1829	Capt. Varsy Hogartie	62	Male	Mariner	France	France	Brig General Gadsden
	Jose Miria Toledo	38	"	Merchant	United States	United States	
	Edward Morris	40	"	Trader	Spain	Spain	Brig New Priscilla
	John Humphreys	25	Male	Merchant	U. States	United States	Sch. Lovely Rizia
	John ditto	78	Male	Farmer	Britain	United States	Ship John Thomas
	James ditto	31	"	"	"	"	
	William ditto	6	"		"	"	
	Agnes ditto	1	"		"	"	
	Sarah ditto	24	Female	None	"	"	
	Hugh Daley	3	"		"	"	
	John Gillilane	30	Male	Farmer	"	"	Ship Robert Kerr
	Samuel Quin	50	"	Merchant	"	"	
	Thomas McBride	30	"	Farmer	"	"	
	Peter do	45	"	Trader	"	"	
	Michael do	22	"	Clerk	"	"	
	James Campbell	15	"	None	"	"	
	Joseph Irvine	38	"	Farmer	"	"	
	James Stuart	45	"	Tailor	"	"	
	James Buttry	46	"	Farmer	"	"	
	R. Achinkson	50	"		"	"	
	Margaret Darwin	45	"	"	"	"	
	Margaret Service	39	Female	None	"	"	
	Thomas Service	30	"		"	"	
	Eliza Service	5	Male		"	"	
	James Hice	3	Female		"	"	
	James Dulin	50	Male	Shoemaker	"	"	
	Pat Hon	28	"	"	"	"	
	James Munro	36	"		"	"	
	J. L. Zutton	39	"	Merchant	United States	"	Ship Perfect
		25	"		"		

145

PASSENGERS ARRIVING AT THE PORT OF CHARLESTON 1820-1829

Quarter ending	Names	Age	Sex	Occupation	Country-belong	Country-inhabit	Vessel
March 31, 1829	E. Vaughn	17	Male	Merchant	United States	United States	
	Rice	50	"	Farmer	"	"	
	Packard	25	"	"	"	"	
	Antonio Eymar	36	"	Trader	Portugal	"	Brig Scion
	J. M. Perez	29	"	"	United States	"	
	Benj. N. Barden	32	"	Merchant	"	"	Brig Stranger
	E. W. Woolsey	28	"	"	"	"	
	Samuel Williams	27	"	"	"	"	
	Edward Emud	12	"	None	"	"	
	J. McRae	25	"	Overseer	Greenock Brit.	"	Brig Margaret Miller
	Barnard Conolly	25	"	Labourer	Belfast	"	Brig Fingall
	Peter do	26	"	"	Britain	"	
	Thomas McWinnie	18	"	Clerk	"	"	Brig Margaret Miller
	John Reid	29	"	None	"	"	Ship Jane
	J. Jellings	44	"	Mechanic	"	"	Ship Nimrod
	James Cox	17	"	None	"	"	Bark Finberry
	William N. Johns	20	"	Mechanic	"	"	
	Greenleaf	29	"	"	"	"	Brig General Gadsden
	L. Rosindale	35	"	"	"	United States	
	H. P. Keizer	20	Male	Mechanic	G. Britain	"	
	J. Drake	23	"	"	"	"	
	G. Drake	26	"	"	"	"	
	James Colhunt	28	"	"	"	"	
	N. Patumble	35	"	Servant	"	"	
	J. M. Arcey	28	"	"	"	"	
	J. Joseph	32	"	Merchant	"	"	Brig Bolivar
	David Guild	44	"	"	"	"	
	Stephen Tolobung	37	"	"	France	"	Brig Emeline
	Antonio Peter Seguin	30	"	"	Britain	"	
	Barking	37	"	"	Zwitzerland	Britain	Schooner Lovely Keziah
	C. Forbade	45	"	Labourer	Britain	United States	Bark Cyrus
	Timothy Dukal	35	"	Mariner	U. States	"	
	Capt. Hall	35	"			"	
	Marion						Brig Catherine
June 30, 1829	James Marlow	70	Male	Farmer	Britain	United States	Brig Rose Bank
	Bridget Marlow	65	Female	None	"	"	
	James Firth	22	Male	"	"	"	
	Sir William Edden	25	"	"	"	"	Brig Genl. Gadsden
	C. W. Stoke	36	"	Merchant	Switzerland	Britain	
	Oliver OHarra	40	"	"	United States	United States	
	M. L. Salandanza	32	"	"	Britain	"	
	James Wiecard	22	"	Servant	Britain	"	

146

PASSENGERS ARRIVING AT THE PORT OF CHARLESTON 1820-1829

Quarter ending	Names	Age	Sex	Occupation	Country-belong	Country-inhabit	Vessel
June 30, 1829	James Porter	27	Male	Trader	Spain	United States	Schooner Richmond Packet
	Antonio Moraga	46	"	"	"	"	
	Adam Weddell	14	"	Clerk	Britain	Britain	Brig Retrench
	James Campbell	20	"	Labourer	Britain	"	
	Eliza Burk	35	Female	None	United States	United States	Schooner Felicity
	Andrew Burk	19	Male	Clerk	"	"	
	T. P. Burk	22	"	Planter	"	"	
	Robt Mechlin	25	"	Lawyer	"	"	
	Robert Miller	24	"	Merchant	"	"	Schooner Lovely Kesia
	Edward Morris	25	"	"	"	"	Brig Stranger
	James S. Mitchell	30	"	Cooper	"	"	Ship Julian
	Antonio Aimar	40	"	Trader	Portugal	"	Felucca Union
	Perez	38	"	"	"	"	
	John W. Henry	28	"	None	Britain	"	Schooner Marion
	Thomas Murray	30	"	Mechanic	"	"	
	Charles Hadden	40	"	Baker	"	"	
	Ann Hadden	35	Female		"	"	Ship Andromachi
	George Carpenter	41	Male	Stone Mason	"	"	
	William Carpenter	11	"	None	"	"	
	John Stoney Jr.	20	"	Clerk	United States	"	Ship Leonidas
	G. G. Crawford	22	"	Surgeon	"	"	
	Mrs. M. Crawford	19	Female	None	"	"	Brig Diligence
	Archibald Campbell	27	Male	"	"	"	
	Mrs. Campbell	25	Female	"	"	"	
	John Capo	28	Male	Merchant	"	"	Brig Mary
	Epharya Capo	24	Female	None	"	"	
	Roger Jones	42	Male	Carpenter	"	"	
	P. Jones	13	"	"	"	"	
	Alex'r Harrang	40	Male	Planter	"	"	Brig James and Isabella
	James Dutch	Boy		None	Britain	Britain	Brig Avis
	Peter McCardle	"		"	"	"	
	Arthur L'Estrange	"		"	"	"	
	Duncan McRea	56	Male	Planter	United States	United States	Brig Atlantic
	A. G. Heldreth	30	"	Mariner	"	"	
	Francis C. Black	39	"	Merchant	"	"	
	E. Dickinson	33	"	Physician	"	"	Brig General Gadsden
	Henry S. Richards	26	"	Attorney at Law	"	"	
	Lewis Ebrentz	38	"	Merchant	"	"	
	O. Sollett	31	"	"	"	"	
	Danely Gilis	29	"	Gentleman	Britain	Britain	Ship Perfect
	Peter Fausan	40	"	Mariner	United States	United States	Schooner Marion
	James Munson	22	"	Mechanic	"	"	Schooner Little William

PASSENGERS ARRIVING AT THE PORT OF CHARLESTON 1820-1829

Quarter ending	Names	Age	Sex	Occupation	Country-belong	Country-inhabit	Vessel
June 30, 1829	James G. Blois	35	Male	Merchant	United States	United States	Schooner United States
	Mrs. Blance	32	Female	None	"	"	
	Julia White	18	"	"	"	"	Brig Lexington
	Joanna White	16	"	"	"	"	
	Catherine White	9	"	"	"	"	
	Timothy White	25	Male	Accomptant	"	"	
	James White	22	"	"	"	"	

148

Canton, D. 103
Cantor, D. 34
Canuet, William 8, 93
Capers, William H. 9, 94
Capo, Ephanza 84
Capo, Epharya 147
Capo, John 84, 147
Caranchal, M-ther 78
Carbajet, C.G. 73, 138
Cardoza, J. 33, 103
Carell, R. 132
Carell, Romero 67
Carler, John 125
Carlisle, James 98
Carlisle, Mary 98
Carlisle, Robert 36
Carlyon, William 80
Carlyon, Wm 144
Carman, Thomas 40
Carmett, Edward 51
Carmett, Mrs. 51
Carne, Mrs. 126
Caron, David 72, 137
Carpenter, George 84, 147
Carpenter, William 147
Carpenter, Wm 84
Carpo, B. 145
Carpo, Bartholomew 83
Carr, Jas 70
Carr, P. 133
Carran, Don Diago 23
Carran, Elizabeth 23
Carraras, John 8, 93
Carrare, Don Diago 96
Carrare, Mrs. Don Diago 96
Carreased, - - - 58
Carreased, D. 117
Carrier, - - - 7, 92
Carroll, James 29, 99
Carroll, Michael 30, 100
Carsdoff, Master 9
Carsinell, James 66, 130
Carslile, Alexander 25
Carslile, James 25
Carslile, James (2) 25
Carslile, John 25
Carslile, Mary 25
Carslile[?], Thomas Henry 25
Carson, Jane 46
Carson, Wm. 127
Carter, Geo. E. 71

Carter, Geo. T. 140
Carter, George E. 136
Carter, George T. 75
Carter, L. 132
Carter, Wm. 73, 138
Cartu, F. 115
Cartu, Felip 55
Cartwright, H.D. 53
Carty, Robert 125
Carvin, Mrs. 58, 118
Cassedy, John J. 120
Cassen, P. 37, 106
Cassidy, Fannie[?] C. 59
Cassidy, John J. 59
Cassidy, Mrs. 120
Castilli, - - - 85
Castino, Christopher 42, 110
Castles, Mary 108
Castles, Thomas 108
Catlett[?], Benjamin 48
Catlin, Henry 74, 139
Cattell, John 28, 95
Caulfield, Henry 25, 49, 98
Caulfield, Mary A. 107
Caulfield, Thomas 107
Caura, F. 109
Caura, Francis 41
Cawon, T. 143
Certagne, L. 85
Certenger, Augustus 62, 121
Chaffer, G. 82
Chaffer, Sof. 82
Chambers, Thaddeus 71, 136
Chambore, James 6, 91
Changuian, A.H.F.L. 109
Chanquion, I.H.F.S. 41
Chanson, Mr. 63, 122
Chapman, Ben 42
Chapman, Benj. 109
Chappels, S. 74, 138
Charles, William 25
Charles, Wm 97
Charters, Preston 59, 120
Charties, Ann 2, 86
Chartran, John 33, 102
Chartran, Louisa 33, 102
Chartran, Thomas 17
Chartrand, J. 74, 139

Chartrand, John 131
Chartrand, Mrs. John 131
Chartrar, John 144
Chastean, L. 129
Chastean, Louis 64
Chatran, S. 62, 122
Chaves, John 34, 103
Chazell, Master 9
Chenee, Bernard 32, 101
Chereugh, Francois 116
Chereugh, Julianna 57, 116
Cherry, J. 72, 137
Chesolm, Mrs. 128
Cheves, R. 97
Cheves, Ramin 24
Child, Robert 5, 90
Chimenard, Madam 8
Chimernard, Madam 93
Chisolm, E. 23, 96
Chisolm, J. 128
Chisolm, Robert 106
Chisolm, S. 128
Choel, Pierce 17
Chresto, Joseph 125
Christie, - - - 65, 129
Christie, William 19
Cinkin, W.J. 130
Ciolan, D. 116
Clannegan, Wm. 126
Clar, D. 133
Clar, Deonicio 67
Clark, - - - 7
Clark, B. 126
Clark, Charles 19
Clark, F. 130
Clark, Henry 66, 132
Clark, John 58, 112, 117
Clark, Joseph W. 94
Clark, Mrs. 59, 118
Clark, William 92
Clarke, John 69, 133
Clary, Nathaniel Green 7, 92
Class, Joseph 71, 136
Claudier, Simon 20
Claxton, G.B. 73, 138
Cleland, Mrs. 73, 138
Clendennen, John 123
Clevenger, John 66, 132
Cleyes, Chauncey 131
Clifford, B. 127
Clifford, Mary 83, 145
Close, Wm 138
Close, Wm. 73